BILLY WRIGHT

BILLY WRIGHT
A Hero for All Seasons

NORMAN GILLER

ROBSON BOOKS

First published in Great Britain in 2002 by Robson Books, 64 Brewery Road, London, N7 9NT

A member of **Chrysalis** Books plc

British Library Cataloguing in Publication Data
A catalogue record for this title is available from the British Library.

ISBN 1 86105 528 5

Typeset by FiSH Books, London
Printed in Great Britain by
Creative Print and Design (Wales), Ebbw Vale

To the memory of Billy Wright,
our hero for all seasons,
and to Joy, who always
brought him joy

And for Eileen, who dialyses four times daily
while the author is at work
and play; and never a single complaint.
Who said women are the
weaker sex?

PREVIOUS BOOKS BY NORMAN GILLER

Banks of England (with Gordon Banks)
The Glory and the Grief (with George Graham)
The Seventies Revisited (with Kevin Keegan)
The Final Score (with Brian Moore)
ABC of Soccer Sense (Tommy Docherty)
The Rat Race (with Tommy Docherty)
Denis Compton (The Untold Stories)
The Book of Rugby Lists (with Gareth Edwards)
The Book of Tennis Lists (with John Newcombe)
The Book of Golf Lists
TV Quiz Trivia
Sports Quiz Trivia
Fighting for Peace (Barry McGuigan biography, with Peter Batt)
Know What I Mean? (with Frank Bruno)
Eye of the Tiger (with Frank Bruno)
From Zero to Hero (with Frank Bruno)
Mike Tyson Biography
Mike Tyson, the Release of Power
(with Reg Gutteridge)
World's Greatest Cricket Matches
World's Greatest Football Matches
Golden Heroes (with Dennis Signy)
The Judge, 1,001 Arguments Settled
Crown of Thorns, the World Heavyweight Championship
(with Neil Duncanson)
The Marathon Kings
The Golden Milers
(with Sir Roger Bannister)
Olympic Heroes (Brendan Foster)
Olympics Handbook 1980
Olympics Handbook 1984
Book of Cricket Lists (with Tom Graveney)
Top Ten Cricket Book (with Tom Graveney)
Cricket Heroes (with Eric Morecambe)
Big Fight Quiz Book
TVIQ Puzzle Book
Lucky the Fox (with Barbara Wright)
Gloria Hunniford's TV Challenge
Watt's My Name (with Jim Watt)
My Most Memorable Fights (with Henry Cooper)
How to Box (with Henry Cooper)
Henry Cooper's 100 Greatest Boxers

Novels:
Carry On Doctor
Carry On England
Carry On Loving
Carry On Up the Khyber
Carry On Abroad
Carry On Henry
A Stolen Life
Mike Baldwin: Mr Heartbreak
Hitlergate

PLUS books in collaboration with JIMMY GREAVES:
This One's On Me
The Final (novel)
The Ball Game (novel)
The Boss (novel)
The Second Half (novel)
World Cup History
GOALS!
Stop the Game, I Want to Get On
The Book of Football Lists
Taking Sides
Sports Quiz Challenge
Sports Quiz Challenge 2
It's A Funny Old Life
Saint & Greavsie's World Cup Special
The Sixties Revisited
Don't Shoot the Manager

Contents

Author's Acknowledgements

I started out writing this alone, and finished with an army in support. My thanks to all those who have so willingly furnished me with memories of Billy Wright, many of whom are mentioned individually in the section called, 'The Things They Say About Billy'.

Most of all I thank Joy Beverley Wright for her encouragement in the writing of this story of the life and times of her beloved Billy. Thanks, too, to Jeremy Robson for being wise enough to publish the book, to Joanne Brooks and Ian Allen at the editing end of Robson/Chrysalis Books, and Richard Mason, who designed the cover.

I wish to thank in particular all those supporters who visited my website at www.billywright.co.uk to add memories and tributes. This website will remain open as a permanent cyber monument to Billy and you are welcome to add your personal contribution to the Memorial Book.

The Wolverhampton *Express & Star*, which claims with some justification to be the number one provincial newspaper, has been a consistent source of help. Sports Editor Steve Gordos and his wife, Lindsay, went beyond the call of duty in making sure I had my facts right, and insisted that I paid their reading fee to the Wolves' Former Players Association, which Billy helped form and for whom honorary secretary Peter Creed is a bottomless mine of knowledge. Vincent Wright also employed his subeditor's eagle eye on my behalf, and I am grateful for the overseas help from Californian-based dyed-in-the-Wolves followers Peter Young and Charles Bamforth, and Swedish fount of Molineux facts and figures, Truls Mansson.

Thanks, too, to Lorraine Hennessy (Wolves communications manager) and Peter Pridmore (Wolves superstore merchandise manager) for their help in getting this project off the ground.

This book would not have been possible without Sir Jack Hayward, the saviour of Wolves who put the spring back into Billy's step by making him a director and giving him back the desire and inspiration to want to talk about the golden days at Molineux. My thanks to Sir Jack and his witty and wise PA and board director Rachael Heyhoe Flint for their cooperation.

Thanks, too, to Michael Giller for his invaluable research work, and, mostly, to *you* for buying the book. I just hope I have done justice to the memory of Billy Wright, our hero for all seasons.

'Billy Wright is our hero. It is his ability to use the inside of his head as well as the outside that has made him so remarkable. Not since Romulus and Remus has there been such a distinguished Wolf.'

Lord Brabazon
On Billy's award of his 100th England cap
1959

'Look around the new Molineux. Billy Wright was the inspiration for all this. He did more than anybody to fire my imagination and my love of Wolves when I was a young man and he was my hero. Yes, a hero for all seasons.'

Sir Jack Hayward
President and Chairman
Wolverhampton Wanderers Football Club
2002

Joy and Billy at their 'secret' 1958 wedding that brought Poole (in Dorset) to a standstill. Billy became the mister who did NOT come between Joy and the Beverley Sisters.

Foreword
by *Joy Beverley Wright*

My Billy was much more than just a wonderful footballer. He was a beautiful human being who always put the needs of others before his own. I have encouraged his old friend Norman Giller to write this biography because he knew him so well, and I know that I can trust him to capture the real Billy Wright.

It is not too far from the truth when people say that Billy and I were the Posh and Becks of our time. He was captain of England and the League champions Wolves when we met, and we Beverley Sisters were enjoying an unbelievable career. However, our wedding in 1958 was somewhat different to David and Victoria's. We decided to keep it quiet, and agreed that Poole in Dorset would be the ideal out-of-the-way place to tie the knot. The twins and I were in the middle of a record-breaking season in Bournemouth, a few miles away. Somehow, our secret leaked out and the town came to a stop, because so many well wishers crowded the streets. Billy and I, along with my two sisters, were mobbed as thousands of people (in the trees, up lampposts, hanging out of windows) surrounded us with their love. Wonderful memories.

All these years later, Norman has discovered how the secret was broken. It is just one of many facts revealed in the book that have come as surprising news to me.

I will never get used to losing Billy to cancer. The third of September 1994, is a date I cannot forget. He was such a shining light in my life, but in our children and grandchildren, the miracle lives on.

I know that my son Vincent, and our daughters, Vicky and Babette, think the same way. Billy was such a unique person who made an amazing contribution to the happiness of others.

In this book Norman has concentrated not only on Billy, the man and footballer, but also the period in which he was captain of both his club and country. Any younger people reading it will not believe the changes in the way the game is played and projected, and those of the older generation will know that every word is true and that they and Billy enjoyed the golden age of football.

What pleases me most about this book is that it features a section contributed by supporters, the people who meant most of all to him. The warmth that has always come through to me from the fans, particularly those at Wolves, is now captured for you all to feel. It remains a great source of comfort to me as I face up to life without Billy.

I am often asked what he would have thought of all the money the modern professionals make. I promise you that the Beckhams of this world will feel no happier, more fulfilled or prouder than Billy was to wear the shirt of Wolves and England.

I think he would have done it for nothing.

Billy was a generous and modest man, and I was so lucky to know him and his loving heart. I hope this book brings back wonderful memories for those who saw him play and serves as an inspiration to those who have only heard of him.

London, summer 2002

Introduction
by *Norman Giller*

This book was originally meant to be called: *Billy Wright, An Autobiography*. Tragically, Billy was beaten by cancer before we could get into print. With the encouragement and blessing of his widow, Joy, I am now able to share Billy's thoughts with you on his life and footballing times.

While preparing the book, I was given privileged access to Billy's private and personal papers and photographs. This has helped me build a biography that I hope does justice to a man who truly was A Hero for All Seasons.

There is a young generation growing up who deserve to know just what loyalty and sportsmanship mean, because they get few examples of it in the modern game. Older people, lucky to have witnessed the way football used to be played, will vouch for the fact that Billy Wright was the perfect role model.

Billy was the David Beckham of his day. He was England captain a record ninety times and the first footballer in the world to win one hundred international caps. In 1958, at the zenith of his career, he married singer Joy Beverley. She was a vivacious member of the Beverley Sisters, who were the Spice Girls of their time. This was Posh and Becks in black and white.

Just one slight difference: David Beckham earns in one week more than Billy Wright picked up as a player throughout his entire footballing career. That is worth repeating: one week of Beckham's wages amounts to more than Billy earned in 21 years with Wolverhampton Wanderers and thirteen years with England.

A Hero for All Seasons is not only the story of Billy Wright the man and the footballer, but also of an age that has disappeared from sight.

Writer LP Hartley memorably began his evocative novel *The Go-Between* with the words, 'The past is a foreign country: they do things differently there.' Never can that be truer than when looking back on a football world that has become just about unrecognisable.

I have Billy as a companion throughout the book, filling in the gaps with quotes that I had collated for what was intended to be his own remarkable story. We had decided that the best way to tell his tale was with a flashback through the seasons that he proudly played for Wolves and England, including a record 70 international selections in succession. I have elected to stick to that route because his 105 caps, collected between 1946 and 1959, capture an era when England were considered the Old Masters of football. Billy was in a beaten side only 21 times, and went six years before he knew what it was like to come second at Wembley; and when it did happen, what an explosion! A 6–3 defeat by Hungary at Wembley in 1953 revolutionised the way England players thought about and played the game.

In my role as the argument-settling Judge of the *Sun* (www. thesportsjudge.co.uk), I receive thousands of questions a year and a large percentage are centred on the 1940s and 1950s era featured in this book. To ensure that it is a complete record of those footballing decades, I include a who-won-what breakdown for every post-war season in which Billy played. Every Championship and FA Cup-winning team is listed, and I also feature the full line-up of every single England team with which he appeared. There will be a lot of dads and granddads out there who will welcome this as a treasure chest of a book, because it will take them back to a time when football had a soul. People of a certain age will know exactly what I mean.

If a young professional player of today – let's say Beckham, for example – was time-machined back to the era when Billy dominated the soccer stage, he would think he had landed on another planet.

They even spoke another language in the soccerland of the forties and fifties. There were wing-halves, inside-forwards, and wingers; two points for a win, and players had to control a thick-laced leather football that weighed a ton when the pitches were muddy. Dubbined football boots reached high above the ankle, and protective shinpads were, out of necessity, as thick as a rolled-up newspaper.

These were the tough days of tackling from behind, and shoulder charges were permitted against goalkeepers battered by combative forwards who would not be allowed to draw breath in today's more subtle and softer game.

Referees did not wave yellow and red cards. They had a little book in which they took names of offending players during an era when football was a game of shuddering physical contact. Gentleman Billy Wright was not booked once throughout a career in which he played 105 times for England and 541 League and Cup games for Wolverhampton Wanderers.

Words and phrases like striker, overlap, workrate, tackling back, centre-back, man-to-man and zonal marking, substitutes and the professional foul had not entered the vocabulary when Billy was playing. Foreign footballers were, well, foreign to the game.

Teams played with five forwards, including two wingers who used the full width of the pitch and were detailed to patrol the touchlines and to supply a stream of crosses. The most common playing formation was 2–3–5: two full-backs, three half-backs and five forwards. The more progressive teams boldly experimented with the 4–2–4 line-up that served Brazil so well when, Pelé-propelled, they won the World Cup for the first time in Sweden in 1958.

On the packed terraces they wore flat caps, rosettes and scarves, waved rattles and cheered, and about the most imaginative chant they stretched to was 'two–four–six–eight ... who do we appreciate.' There was not a football hooligan in sight.

Press boxes resounded to the rat-a-tat-tat of clattering typewriters, Raymond Glendenning roared into a BBC wireless microphone in his unchallenged role as the Voice of Football, and half-time entertainment was provided by the local brass band or, if you were at Highbury, the Metropolitan Police Band.

These were the 'good old days' when we still had threepenny bits and tanner coins, and it cost just a couple of bob (two shillings, 10p) to stand on the terraces to watch your favourite First Division team, and for an Oxford scholar (a dollar...five shillings...25p) you could sit in comfort in the stand.

A programme cost you between twopence and sixpence, and you could expect long queues at the turnstiles because average First Division attendances in the immediate post-war years stood at 36,000. It was nothing unusual to see more than 70,000 crammed into Maine Road (where Manchester United played their matches because of bomb damage at Old Trafford), Goodison, Highbury, The Valley and Stamford Bridge.

Floodlit football was just seeing the light of day, and Saturday was the big football focal point when millions of listeners would tune into Sports Report on the BBC wireless Light Programme on which Eamonn Andrews introduced the five-o'clock results and reports. Television hardly got a look-in, and it was considered blasphemous to even think of a League football programme on a Sunday.

These were ration-book days of austerity, with food, clothes and petrol limited in supply. It was the people's game of football that brought the brightest shaft of light to a country still severely wounded by war.

The game, it was claimed, was going off its head when in 1950 Sunderland paid a British record £30,000 for Aston Villa's skilled and powerful Welsh international centre-forward Trevor Ford. A reader's letter in *The Times* thundered: 'This is an obscene amount of money to pay for somebody adept only at kicking a lump of leather around a grassy field. What on earth is the world coming to?'

The new millennium footballer would most feel the difference between the two worlds in his pocket. The maximum wage that a player could earn at the peak of Billy's career was £17 a week, regardless of how talented he might have been. Thousands flocked to watch the likes of Stanley Matthews and Tom Finney perform their wizardry, but their weekly wage was still the same £17 as paid to an average player down in the Third Division North or South.

This, then, was the stage on which Billy Wright performed with style, strength and distinction. Now it is my privilege to paint an affectionate and, hopefully, accurate word portrait of the man who from humble beginnings grew into a football folk-hero. Helping me complete the picture are the team-mates, friends, family, sports writers and, the most important people of all in the world of Billy Wright, the supporters who were witnesses to his long playing career. You, too, can give a view by visiting our special website tribute pages at www.billywright.co.uk.

Let me give my credentials for being trusted with this biography. During Billy's generally tortured period as manager of Arsenal in the early 1960s, I ghosted his column for him in my then position as a football writer with the *Daily Express*. We remained firm friends when he switched to an executive role in Midlands television, and I scripted Michael Aspel's *This Is Your Life* tribute to him in 1989.

There were tears in Billy's eyes as he stood on the *This Is Your Life* set cuddling the famous red book that had just been presented to him. He was surrounded by old England and Wolves team-mates, friends and colleagues from his days in television, his daughters, Victoria and Babette, and by the Beverley Sisters, led, of course, by his wife Joy. Alongside him stood the legendary Russian goalkeeper Lev Yashin, Billy's rival in several intense and memorable international battles, who had recently had a leg amputated.

It was the appearance of Yashin as a surprise last guest that had finally broken Billy, who was close to tears throughout an emotional show. What only he and a handful of us knew was that both he and Yashin had recently conquered drink problems that had crept up on them in middle age. This is the only dark side in the Billy Wright story, and one that his widow Joy is happy for me to mention because she wants this to be an honest portrayal of her hero. Billy confided that beating the bottle was his greatest victory. He was always a winner.

As the cameras and microphones were switched off on the *This Is Your Life* set he said to me: 'My life has been like a fairytale. Who would have believed all this could have happened to a lad from Ironbridge?'

And that is where our journey starts, in Ironbridge. I invite you to climb into my time-machine and come back with me into another football age to meet A Hero for All Seasons...

SEASON 1938–39:
Man of Iron

It is somehow fitting that William Ambrose Wright should have been born in Ironbridge, the small Shropshire town which is generally accepted as the starting point for the Industrial Revolution. Industrious is a word that always fitted comfortably on Billy's powerful shoulders, and he showed an iron will throughout his glorious League and international career.

He got his first kick of life on 6 February 1924, and the small terraced house at 33 Belmont Road, Ironbridge where he grew up now carries a plaque to tell future generations that footballing legend Billy Wright lived here. The house overlooks the historic bridge that straddles the gorge and the River Severn. Spanning one hundred feet, it was the first iron bridge ever built and beneath it, in 1787, the first iron ship was launched. Yes, iron was definitely in Billy's blood.

It was not iron but milk which was a problem for Billy when he was born. He weighed just five pounds at birth and his mother, Annie, had to feed him his first drops of milk from a fountain pen.

His father, Tommy, worked in the local Coalbrookdale iron foundry, and there is no question that Billy – the eldest of two sons – would have followed him into the smelting business but for the fact that a schoolmaster spotted his footballing talent.

BILLY: I was only a nipper, but the sports master at the Madeley Senior School where I was a pupil decided I was best suited to leading the attack. In my debut at centre-forward against Bewdley

1

School we won 13–0 and I helped myself to ten goals. The master, a Norman Simpson, kept a close eye on me from then on and suggested that I could make the grade in professional football even though I was short for my age. My dream was to play for the Arsenal, but Mr Simpson noticed that Wolves were advertising for groundstaff boys and he recommended that I apply. In fact, as I recall, he wrote to Wolves saying that I was an outstanding prospect. I was interviewed and accepted and I went to Molineux five months after my fourteenth birthday and just before the kick-off to the 1938–39 season. My Dad, who was well known in Ironbridge for being a good-quality club footballer, just said, 'Well it certainly beats working in an iron foundry.'

The exact date of Billy's arrival at Molineux was Monday 11 July 1938. I can be specific because of a letter in the first of the cuttings books to which Joy Beverley Wright kindly gave me access. The letter, reproduced in the first photo-album section, was sent to schoolmaster Norman Simpson. It was signed by the legendary manager, Major Frank Buckley, and instructed: 'Please arrange for the lad Wright to be at the above address [Molineux] on the morning of Monday July the 11th ready to start on the ground.'

Billy Wright's career was about to kick-off, literally, at grass roots level.

I spent hours with Joy looking through the cuttings books that Billy used to keep. The first, started in 1938 and captioned in blue ink with a neat, schoolboyish hand, revealed that he used to call himself Bill Wright. It was the press who turned him into Billy. He was an avid autograph hunter, and every match programme of his early representative games are signed by his team-mates. The past comes rumbling to life as you look at the handwritten signatures of such illustrious names as Stanley Matthews, Tommy Lawton, Tom Finney and just about every major England football international of the 1940s. Pasted into his wartime cuttings book are special passes from his camp commandant, giving him permission to travel to games across the country. His collection of wartime match programmes, many just typewritten sheets, chart his progress as a physical training instructor.

He is first listed as Private Wright, then corporal and, in his last year in the Army, as a sergeant.

There is no reference in the cuttings books as to why Billy had the middle name Ambrose, the most famous second name in British football. Joy did not know the answer, and she said that Billy used to shrug and say it was just a name. Eventually it was Gwyneth Wright, charming widow of Billy's late brother Laurence, who solved the enigma. She told Joy that Ambrose had been passed down the line of Wrights as a traditional family name. There is stark evidence on a Shropshire war memorial that reads: 'William Ambrose Wright, killed in action on the Somme, 1916.'

Neil Wright, Billy's nephew and son of Laurence, told me: 'This was Billy's and my dad's paternal grandfather. He was killed in the First World War and left a widow and seven children.'

Just a few facts here to put 1938 and the start of Billy's life in football into historical context. Just weeks before Billy was invited to join Wolves, Adolf Hitler appointed himself supreme commander of the German armed forces, and in London Anthony Eden resigned as foreign secretary in protest at Prime Minister Neville Chamberlain's appeasement policies. Billy was settled in at Molineux and cleaning boots and sweeping terraces when Chamberlain flew home from a meeting with Hitler in Munich waving a piece of paper and promising 'peace for our time'.

Walt Disney had recently released *Snow White and the Seven Dwarfs* as his first feature-length cartoon; Italy retained the World Cup (after their players received a 'Win or die' telegram of encouragement from Mussolini); Len Hutton scored a world record 364 Test runs against Australia at the Oval; Joe Louis smashed Max Schmeling to a one round defeat; Helen Moody won her eighth Wimbledon title; a George Mutch penalty in the last minute of extra-time had given Preston North End a 1–0 1938 FA Cup final victory over Huddersfield Town and Arsenal pipped Wolves for the League championship by one point.

Billy was paid £2 a week for his groundstaff work, and thirty shillings of that went to his landlady. He sent five shillings a week home to his mother, and allowed himself five shillings pocket money; this at a time when you could get a cup of tea for a penny, a packet of cigarettes for a shilling and a pint of beer for twopence. He travelled everywhere by bus or train in an era when even the established first-team professionals, earning £8 a week, could not afford to run a motorcar.

Molineux in 1938 was under the autocratic rule of Major Buckley, who had kept his rank from the First World War and never got out of the habit of demanding parade-ground discipline. He had the appearance more of a retired gentleman farmer than a football manager, with a penchant for tweed suits and plus fours. He often had a couple of his favourite Airedale dogs snapping at his heels as he walked around Molineux as if in estate grounds. The major could have clambered out of the pages of a PG Wodehouse novel. He looked at the world through thick horn-rimmed spectacles (whipped off if any press photographers were within shooting range), and he put the fear of God into battle-hardened professional footballers with his abrupt manner. The players were called by their surnames, and the many youngsters on the staff were always 'laddie' or 'sonny', mainly because he could not remember all their names. Naturally, the groundstaff boys were terrified of him.

So it was with fear and trepidation that Billy answered a summons to the manager's office near the end of his six months' trial as an apprentice. The Major did not waste time getting to the point. 'Sonny,' he told Billy, 'this is not working out. You are far too small to ever make the grade as a professional footballer. I am sending you home.'

BILLY: I was devastated. All I could think was that I was a failure, and I walked out of the major's office without a word. I was too choked with tears to be able to say anything. The club groundsman Albert Tye saw me, and guessed what had happened. Twenty minutes later, as I was getting my things together, I was called back into the manager's office. Our trainer Jack Davies stood alongside him. 'I have been persuaded to change my mind,' the major said. He got up out of his seat and walked over to me. He pushed a finger at my chest and said, 'I am assured that you are big here where it really matters. In the heart. You can stay.' It must have been one of the shortest sackings of all time. In truth, I think one of the main reasons I was kept on was because I was so good with a broom and at cleaning boots! The club got me

lodgings in a real home at Tettenhall and with a real family. Mr
and Mrs Arthur Colley became like a second mum and dad to me,
and their son, Arthur, was like the brother Laurence I had left
behind in Ironbridge. Along with my club team-mate Alan Steen,
I moved in with them and immediately felt settled. Over the next
two to three years I shot up from five foot three to just over five
foot eight, and nobody ever called me 'Shorty' again.

It is worth taking a closer look at Major Buckley, because he played
such an influential part in the shaping of the young Billy Wright in the
days when he was known as 'Snowy' because of his blonder-than-
blond shock of hair.

Franklin Charles Buckley was born in Urmston, Manchester, in
1883. He was one of five footballing brothers, one of whom – Chris –
played at centre-half for Arsenal and Aston Villa, and later became
chairman at Villa Park.

As a teenager, Frank fought as a volunteer in the Boer War before
playing as a centre-half for a string of clubs including Birmingham
City, Derby County, Aston Villa, Brighton, Bradford City and both
Manchester United and Manchester City. He had just made the breakthrough at international level with one cap for England against Ireland
in 1914 when the First World War started. He became a major while
serving with the 17th Middlesex Regiment, commanding what became
known as the 'Footballers' Battalion' because there were so many
professional players in the squad.

Major Buckley insisted on people continuing to use his rank after the
war when he went into football management, first with Norwich City
and then with Blackpool. He also tried his hand on the road as a
commercial traveller before taking over as manager at Wolverhampton
in 1927, arriving at Molineux with the club struggling in the Second
Division.

They were close to relegation in both 1928 and 1929 before the
Buckley youth-first policy began to pay off. Wolves won the Second
Division title in 1931–32, Buckley keeping the club solvent by selling
a procession of star players while developing the 'Wolves Cubs'.

He had Victorian values and believed in the three Ds – discipline,

discipline, discipline. Any player who slacked in training was quickly shown the door because Buckley was convinced that fitness was the vital ingredient for any team.

BILLY: The influence of Major Buckley on me lasted throughout my career. I never smoked and rarely drank as a player because he planted it in my head how harmful it was, and I always trained until I was exhausted. It was well known throughout the game that Wolves' players were the fittest in the land. I could not say that the major was likeable because he was too aloof for that, but he had everybody's full respect. In fact, I would say many players were frightened of him and the fear factor played a big part in his style of management. I know when I was a young lad I was petrified of him. He always wore brogues, and at the sound of him walking through the corridors you were wise to make yourself busy or get a flea in the ear. I have to thank the major for drumming into me the importance of being disciplined, but I think I must have subconsciously made a decision then that if I ever became a manager I would not have the players living in fear of me. I have never seen the point of being deliberately nasty to people. Life is too short.

Among the established professionals who developed under Buckley was Stan Cullis, who was eventually to have the biggest influence of all on Billy's career. He became one of England's finest ever centre-halves, and more than anybody learned from the major's managerial skills in setting up a scouting network, giving young players their chance and putting huge emphasis on discipline and fitness.

Buckley put Cullis into the centre of the Wolves defence when he was seventeen, and made him captain at nineteen. By the time he was twenty-two Cullis was skippering England. And here's something for the new millennium footballer to chew on: his wage was £8 a week in the season and £6 in the summer months.

Billy revealed that it was Cullis who claimed to have been the first to come up with one of football's oldest punchlines. At the start of each season players would queue at the major's office to discuss their terms for the following year. As they came out, each player whispered what they had got. It ranged from a maximum £8 a week in the season, reduced to £6 a week in the summer for the top players, down to £5 and £4 for the less-established players. When Cullis was offered £8 in the winter and only £5 in the summer, he protested. 'You are paying Dennis Westcott £8 in the winter and £6 in the summer.'

'That,' said Major Buckley, 'is because he is a better player than you.'

'Not in the flipping summer he's not,' said Cullis – and got his £1 rise.

When Frank Buckley passed on in 1964 at the age of 81, I put together a hurried obituary for the *Daily Herald*, the newspaper from which I was earning my daily bread. He had resigned from Wolves in 1944, and later managed Notts County, Hull City, Leeds United and Walsall. I was grateful to Leeds and England centre-half Jack Charlton for this anecdote that showed another side to the man best remembered as the Martinet of Molineux: 'The major took me on the Elland Road groundstaff, and we all feared him because his bite was just as bad as his bark. But deep down there was a kind man. He hauled me over the coals one day because of the state of my shoes, and I told him they were the only pair I had. When he called me into his office the next day I thought I was in for another rollicking. He pointed to a box on his desk and said, 'Here you are, Sonny. Take these, and remember that scruffiness breeds bad discipline.' Inside the box were a pair of Irish brogues, the sort the major famously wore himself. They were the finest and strongest pair of shoes I had ever clapped eyes on, and I wore them with pride for years. The major was hard, but his heart was in the right place.'

The major was also a master publicist, as young Billy Wright was to see at first hand in the memorable 1938–39 season when Wolves went all the way to Wembley.

Buckley knew how to generate headlines that kept Wolves in the news, and Billy had a ringside seat as the major drummed up publicity that helped attract huge crowds to Molineux. It was in this season of 1938–39 that the ground record of 61,315 was set, a record that will never be beaten in today's all-seater age. The magnetic game was a home fifth-round FA Cup tie against Liverpool on 11 February 1939.

Buckley had started the season by infuriating the fans when he sold Welsh international inside-forward Bryn Jones to Arsenal for what was then a world record £14,000. He had plucked Jones out of the relative obscurity of Welsh League football, and he quickly became a match-winning favourite with the Molineux supporters. Threats were made against Buckley, and the club arranged for him to have a police bodyguard but the war veteran sent the constable packing with the words: 'The day I cannot defend myself is the day I give up.'

While the major was considered a villain on the terraces, he was rated a hero in the boardroom. The Jones sale took the income from transfers to £110,000 over three years, which was a fortune by 1930s standards.

Buckley shut up his critics in the best possible way by guiding his team to within shooting range of the elusive League championship and FA Cup double.

BILLY: That was an extraordinary season, and I watched everything going on with an open mouth. It was amazing. The major got acres of newspaper space by convincing journalists that the reason Wolves were doing so well was because the players were having monkey-gland treatment. Actually, it was probably no more than a new form of immunisation against the common cold but the major made such a thing of it that even overseas journalists were visiting the ground to write about the great medical revolution. We groundstaff boys were spared the needle, and had our treatment given to us in tablet form. I hated the taste of them and secretly fed my tablets to Mrs Colley's tomcat, who I have to say took on a new sheen and swaggered around as though he owned the place. The publicity stunt almost backfired on the major when several of the players refused to have any more injections because they were concerned about the long-term effects. They had believed the monkey-gland stories! He also brought in a psychologist to give the players what he called 'couch coaching'. Many people thought the major was something of a crank, but he was ahead of his time with many of his ideas and theories.

After making his club debut in a number nine Wolves shirt in a Minor League match against Walsall Wood, Billy was promoted to 'chief kit boy', which meant that he had the responsibility for preparing the skip containing the first-team boots, shirts and socks. He carried the skip in and out of the dressing-room in harness with a teenage winger from Newcastle called Jimmy Mullen, who had joined the Wolves groundstaff just a few months ahead of Billy. The senior players considered them lucky mascots as they made their bold bid for the League championship and FA Cup double.

For the second successive season they had to be content with runners-up place in the First Division, losing out to Everton for whom England centre-forward Tommy Lawton crashed in 35 goals. The shock result of the season was the 7–1 drubbing of Everton by Wolves on a mud-heap of a pitch at Molineux. Secretly, for three days before the match, Major Buckley had Billy and the other groundstaff boys helping groundsman Albert Tye swamp the pitch with gallons of water. They became known as the 'Hosepipe Gang'. Buckley knew that Everton were the better footballing side and wanted to sabotage their neat passing game.

It was in the FA Cup that everybody expected Wolves to win their first major trophy for 31 years. Their last day of glory had been a 3–1 FA Cup final victory against Newcastle United at Crystal Palace in 1908. Sixteen-year-old Mullen went from handing out the kit to wearing it in the FA Cup semi-final, helping Wolves to a 5–0 victory over Grimsby. Deadeye Dennis Westcott scored four of the goals. In earlier ties the Molineux machine had accounted for Bradford (3–1), Leicester City (5–1), Liverpool (4–1) and eventual Football League champions Everton (2–0).

Wolves were just about the warmest favourites there had ever been at Wembley. Their opponents, Portsmouth, were struggling in the relegation zone of the First Division and looked outgunned on paper. It was a different story on the pitch.

BILLY: I was in tears that day. As the kit boy, I had got very close to the players and was willing them to win. I waved them off from Molineux that morning, and then joined the 'A' team for a

Saturday morning match. I listened to the game on the wireless. The Portsmouth manager Jack Tinn wore his lucky spats, and walking alongside him was the major in full morning dress and carrying a top hat. King George VI was in the Royal Box waiting to hand over the cup. We just froze and never got into the game. Pompey hammered us 4–1, and Tinn said afterwards that he knew we were beaten before a ball was kicked. An official autograph book, that was to be signed by both teams, arrived in the Pompey dressing-room twenty minutes before the kick-off, and Tinn saw that the handwriting of the Wolves players was so shaky with nerves that he could not read the signatures. He showed the shaky signatures to his team and said, 'Look, they are frightened stiff.'

Skipper Stan Cullis tried to cheer up his depressed team-mates after the demoralising defeat with the promise, 'We'll be back next year and will come away with the cup.'

But no football promises were kept the next year. A match with Adolf Hitler took all the attention ... and Billy Wright's career started for real.

SEASONS 1939–46:
Wartime Footballer

No lives were untouched when Prime Minister Neville Chamberlain made his historic broadcast on 3 September 1939: 'A state of war now exists...' For fifteen-year-old Billy Wright, the immediate result was a rapid promotion to first-team status.

With many of the senior squad called up for active service, Billy was selected as a right-winger for his first-team debut against Notts County at Meadow Lane in October 1939. Jimmy Mullen played on the opposite wing, and Wolves won the wartime League match 2–1.

Then Billy's world came apart after four more games when both he and Mullen were told by Major Buckley that all groundstaff boys were being released. They were given jobs at a local tyre-manufacturing company, and a return to playing at Molineux seemed a forlorn hope when Wolves announced they would not be competing in the 1940–41 wartime League.

Now here's a question worth a place in trivia quizzes: In which colour shirt did Billy Wright win his first trophy? The answer is the blue of Leicester City. He and his close pal Mullen were recalled from labouring with tyres and loaned to Leicester as guest players throughout the 1940–41 season.

BILLY: Jimmy and I had the time of our lives at Leicester. Between us we scored 23 goals, fourteen of them coming from Jimmy who was like greased lightning on the left wing. I doubt if any youngster had a harder left foot shot. We reached the final of the

Midland War Cup and beat Walsall 2–0. Jimmy scored the first goal from my cross, and then he returned the compliment for me to score the second. We were presented with a miniature cup each, and felt like World Cup winners. Jimmy and I used to travel together three or four times a week to Leicester, catching the Midland Red to the Bull Ring, then to Leicester by way of Coventry. It's funny how the pair of us clicked, because we were sworn enemies for a time. Jimmy made a sarcastic remark about me in the dressing-room soon after I had joined the club. For once in my life I lost my rag and lashed out at him. I swung my left fist, my strongest hand, and it landed on his nose and sent blood spurting over his face. He reacted by throwing me across the dressing-room and my head was cut as I crashed against the wall. We both had to go and get first aid, and as we came out of the treatment room with plasters on us we broke out laughing, shook hands and became firm, lifelong friends. It's just as well the major was not around to see us having our little dust up, otherwise we would both have been on the carpet.

Wolves recalled both Billy and Jimmy when they returned to the Wartime League for the 1941–42 season, competing in the Southern section. Billy officially signed professional forms soon after his seventeenth birthday, and received the statutory £10 signing-on fee that he paid into his post-office account. He felt like a millionaire.

Major Buckley did not seem to know quite what to do with Billy. He was one of the fastest sprinters in the club, but he did not have the ball-dribbling skills traditionally shown by wingers. Although he was sprouting up, he was still too short for the role of centre-forward that required strength in the air and an animal aggression that was not in Billy's nature (although Jimmy Mullen might have disagreed). The major played him in all five forward positions, gave him a run at centre-half and then switched him to left-half.

BILLY: I did not have a clue which position I would be playing in from one game to the next. Then when the great Frank Broome joined the club as a guest player I was given a role that I found suited me best of all. The Major played me at right-half, supporting Frank on the right wing. He had played in four different forward positions for England in the two seasons immediately before the war, and I learned an enormous amount from him about support play and positioning. Frank felt like a grandfather in our team because most of the rest of us were in our teens, and the newspapers dubbed us Buckley's Babes. I remember a cartoon that showed us running out on to the pitch with baby's dummies in our mouths. Much later, I would be the father-figure for the Cullis Cubs!

With the Wright–Broome partnership working to perfection, Wolves won the 1941–42 League Cup. They beat Sunderland 6–3 on aggregate in the two-legged final, but Billy played no part in it. He hobbled off with a twisted right ankle in the second match of the semi-final against West Bromwich Albion, which Wolves won 4–0 to complete a 7–0 aggregate victory. An x-ray the next day revealed that the ankle was fractured.

There were fears that his career was over almost before it had started, and Mrs Colley reported that Major Buckley had tears in his eyes when he told her, out of Billy's hearing: 'That's it for the lad, I'm afraid. He was such an excellent prospect. Nobody plays again after breaking an ankle. It is the worst of all injuries.'

Tears from the major? Proof that the Ice Man had a heart.

A Wolverhampton surgeon called Ernest Freeman suggested what was then a revolutionary operation that involved putting a pin into the ankle. While researching Billy's early life, I tracked down the nurse who was on duty when he was brought in to the Queen Victoria nursing home in Bath Road, Wolverhampton. Mrs Gwen Edwards, now living in Shrewsbury, told me: 'I was just starting out on my nursing career and will never forget preparing Billy for the theatre. He was quite terrified, and I had to keep reassuring him that he could not be in better hands. Mr Freeman was a renowned surgeon, and was confident that the new technique would do the trick. I was with Billy when he came round in the recovery room, and he was very concerned about whether he would be able to play again. I sat and chatted with him, and managed to convince him he would soon be back playing for Wolves.'

The operation was a success and Major Buckley took a personal hand in getting Billy back to full fitness. Billy had lost the confidence to shoot with his right foot or to make a telling tackle. The no-nonsense Buckley method of recovery was to set up special training sessions in which Billy was instructed to kick the ball only with his right foot, and the club's most combative defenders were told to tackle him at every opportunity. In no time at all Billy was back to believing in himself and being a two-footed player, inspired by the major standing on the touchline barking: 'Right, Wright... right, Wright.'

Billy found himself on the receiving end of the major's blistering tongue when he was in the Wolves 'B' side that suffered a 6–1 defeat at Dewsbury, a result that enraged the major. On the morning after the setback, Buckley summoned the entire team to a meeting in the Molineux dressing-room.

BILLY: We were read the riot act, the major going almost purple with anger. 'Wright,' he said to me, 'do you go dancing?' I felt my face colouring, thinking he believed I was becoming something of a playboy. 'Never, sir,' I said. 'Don't sir me, boy!' he barked. 'It's major.' He then waltzed around the dressing-room, with the other lads not daring to laugh. 'You lack balance, laddie,' he said. 'Learn to dance. It will help your balance and also teach you to change step.' Then he turned on poor Jimmy Mullen. 'You, sonny,' he said, 'have got so big headed that your head would not fit into the wastepaper basket in my office. The fact that I picked you for an FA Cup semi-final does not mean you're the be all and end all. Come down to earth, or you'll be out on your ear.' I took the major's advice and learned how to dance, and I truly do believe that it helped make me better balanced.

In the summer of 1942 eighteen-year-old Billy was enlisted in the army, after requesting a place in the Royal Navy. He was assigned to the General Service Corps and was then switched to the Infantry Training Centre where he became a physical training instructor. He was based first of all in the Midlands and then in Aldershot, where he was listed as Corporal WA Wright, of the Shropshire Light Infantry. He became a regular in the Army side, with Frank Swift, Johnny Hancocks, Tommy Lawton and Jimmy Mullen among his team-mates. But his main attention was on getting soldiers fit for the looming invasion of Europe on D-Day 1944.

BILLY: We had an officer, Major Beecher-Stow, who knew AE Housman's 'A Shropshire Lad' by heart and he could bring us lads close to tears. 'From Clee to heaven the beacon burns,/ The shires have seen it plain,/ From north and south the sign returns/And the beacons burn again... That is the land of last content, I see it shining plain, The happy highways where I went/And cannot come again.' You can just imagine the effect that had on us Shropshire lads. There were times when I felt guilty that I was not involved in the thick of the war, but our commanding officer stressed to us that we physical training instructors were doing an invaluable job getting our fighting force fit for overseas duty. I used to say to the lads who came to me for fitness drills, 'You will leave me with Wolves fitness, and you cannot do better than that!'

There was undisguised resentment that footballers seemed to be given a soft ride during the war, but the fact that more than ninety professional players lost their lives in action is chilling evidence that this was a myth. Prime Minister Winston Churchill saw football as a morale-booster for Britain's war-weary public, and he actively encouraged its promotion by attending games at Wembley.

Billy's football was confined mostly to Army and Combined Services matches, with games fitted in for Wolves when he could get home on leave. In one visit back to Molineux he scored a hat-trick inside seventeen minutes against Nottingham Forest, and new manager Ted Vizard decided that his best position was inside-left. This was at a time when professional players were restricted to maximum appearance money of 30 shillings a game. All contracts had been cancelled within weeks of war being declared, and the suddenly freelance players grabbed games where and when they could in the regionalised leagues. Many of them made guest appearances for the clubs to which they were most closely stationed, and spectators would turn up not knowing who they were likely to see play. It could be somebody as illustrious as Tommy Lawton filling the number nine shirt or it could be Bill the local butcher.

Lawton, arguably the biggest box office draw at the time, epitomised the have-boots-will-travel attitude that players were forced to adopt. During the five years of the war he played for Everton, Tranmere, Aldershot and Chelsea. He also turned out for Morton while honeymooning in Scotland and appeared twice in a Christmas Day programme. He played for Everton in the morning, helping them to a 3–1 victory over Liverpool, and then scored twice for Tranmere in their 2–2 draw at Crewe in the afternoon. In all during this wartime period Lawton scored 212 goals, which put him third on the top marksman list behind Albert Stubbins (Newcastle, 226) and Jock Dodds (Blackpool, 221).

This prolific goal scoring never finds its way into official records, and Lawton is credited with 'only' 231 career League goals. Like so many of that generation, the peak years of his playing days were lost to the war. He represented England in 23 unofficial international matches, with only Joe Mercer (27) and Stanley Matthews (29) making more appearances.

Lawton was leading the attack when 21-year-old Billy was picked for his first Victory International for England against Belgium at Wembley on Saturday 19 January 1946. There is a perfect illustration in Billy's personal files of the master–servant attitudes of the time. The letter from FA secretary Stanley Rous, informing him that he had been selected, began, 'Dear Wright'; no mister, and certainly no Billy. For an earlier call-up in October 1945, Billy learned he had been 'selceted' (sic) as a travelling reserve for the England–Wales Victory International. The letter, reproduced in the first photo-album section, exposes the amateurishness of the Football Association of the time. It was typed, no doubt with two fingers, on a clapped-out typewriter. But Billy could not have cared less had it been written in pencil on the back of an envelope.

The players were allowed to charge third-class fares on their expenses. I travelled many miles going to the same international matches as Sir Stanley Rous, and I never knew him travel anything but first class.

Billy's match against the Belgians signalled his Wembley debut, and he arrived in his Army uniform, travelling on a soldier's travel warrant.

BILLY: I was due to partner Jimmy Mullen on the left wing against Belgium, but Frank Soo failed a late fitness test and I was switched to right-half. This meant I was playing a supporting role to the one and only Stanley Matthews. I was surprised when Stan told me that he wanted me to play the ball to his feet, not ahead of him. I concentrated on sending side-footed passes direct to him and he teased and tormented the Belgians with unbelievable dribbling runs, despite the fact that he had got out of a 'flu bed to play. We won 2–0, and it could easily have been 6/7–0. It was my first visit to Wembley and I remember being nearly sick with nerves before we left the dressing-room. That's how I felt before all major matches. It meant that I was really 'up' for the game. Our skipper Joe Mercer saw that I was white with nerves, and he took me for a walk out in the middle of the Wembley pitch. He mimed as if making a side-footed pass, and said, 'You will find this is like playing on a snooker table. Every ball runs true. It's the greatest pitch you'll ever play on. All you've got to do is give the ball to Stanley and leave the rest to him.' Joe really made me feel at ease, and I learned a lot from him about how to make team-mates relax and enjoy the challenge of international football. That's an important part of captaincy, making sure your team-mates feel right. Joe was a master at it. The oddest thing about that game against Belgium is that a fog dropped on to the ground in the second half, and visibility was down to just a few yards. It began to lift near the end of the game, and we found that half the 85,000 crowd had left. It was really eerie. My future Wolves clubmate Jesse Pye, who was then with Notts County, scored one of the two goals against the Belgians. At the after-match banquet, all the players were presented with cut-glass ashtrays as a memento. It seemed an odd choice of gift, because only a couple of the players smoked.

Billy had been promoted to Sergeant Wright by the time the last shots of the war were fired, and continued to serve in the Army while helping Wolves launch a stirring challenge for the League championship in the first full post-war season of 1946–47. It was also the season in which he started one of the most consistent international records in footballing history. He was about to become an England player for the remainder of his career.

THE WARTIME WINNERS

1939–40: South 'A' – Arsenal; South 'B' – Queen's Park Rangers
South 'C' Tottenham Hotspur; South 'D' – Crystal Palace
Western – Stoke City; South-Western – Plymouth Argyle
Midland – Wolverhampton Wanderers; East Midland – Chesterfield
North-West – Bury; North-East – Huddersfield Town.
1940–41: South – Crystal Palace; North – Preston North End.
1941–42: South – Leicester City; North – Blackpool; London League –
   Arsenal.
1942–43: South – Arsenal; North – Blackpool; West: – Lovells Athletic.
1943–44: South – Tottenham Hotspur; North – Blackpool; West – Lovells
   Athletic.
1944–45: South – Tottenham; North – Huddersfield Town; West – Cardiff
   City.
1945–46: South – Birmingham City; North – Sheffield United.

WAR LEAGUE CUP FINALS

1939–40: West Ham 1, Blackburn Rovers 0
1940–41: Preston 1, Arsenal 1 (Preston won the replay 2–1 at Ewood Park)
   Midland – Leicester City 2, Walsall 0
1941–42: Wolves (2) 4, Sunderland (2) 1 (Wolves won 6–3 on aggregate)
1942–43: South – Arsenal 7, Charlton 1
   North – Blackpool 2, Sheffield Wednesday 1 (replay)
   National final at Stamford Bridge: Blackpool 4, Arsenal 2

1943–44: South – Charlton 3, Chelsea 1

North – Aston Villa (1) 4, Blackpool (2) 2 (5–4 on aggregate)

Midland – West Bromwich 6, Nottingham Forest 5 (aggregate)

1944–45: South – Chelsea 2, Millwall 0

North – Bolton 3, Manchester United 2 (aggregate, 1–0 and 2–2)

National final at Stamford Bridge: Chelsea 1, Bolton 2

1945–46: FA Cup final at Wembley – Derby County 4, Charlton Athetic 1

(after extra-time, the rounds up to the final were on a two-leg basis)

Derby County: Woodley, Nicholas, Howe, Bullions, Leuty, Musson, Harrison, Carter, Stamps[2], Doherty[1], Duncan +1 own goal

Charlton Athletic: Bartram; Phipps, Shreeve; Turner H[1], Oakes, Johnson, Fell, Brown, Turner AA, Welsh, Duffy.

SEASON 1946–47:
First of the Caps

There is not a lot of flesh on the skeletal character that I have sketched so far of our hero. What was the young Billy Wright like, and how had his army experiences changed him? For the answers, I went to the man who knew him better than anybody else: the redoubtable Stan Cullis.

When I was commissioned to script Michael Aspel's *This Is Your Life* tribute to Billy in 1989, I journeyed to the Worcestershire retirement home of Cullis, who in Wolverhampton football folklore stands just as big a giant as Billy himself. I made the trip with some apprehension, because in my young reporting days I used to go in fear and trembling to interview 'Mr Cullis' in his oak-panelled office at Molineux.

He had the reputation for eating young reporters for breakfast, and in the early 1960s I found him an intimidating subject at a time when Wolves were, quite shamefully, plotting his removal. But nearly 30 years on the Cullis I found, seated and relaxed in his favourite armchair and looking out at a beautifully manicured garden, was mellowed almost beyond recognition. When I brought up the name of Billy Wright he beamed as a myriad of memories queued for attention. 'A lovely, lovely man,' was his instant appraisal.

'You were captain of Wolves when he first arrived at Molineux as a groundstaff boy in 1938,' I reminded him. 'What was the young Billy like?'

'He was as quiet as a church mouse and you wouldn't have known he was there if it had not been for his distinctive blond thatch,' Cullis

21

said, almost instinctively rubbing his own famous bald dome that had been as much a trademark as Billy's blond hair. 'We nicknamed him Snowy. He was just a shrimp of a lad, and it was no surprise to find Major Buckley had doubts about whether he would be big enough to make it as a professional footballer. The Major liked his footballers to have height and muscle.'

'What changed the Major's mind?'

'Our trainer Jack Davies told him that Billy might have a small frame but inside was a giant heart. That's all the Major wanted to hear. I could name you a hundred players who had more natural footballing talent than Billy, but not one who could match him for enthusiasm and endeavour. He didn't know how to give less than one hundred per cent. That's infectious you know, and it explains why he made such an outstanding captain.'

'What sort of person was Billy in those early days at Molineux?'

'I remember him as being cheerful, extremely polite, respectful, very shy, a great blusher and able to take the leg pulling from the senior players without going into a sulk. I would not describe him as one of the lads. He was always well behaved, and eager to learn.'

Cullis had been a magnificent centre-half for Wolves and England, and when he briefly resumed his career after the war Billy was a team-mate.

'What changes did you notice in Billy when he reported back to Molineux after the war?'

'The most obvious one,' said Cullis, 'was his size. The little shrimp had become a powerfully built young man, perhaps two or three inches shorter than he would have liked but still somebody who could have a strong physical presence on the pitch. He had also grown in confidence as a person, and all his work as a physical training instructor meant he was positively glowing with strength and good health. Like me, he did not touch alcohol or the dreaded weed, and was a wonderful advertisement for good living.'

The commentating poet John Arlott famously and accurately dubbed Cullis the 'Passionate Puritan'. He set standards of behaviour and discipline that he expected his players to match when he became the League's youngest manager at just 31. The 'Iron Chancellor', as he was known, would have come down like a ton of Black Country slate on a George Best or a Gazza in a long-gone era when Army-style discipline was part and parcel of a professional footballer's life. Billy was the chief Cullis disciple and always followed his code of conduct.

In a biography like this it helps with the writing and the sales if the central character has led at least part of his life on the wild side, and I speak as somebody who has written seventeen books in harness with the irrepressible Jimmy Greaves. But looking for warts on our hero Billy in his young playing days is like trying to drag up skeletons from the cupboard of Mother Theresa. One of his career-long journalist friends, John Graydon, summed him up perfectly as 'the Boy Scout' of football.

Billy really was the archetypal pint-of-milk-a-day man, rarely up later than 10.30 p.m. and usually keeping girls at arm's length right up until his late twenties. He used to go to local dances to practise what Major Buckley had preached, but it was strictly orange juice and departure before the last waltz. His clubmate and close pal Sammy Smyth confirms: 'Billy always left the Civic Hall dance in time to catch the last 10.30 bus home to his digs in Claregate.'

There were two girls he regularly dated before Joy captured his heart. The first was Alice Tudor, who lived within goal-kicking distance of Molineux in North Street. Billy met her through her brother, John, who was in the intelligence corps of the Coldstream Guards as an instructor. 'Billy and I used to meet in the sergeant's mess at Aldershot and would chat about all things Wolverhampton,' he told me. 'He was the most charming fellow you could wish to meet, and was completely dedicated to football and to physical fitness. He used to walk my sister home from school and they became very close until she joined the Navy as a Wren.'

Alice, who later married and emigrated with her husband to Australia, contacted me from Brisbane to tell me: 'Billy gave me the black and yellow ribbon from the FA Cup that Wolves won in 1949. I treasure the memories of having known him. He was a lovely young man.'

Maria Scott, a former dancer from High Wycombe, Bucks, provided the background of Billy's second serious romance: 'My late sister, Jane Gray, met Billy in the early 1950s when she was a dancer at the Latin

Quarter in London. They went steady for quite a while and were very fond of each other. She described him as being a true gentleman; sincere, sensitive, gentle, considerate and quite naive in a nice way. They were once at the cinema together holding hands when one of her false nails came off. Billy thought she was seriously hurt and wanted to take her to hospital! Their romance was over long before Billy met Joy Beverley when he obviously found the love of his life. Neither my sister nor I knew a thing about football, and Billy never used to boast about just how big a star he was. She always thought how lucky Joy was, and she was delighted that Billy had found such happiness.'

Before Maria came into his life, he used to occasionally walk girls home but his dedication to football stopped him getting too romantically involved. His idea of a wild night out was a trip to the pictures with his landlady Mrs Colley, and his hobby was – wait for it, a drum roll for effect – rug-making. He enjoyed playing dominoes, swimming in the local indoor pool, was a forceful batsman at cricket, a naturally gifted single-handicap golfer, and he did most things left handed despite attempts by his schoolteachers to make him orthodox. I will return to the rug-making later in the story.

Billy was always seeking self-improvement, and on the advice of Arthur Oakley, then a Wolves director and a vice-president of the Football League, he used to attend a daytime educational institute. He studied English and the basics of engineering in a bid to make up for all that he had missed by leaving school at fourteen. Mr Oakley was also an England selector, and it was he who first alerted his colleagues that Billy was worth close monitoring.

There was the rare beer and a few experimental puffs, but any time he had a glass or cigarette in his hand he had pangs of conscience. A creature of habit, he stayed with the same landlady, Mrs Colley, virtually throughout his playing career until marrying Joy at the age of 34. Mrs Colley's influence on him became stronger when his mother died of cancer in her early forties. Several girls who tried to get into Billy's life found the Colley doorstep the nearest they could get to him. She was as protective as a mother hen.

But Billy loved what he considered the security of the Colley home. He was eaten up with football, football, football, and – almost fanatically – followed the gospel according to Stan Cullis: 'Early to bed, early to rise ... get out there training and strengthen those thighs.'

Few players were more hurt by the war than Cullis. He had captained England and was at the very peak of his playing powers when it all came to an abrupt halt. There was evidence of what might have been in the unofficial wartime internationals when, along with Cliff Britton and Joe Mercer, he formed what was arguably England's finest ever half-back line. By the time he resumed his League career he was suffering the after-effects of a succession of concussions, but his greatest days were ahead of him as a manager who had few equals.

Now docile in retirement, he looked out of the window at the lawn as if it was the Molineux pitch on which he and his teams tasted such heady wine of success. 'I'm sorry,' he said, 'I know I'm not giving you the material you need. It would be better for your television programme if I could come up with some startling stories about Billy, but he was a model professional. What I can tell you is that Wolves and England had no greater servant. He gave one hundred and ten per cent.'

The great man's speech was just starting to slow, heralding the illness to which he would finally succumb at the age of 84 in February 2001. 'I am paying the price for all that heading of a muddy leather ball and physical wars with centre-forwards,' he said. 'But I would not change a thing. There was nothing to beat playing the game at the top level. I had a lot of success as a manager with Wolverhampton, but doing it out on the pitch was much more satisfying than planning it.'

Suddenly his eyes lit up as he plucked a memory from the cellar of his mind. 'I think I have a Billy Wright anecdote for you,' he said, almost in triumph. 'We had held Real Madrid to a 2–2 draw at the Bernabeu in 1957 when Real were the virtually unchallenged kings of Europe. There was an after-match banquet and I ordered the players to be on the team coach immediately afterwards, but half a dozen were missing when we returned to our hotel, including the captain. I confronted him at breakfast the next morning and demanded to know why they had missed the coach. 'We noticed there was a night club show in the hotel where the banquet was held,' he said, 'and decided on the spur of the moment to go and watch it.' Billy was braced for a volley from me, and I think you could say he was speechless when I replied, 'I'm really hurt that you didn't tell me because I would liked to have seen the show, too.'

He laughed out loud at the suddenly uncorked memory. Mr Cullis – I could never bring myself to call him Stan – in a night club? It was like trying to imagine the Archbishop of Canterbury in a Soho strip joint. This was the nearest he and I could get to evidence of Billy Wright the footballer misbehaving.

There was a parting shot from the old Master of Molineux. 'I knew Billy wouldn't make it as a manager,' he confided. 'He was far too nice. You need a ruthless streak and the skin of a rhinoceros. Billy liked to be liked, but you just cannot be a football manager and also popular with everybody. The players will eat you alive if you are too nice.'

So Billy *did* have warts. He was too nice. Hold the front page!

The Cullis contribution to Billy's *This Is Your Life* ended up as a 30-second tribute to camera, but he was so sincere with his comments that Billy could not stop tears welling in his eyes. 'I owe that man so much,' he told Michael Aspel. 'He was Mr Wolves.'

* * *

We now come to the main thrust of the book: the games that Billy played, starting with this first post-war season. Billy was the first footballer in the world to win 100 caps, and I took him through each of his 105 England games in the hope of unearthing memory pearls that were lying undiscovered. Like so many old footballers he could, when prompted, remember moments from each individual match as he replayed them on his memory screen.

CAP NO 1

Northern Ireland, Windsor Park, 28.9.46. England won 7–2
Swift   Scott   Hardwick*   Wright   Franklin   Cockburn
Finney[1]   Carter[1]   Lawton[1]   Mannion[3]   Langton[1]
* denotes captain

Highlights: Raich Carter scored in the first minute of what was a memorable match for Middlesbrough team-mates Wilf Mannion and George Hardwick. Mannion illuminated his debut with a hat-trick, and Hardwick was made skipper in his first official international. He was to make thirteen successive appearances for England, all as captain. There was a record Windsor Park crowd of 57,000 for this first home international match since 1939. England were 3–0 up at half-time. *The Wright Cuttings Book* (*The Times*): 'Wright had an absolutely flawless match, giving England drive and inspiration with his enthusiastic performance. He can look forward to a long international career.'

BILLY: All but Tommy Lawton and Raich Carter were making their England debuts. George Hardwick, with his Ronald Colman moustache, had the looks of a Hollywood film star. He was one of the most handsome footballers you could ever imagine, and he played the game with a poise that made him stand out in defence. We wondered whether we would get the game started because Windsor Park was full to the rafters and there were hundreds of spectators spilling on to the pitch. As police and stewards were shepherding them back on to the terraces, George was giving us a pep talk. 'The only way we'll shut up this crowd is with an early goal,' he said. He crossed the ball in the first minute and Raich Carter pounced to score. What a start! We ran them silly after that, with Tom Finney and Wilf Mannion just about untouchable. It could easily have been ten. Wilf became a good pal, and was on my *This Is Your Life* show more than forty years later. If it had not been for the war delaying his international career, he would have won at least double his 26 caps. He would be worth ten million pounds in the modern game.

This was England's first game under the stewardship of Walter Winterbottom, a former Manchester United centre-half and a university-educated intellectual whose depth of knowledge about the tactics and techniques of the game were unequalled. He was shackled and stifled by a team selection policy that put all the responsibility on his shoulders but most of the power in the hands of amateur selectors.

In the immediate post-war years the game was in the throttling grip of the barons of the Football League, the club chairmen who put club before country at every turn. Winterbottom was lucky if he got his players together a day before an international match, and often they would arrive just a few hours before the kick-off. It was nothing unusual for England team-mates to meet each other for the first time in the dressing-room shortly before going out to play. Winterbottom and Wright were to form an alliance that would last for more than ten years.

After his seven-goal bonanza start, there was a scare waiting for the new England boss in Dublin just two days later.

CAP NO 2
Republic of Ireland, Dalymount Park, 30.9.46. England won 1–0
Swift   Scott   Hardwick*   Wright   Franklin   Cockburn
Finney¹   Carter   Lawton   Mannion   Langton

Highlights: Tom Finney saved England's blushes with a scrambled winner eight minutes from the end as the light started to fade in this Monday evening match. It was England's first ever game against the Republic of Ireland. There was a persistent drizzle throughout the game, and conditions handicapped the ball-playing England inside-forwards. The O'Flanagan brothers – right-wing partners Dr Kevin and Michael – were outstanding for Ireland. Both were also Irish rugby internationals. Manchester City left-half Billy Walsh, playing for Ireland, had been capped by England as a schoolboy. The team was skippered by John Carey, who played for both Northern and Southern Ireland and who was to become an outstanding captain of Manchester United. *The Wright Cuttings Book* (*Daily Telegraph*): 'Wright will have better matches than this in an England shirt. He was the most authoritative of the England half-back line, but much of his work was wasted by forwards who struggled to find a way through a defiant Irish defence.'

BILLY: It's daft to make excuses at this distance, but we were honestly nobbled in the nicest possible way by the Irish. Their hospitality was unbelievable. You have to remember that we were living in an age of severe austerity in England, and to arrive in ration-free Dublin was for us like starving men being let loose at a banquet. I don't think food has ever tasted as good as the eight-course lunch that we were served in the luxurious Gresham Hotel. Yes, I did say eight-course. I remember I had a steak that was so big you could have used it to saddle a horse. It would have eaten up a week's rations allowance at home. We then enjoyed more hospitality at Government House, where we were each introduced to legendary Irish Prime Minister Eamon de Valera. By the time we played the game I think all of us had put on several pounds, and our performance was very sluggish. The Irish played some exceptional football and we were very, very lucky to get away with a win. I remember that trip more for the food than the football!

Billy was now into what were relatively affluent times. He was earning the maximum £10 a week in the season with Wolves, and £7 a week in the summer. This was supplemented by his £20 appearance fees for England. Minimum prices to stand on the terraces at First Division games had been raised to one shilling and sixpence (7.5p). The weekly wage for footballers was gradually (and grudgingly) increased season by season until in 1958–59 it was capped at £20 a week and £17 in the summer. Only in that final season did Billy earn a princely £20 a week, of which £3 went straight to the taxman. These were the days when players were handed their wages in a brown envelope. Imagine that today. Many Premiership players would need a sack!

Including average £4 win bonuses (£2 for a draw), Billy earned around £15,000 in thirteen years post-war League football with Wolves. Added to this were three loyalty benefit cheques, two for £750 and a final one of £1,000, plus an estimated £2,000 trophy-winning bonuses and a £1,500 Provident Fund payout on his retirement.

It was no secret that some clubs rewarded star players with back handers to keep them sweet, but there was none of that pocket-lining at Wolves. The chances of 'Honest Stan' Cullis giving under-the-counter payments was as likely as Roy Rogers having his white stetson knocked off in a fight. The nearest Billy got to a perk was a free haircut at his local barber's shop, and he had the occasional free suit in return for his picture in the tailor's window. He was about as commercially minded as the tailor's dummy.

The most Billy earned playing for England was £50, and his total income from all 105 internationals was less than £4,000. Yet Billy was better off than most of his colleagues, and during the course of his career collected around £10,000 from various sponsorship contracts and another £6,000 from publishing deals. His total earnings – repeat, *total* earnings – while skippering one of the most successful clubs in the land and captaining his country in 90 of 105 matches amounted to just over £40,000, and that includes the commercial extras. Several Premiership footballers today earn more than that in a week. I know everything is relative and that in 'old money' terms Billy didn't do badly, but let's remember it came from a thirteen-year post-war slog.

In this era of innocence, you could count football agents on the fingers of a one-armed bandit. Bagenal Harvey was a respected forerunner of what has now become a rash of 'players' representatives', and he started off with Denis Compton. He negotiated the famous 'Brylcreem' advertisement, for which 'Compo' received £1,000 a year; hardly a king's ransom but very tasty at a time when Billy was lending his name to commercial ventures for small one-off payments.

Douglas Cox, managing director of Purity Soft Drinks for more than 50 years, revealed that he arranged for Billy to endorse his products in the 1950s when he was captain of both Wolves and England. His name and image were printed on thousands of table coasters. 'Billy brought Mrs Colley along to negotiate with me,' Douglas told me. 'We agreed a fee of twenty pounds, of which I know Billy gave half to his landlady.'

Many people would have felt bitter at such poor returns. But there was not a bitter bone in Billy's body. 'I was never ever motivated by money,' he said. 'It sounds corny, but I would honestly have played for England for nothing. You could not beat the moment of pulling on the England shirt and leading the team out. For me, it was all about pride. I loved every second of it.'

I promise that this is the way that Billy talked. A tattoo of the three lions would not have looked out of place on his chest...along, of course, with a Molineux wolf.

The Home International championship was considered the most important tournament on the football calendar, and nearly 60,000 fans attended Maine Road on a windy Wednesday afternoon in October 1946 to watch England against Wales.

CAP NO 3
Wales, Maine Road, 13.10.46. England won 3–0
Swift   Scott   Hardwick*   Wright   Franklin   Cockburn
Finney   Carter   Lawton[1]   Mannion[2]   Langton

Highlights: 'Will-o'-the-wisp' Wilf Mannion scored two and laid on the pass for a Tommy Lawton goal against a Welsh defence in which Alf Sherwood was making his full international debut at right-back. Over the next ten years he missed only one match for Wales. Frank Swift, playing in goal on his home Manchester City ground, made half a dozen outstanding saves to break the hearts of the Welsh forwards. *The Wright Cuttings Book* (*Daily Mirror*): 'While it was the forwards who took the eye, let us not forget the spade work of Billy Wright. Conspicuous by his blond hair, he also stood out like a beacon with his tackling and neat distribution.'

BILLY: Most of the England matches then were staged at League club grounds. Floodlit football was a thing of the future and we played on midweek afternoons to avoid clashing with the Saturday fixtures. This was because clubs were not allowed to postpone matches if they had players on international duty. Questions were asked in the House about the effects this had on absenteeism from work, and it was noted that more grandmothers were allegedly buried on any day that England were playing a midweek international. We were nearly always in command against the Welsh, but when they did break through Frank Swift showed just why he was rated one of the world's great goalkeepers. Swiftie! What a player, and what a man. He had huge hands like shovels and often used to walk around the penalty area holding the ball with one hand as if it was a tennis ball. His reflexes were exceptionally quick for such a big man, and his positioning was just about perfect. They say all goalkeepers are crazy, and Frank certainly came into that category when he used to dive head first at the feet of oncoming forwards. He was the bravest of the brave, and had the full respect of not only his team-mates but also of opponents. Off the pitch he was as funny as a music-hall comedian, and he and Tommy Lawton had a great double act that used to keep the rest of the team in fits. I cried my heart out when Swiftie died in the Manchester United air crash at Munich. My tears were for all the United players who perished, and for my old pal Frank who was travelling as a journalist. I promise that when they made him they threw away the mould.

Sergeant Wright was able to give all his concentration to playing for Wolves and England following his release from the Army after four years. His proudest possession was a demob suit that was brown with chalk stripes. 'I really felt the business in that suit,' Billy told me. 'I had always been a sports jacket and slacks man, but after four years of wearing a khaki uniform it was a delight to feel individual again. Not that I was ever unhappy in the Army. I look back on those wartime years as among my best for companionship and achievement. I was just a boy when I went in and a man when I came out, a sergeant with three stripes on my sleeve. Quite honestly, I have to say that the Army was the making of me.'

Ted Vizard, the new Molineux manager who had made his name as a player with Bolton and Wales, took time to concede that right-half was the position from where Billy could have most influence on a match. Tom Galley, capped by England in 1937, was preferred in the number four shirt for most of the immediate post-war season in this line-up that will pluck nostalgia strings for golden oldie Wolves fans: Williams; McLean, Crook; Galley, Cullis (captain), Wright; Hancocks, Pye, Westcott, Forbes, Mullen.

Wolves started the season with a 6–1 home drubbing of Arsenal, and maintained a bold challenge for the title. Billy, meantime, was also becoming a permanent fixture in the England team.

CAP NO 4

Holland, Huddersfield, 27.11.46. England won 8–2
Swift Scott Hardwick* Wright Franklin Johnston
Finney[1] Carter[2] Lawton[4] Mannion[1] Langton

Highlights: Lawton scored four goals and might have had eight against a Dutch defence that had no answer to his all-round power. The selectors made their first change since Walter Winterbottom had taken over as manager, bringing in Blackpool skipper Harry Johnston for his England debut at left-half in place of Henry Cockburn. The Dutch held their own for the first 24 minutes on a rain-saturated pitch, but were then devastated by a six-goal storm in twenty minutes that included a Lawton hat-trick. During this spell, skipper George Hardwick missed from the penalty spot and Holland managed to pull a goal back to make it 6–1 at half-time. England took their foot off the accelerator in the second half before Raich Carter scored his second goal and Lawton his fourth. Outgunned Holland notched a late second consolation goal. Appalling weather restricted the Leeds Road attendance to 32,500. *The Wright Cuttings Book* (*Daily Express*): 'While this was a match that belongs to Lawton, Billy Wright also deserves to be singled out for a performance that was both gritty and glittering... gritty in the way he tackled the Dutch forwards, and glittering in his work as an auxiliary attacker.'

BILLY: Dutch FA President Karel Lotsy told Tommy Lawton after the game: 'You are the world's greatest centre-forward.' Anybody who saw his amazing performance will have agreed. In fairness, it should be pointed out that Holland were still finding their way as a football nation, and looked up to England as the Old Masters. They went home convinced we were still the kings. There had been nonstop rain leading up to the kick-off, and the pitch was reduced to a treacherous mud heap. It was difficult to stand, let alone run. I would have hated to have been trying to mark Tommy Lawton that day. Even a tank could not have stopped him. One odd thing I recall is that Draeger, the Dutch outside-right, wore a hairnet to keep the hair out of his eyes. You can just imagine the terrible stick he got from the Yorkshire spectators.

Away from the international arena, Billy had established himself as a powerhouse in midfield for Wolves. They ran neck-and-neck with Manchester United, Liverpool and Stoke City for the first post-war championship. United, who were playing their home matches at Maine

Road because of bomb damage to Old Trafford, were top of the table on 56 points after finishing their 42-game programme. Wolves, with an inferior goal average to United, also had 56 points and had one game left to play. That was a home match against Liverpool, who were lying in third place on 55 points. Stoke, with one game to come the following week, were also on 55 points in fourth.

To add to the drama, Stan Cullis announced before the kick-off to the vital match against Liverpool that this would be the final game of his illustrious career. He was hanging up his boots and taking a coaching job at Molineux.

BILLY: We desperately wanted to win the match and the title for Stan. He had been such a great servant to the club, and I am sure that only the war stopped him winning a stack of medals. But Liverpool, with Billy Liddell in blinding form, beat us 2–1 to leapfrog to the top of the table. Stoke could still have won the title because they had a better goal average than Liverpool. They went down 3–0 against Sheffield United at Bramall Lane, so the championship finished up at Anfield. We finished third, and my share of the merit bonus was £10, which went into the first bank account that I had opened. I now had my own chequebook, and felt like a millionaire!

The biggest match of any season in the immediate post-war years was the annual England–Scotland fixture. A crowd of 98,250 gathered for this first post-war international at Wembley. Victory or a draw would give England the Home Championship.

CAP NO 5
Scotland, Wembley Stadium, 12.4.47. Drew 1–1
Swift   Scott   Hardwick*   Wright   Franklin   Johnston
Matthews   Carter[1]   Lawton   Mannion   Mullen

Highlights: Scotland were the superior side in the first half and deserved their 1–0 half-time lead from a goal by Preston inside-right Andy McLaren. England equalised in the 56th minute when Raich Carter finished off a sweeping movement involving Tommy Lawton and Wilf

Mannion. With the score deadlocked at 1–1, Carter was racing unchallenged towards the Scottish goal in the dying moments when he heard a whistle and pulled up. The whistle had come from the crowd. Jimmy Mullen made his debut on the left wing, and Stanley Matthews was preferred to Tom Finney on the right wing. It was Stanley's eighteenth peacetime international appearance and his first since before the war. *The Wright Cuttings Book (News of the World)*: 'Billy Wright was quietly assertive at right-half alongside Neil Franklin, who was his usual tower of strength. Wright and Franklin are developing into the Britton and Cullis of peacetime football. There can be no higher praise.'

BILLY: This match saw the start of the Matthews-or-Finney controversy that lasted throughout their careers. The selectors never seemed quite sure which to pick. They were both exceptionally gifted players, but it was considered it would be too much of a luxury to play them both. It started long arguments between fans, whipped up by newspapers, as to which of them should wear the number seven shirt. I always thought it would have made most sense to play them both, but in those days only the selectors decided the line-up. As a mere player, you were expected to keep out of it. In all my years playing for England, there were only a handful of times when the selectors asked my opinion on the little matter of which players should be in the side. It was an era when you spoke only when spoken to. The selectors meant well, but they should have let Walter get on with managing the team without interference. Walter was allowed an opinion at selection meetings, but would often be asked to leave the room when the final team was picked. It was a crazy way to run the national team.

CAP NO 6
France, Highbury, 3.5.47. England won 3–0
Swift   Scott   Hardwick*   Wright   Franklin   Lowe
Finney¹   Carter¹   Lawton   Mannion¹   Langton

Highlights: The selectors continued to dither over whether to play Matthews or Finney. The Preston plumber got the nod this time, making his mark with the first goal in a 3–0 canter against a French team whistled and jeered for their shirt-pulling and spoiling tactics. Wilf Mannion scored the second goal with a delightful lob over French goalkeeper Da Rui, who had kept a blank sheet in the first half with a series of spectacular and unconventional saves. Eddie Lowe, making his debut at left-half, sent three defenders the wrong way with an outrageous dummy before passing the ball into the path of Raich Carter, who coolly slotted home England's third goal. *The Wright Cuttings Book (London Evening News)*: 'Wright was at the heart of most England attacks, delivering the ball with simple but productive passes. He was free to help the forwards because there was not much coming in the way of attacking football from the temperamental Frenchmen.'

BILLY: Playing at Highbury was something I always looked forward to, and to walk out on to the Highbury pitch in an England shirt was beyond my wildest dreams. They had the best facilities in the League at the time. I had been a long-distance supporter of the great Herbert Chapman sides in my schoolboy days. In fact the first game of professional football I ever saw was Arsenal against Wolves at Molineux when I was eleven. My father was a very good club footballer and supported Aston Villa, but he took me to Molineux as a special treat. To this day I can recall the thrill of it all, and seeing Cliff 'Boy' Bastin smashing a 35-yard drive against a post in a game that finished drawn. I remember standing in the Marble Halls with Arsenal full-back Laurie Scott before the game against France and looking at the bust of Chapman. 'You can feel the history in the place,' I said to Laurie. 'Yes,' he said, 'and when you play for Arsenal you can feel the history on your back. The supporters have been spoiled by the Chapman years and expect a trophy every season.' Little did I know that one day I would manage Arsenal and would find out exactly what Laurie meant.

Who won what in 1946–47

First Division: Liverpool, 57pts. Runners-up: Manchester United, 56pts.

Liverpool record: P42 W25 D7 L10 F84 A52 Pts57

Liverpool squad: Sidlow, Lambert, Spicer, Taylor, Hughes, Jones (Paisley), (from) Priday, Balmer, Stubbins, Fagan*, Liddell, Done. Top scorers: Balmer (24) and Stubbins (24). Manager: George Kay.

Second Division: Manchester City, 62pts. Runners-up: Burnley, 58pts.

Third Division (South): Cardiff City, 66pts. Runners-up: QPR, 57pts.

Third Division (North): Doncaster Rovers, 72pts. Runners-up: Rotherham United, 64pts.

FA Cup final: Charlton Athletic 1, Burnley 0 (after extra-time).

Charlton: Bartram: Croker, Shreeve; Johnson, Phipps, Whittaker; Hurst, Dawson, Robinson, Welsh, Duffy[1].

Burnley: Strong; Woodruff, Mather; Attwell, Brown, Bray; Chew, Morris, Harrison, Potts, Kippax.

Top First Division marksman: Dennis Westcott (Wolves), 38 goals*.

Scottish champions: Rangers, 46pts. Runners-up: Hibernian, 44pts.

Scottish Cup final: Aberdeen 2, Hibernian 1

Several record books credit Westcott with 37 goals, but good detective work by Express & Star *Sports Editor Steve Gordos uncovered that a goal originally marked down to Jimmy Mullen was in fact touched into the net by Westcott. This remains the Wolves individual goalscoring record for a season.*

SEASON 1947–48:
The Winterbottom Factor

It is impossible to paint an accurate picture of the footballing life and times of Billy Wright without positioning prominently in the foreground the donnish figure of Walter Winterbottom. Billy was an extension of Walter out on the pitch, carrying his orders and encouraging his team-mates to put into practice all the things that the England manager preached. Writing about Walter becomes particularly poignant and pertinent because as I prepare this biography for the publisher the sad news has just broken of his passing on at the age of 89. He had talked so warmly to me about Billy when I first started laying the foundations for the book, and his departure is yet another break with a footballing past that is quickly vanishing from sight.

Winterbottom and Wright were about as alike as grass and granite. Billy, though quietly intelligent, was hardly an academic after leaving school at fourteen, and he would have worked in an iron foundry if it had not been for football. Walter, educated at Oldham Grammar School and then Chester College, combined a teaching job with playing football as an amateur for Royston and Mossley. In 1934 he signed professional for Manchester United, a playing career cut short by a spinal injury.

He became a college lecturer, and then, on the outbreak of war, Walter qualified as a wing commander in the RAF and was seconded to the Air Ministry where he was appointed head of physical training. He resumed his playing career as a guest for Chelsea and was twice called up as an England reserve for wartime international matches, understudying master centre-half Stan Cullis.

Walter had arranged to return to teaching after the war when he got a call from Football Association secretary Sir Stanley Rous inviting him to take over as the supremo of English football, responsible for the development of the game at all levels. He was just 33.

In the first half of his sixteen-year reign as England's first full-time manager Walter was given access to arguably the greatest English footballers of all time. As well as our hero for all seasons Billy Wright, the names of the prominent players of that era echo like a roll call of footballing gods: Stanley Matthews, Tom Finney, Tommy Lawton, Raich Carter, Len Shackleton, Wilf Mannion, Nat Lofthouse, Stan Mortensen, Jackie Milburn, Frank Swift, and a poised and purposeful right-back called Alf Ramsey.

With players of that quality to call on, England should have cemented their traditionally held reputation as the masters of world football. It is an indictment of the overall system rather than Winterbottom's management that even with all this talent on tap English international football went into a decline.

Despite the stature of his job, the bespectacled, scholarly-looking Winterbottom managed to keep a low public profile. The only time he used to make it into the headlines was when the football writers lined up like a firing squad following any defeat. It was a standing joke in Fleet Street that the sports desks of the national newspapers had *'Winterbottom Must Go'* headlines set up for every match. He would shrug off the searing criticism and get on with his job as if nothing had been said, and he would greet the journalists who had been sniping at him with friendly courtesy. Walter, like Billy, was a true gentleman.

His influence on post-war English football is greater than almost anybody's, yet to the man in the street (and on the terraces) he was a little-known figure. It was as a coach that he made his most telling contribution, combining the role of England manager with that of what he saw as the more important job of the Football Association's Director of Coaching. In fact it was made clear to him right from the off that he was the FA coach first and England manager second. The forward-looking Sir Stanley Rous said: 'Most of the FA councillors did not want a national team manager, but I persuaded them to, rather reluctantly, appoint one. They gave Walter the responsibility, but saw to it that they retained the power. Anybody assessing what Walter achieved for English football must think of him first and foremost as a coach and an organiser *extraordinaire.*'

Winterbottom was the 'Father' of English coaching. He set up a nationwide network of FA coaching schools, and among his many disciples you will find outstanding coaches such as Ron Greenwood, Bill Nicholson, Bobby Robson, Dave Sexton, Malcolm Allison, Don Howe and a young bearded Fulham forward called Jimmy Hill. Billy Wright was another regular at his 'coaching for the coaches' sessions.

Sir Stanley, who later became the all-powerful president of the world-governing body, FIFA, had been impressed by Winterbottom when they met on an experimental coaching course that the visionary Rous had set up in 1937. They formed a strong alliance that had a wide-ranging impact on post-war English football.

Winterbottom, knighted for his services to sport in his 1970s role as chairman of the Central Council for Physical Recreation, was handcuffed throughout his sixteen-year reign as England manager by amateur selectors, most of whom had vested interest in their selections because of their allegiance to various League clubs and local associations. 'When I first took the job,' he told me, 'each selector would arrive at our meetings with his personal list of who should play. We used to discuss and discuss until we were down to, say, two goalkeepers and then a straight vote would decide. Then on to the next position, and so on through the team. Before they made their final decision I would be asked to leave the room while they deliberated. I would be called back in and told the line-up. It was asking almost the impossible to get the right blend with this way of selecting a team. At least in the later years I was able to present my team and then let them try to argue me out of it. The trick of it was to stick to the men who were most important, and to make concessions to the committee where it didn't matter so much.'

While gathering material for Billy's *This Is Your Life* tribute, I asked Sir Walter for his assessment of the man he selected as captain 90 times. 'Well,' he said, 'for a start let me say that I considered myself fortunate to have Billy to call on so often. He had a heart of oak, and was the most reliable of men. He filled the players around him with confidence and enthusiasm. Billy was a good listener and could take on board tactical plans, and then help to put them into operation out on the pitch. You could count his below-par performances in one hundred and five international matches on the fingers of one hand. He was an authoritative right-half and then, because his country needed him, he moulded himself into an exceptional centre-half. English football has not had a better servant.'

During the summer of 1947, Walter took his squad on a European tour that touched the dismal depths and dizzy heights of football emotions. It started with England's first defeat under the Winterbottom banner.

CAP NO 7

Switzerland, Zurich, 18.5.47. England lost 1–0
Swift   Scott   Hardwick*   Wright   Franklin   Lowe
Matthews   Carter   Lawton   Mannion   Langton

Highlights: England's famed and feared attack ran into a Swiss wall defence known as 'The Redoubt'. Switzerland introduced the deep-lying centre-forward tactic that completely baffled England's defenders. Left-winger Jacques Fatton scored the only goal in the 27th minute. Tommy Lawton celebrated what he thought was a second-half equaliser, but the referee ruled it offside. Once the Swiss were in front, they stifled England with a mass defence that was both disciplined and rock solid. It was 33-year-old Raich Carter's final match for England after an international career that stretched back to 1934. *The Wright Cuttings Book (Daily Mail)*: 'Even Billy Wright, that most consistent of players, was caught up in the web of complacency that wrapped itself around England. Like his team-mates, he seemed to think this was going to be easy, but the Swiss were like clockwork and time was up for England.'

BILLY: The small ground was so packed that they put seats alongside the touchline to cater for an overflow of spectators. This meant it was so cramped on the wings that we could not play to the strength of Stanley Matthews and Bobby Langton. What really threw us was the Swiss ploy of dropping their number nine back into the midfield, and it took us much of the first half working out just which players each of us should be marking. It was a sad way for Raich Carter to end his wonderful run as an England player. He was the finest positional player I ever saw, and always knew exactly where to be to get the best out of any situation. He could pass with great precision and had an accurate shot. In short, Raich was the perfect inside-forward.

The defeat by Switzerland panicked the selectors into at last agreeing that they should play their two aces, Matthews and Finney, in the same attack against Portugal in Lisbon a week later. The effect was sensational.

CAP NO 8
Portugal, Lisbon, 25.5.47. England won 10–0.
Swift   Scott   Hardwick*   Wright   Franklin   Lowe
Matthews¹   Mortensen⁴   Lawton⁴   Mannion   Finney¹

Highlights: England paralysed Portugal with two goals inside the first two minutes through debutant Stan Mortensen and Tommy Lawton. Matthews and Finney ran down the wings as if they owned them, and the Portuguese defence just caved in under the nonstop pressure. England were 5–0 up at half-time and then repeated the dose in the second half after Portugal had substituted their goalkeeper, who went off in tears. Morty and Lawton scored four goals each, and Matthews and Finney got on the scoresheet. Wilf Mannion was the only forward who did not score, but his passes were an important part of the goals banquet. *The Wright Cuttings Book* (*The Times*): 'Billy Wright had nothing to do in a defensive capacity, and just concentrated on keeping the forwards supplied with neat, telling passes.'

BILLY: I can honestly say that this was the closest thing I ever saw to perfection on the football field. Everything we tried came off, and Portugal just didn't know what had hit them. There was a dispute before the game over which ball should be used. Walter demanded the usual full-size ball that was common to most international matches, but the Portuguese coach wanted a size-four ball, the type used in our schoolboy football. The referee ordered that we should play with the full-size ball, and we had it in the back of their net within twenty seconds of the kick-off. It seemed to take the goalkeeper an age to retrieve the ball, and he was fiddling around on his knees appearing to be trying to disentangle it from the corner of the netting. We were in possession within seconds of the restart and realised the goalkeeper had switched the ball for the smaller one, and a minute later he was also fishing that out of the back of the net! I doubt if there has ever been a more astonishing debut than Stanley Mortensen's. A goal inside the first minute and four in all! Incredible. Stan was a real miracle man. Only two years earlier he had been dragged unconscious from a crashed bomber that he had been piloting, and had head injuries that threatened to end his life, let alone his football career. He and his Blackpool team-mate Stanley Matthews were magical together. This was the match in which Tommy Lawton jokingly complained to Stanley Matthews that the lace was facing the wrong way when he centred it.

Billy returned from the tour to be told by manager Ted Vizard that he had been appointed Wolves skipper in succession to Stan Cullis, who was now assistant manager at Molineux. Billy's first game as captain was a home First Division match against Manchester City, skippered by Frank Swift. Wolves lost 4–3 in a game that Billy recalled as one of the most exciting in which he ever played. 'I was completely shattered at the end of it, and it was only when Stan Cullis pulled me to one side that I realised why,' Billy said. 'I had been so determined to impress as captain that I raced everywhere and hardly stopped for a breather. Stan quietly told me that I should play my normal game, and inspire my team-mates by example and not by running myself into the ground.'

Football crowds had never been so vast as in this second full season after the war. The total attendance for all League games topped 40 million for the first time. That's a little matter of around 14 million more than watch the fat-cat new millennium footballers. Newcastle, for example, averaged a remarkable 56,000 on their way up from the Second Division. The Professional Footballers' Association seized on the increase in gate receipts to negotiate a rise for their members. Billy Wright in the First Division and Tommy Lawton, sold by Chelsea to Notts County in the Third Division South for a record £20,000, would now be able to earn £12 a week in the season and £10 in the summer.

CAP NO 9
Belgium, Brussels, 21.9.47. England won 5–2
Swift   Scott   Hardwick*   Ward   Franklin   Wright
Matthews   Mortensen[1]   Lawton[2]   Mannion   Finney[2]

Highlights: Many observers considered this the finest match Stanley Matthews ever played for England. The 'Wizard of Dribble' laid on all five goals and at the final whistle got a standing ovation from the Belgian crowd. Stanley started the slaughter after just 35 seconds when he centred for Tommy Lawton to score with one of his typical headers. It was raining cats and dogs and goals as England raced 3–0 clear before the Belgians pulled one back just before half-time. Belgium began to get a grip on the game as the sun came out in the second half, and they made it 3–2 before Matthews took over again, laying on decisive goals for first Tom Finney and – finishing as he had started – crossing the ball for Lawton to head his second goal and England's fifth. Derby County right-half Tim Ward made his debut, with Billy playing in the number six shirt. *The Wright Cuttings Book* (*Daily Mirror*): 'How lucky England are to have such a versatile half-back as Billy Wright. He was switched to the left side of the field to let in Tim Ward for his debut, and he was just as vigilant, just as vigorous and just as victorious as when wearing the No 4 shirt. He was the perfect partner on the left for the tantalising Tom Finney.'

BILLY: We played at the Heysel Stadium, the scene of the tragic crowd disaster during the 1985 European Cup final between Liverpool and Juventus. The ground had been used as a park for German tanks during the war and the pitch had been relaid. It started to cut up in the downpour. The Belgian defenders were slipping and sliding all over the place as Stanley ran rings round them. It was an astonishing performance by the Maestro. Five Belgians tried to get the ball off him when he set up the fourth goal. He beat each one of them, then dribbled round another for a second time before passing to Tom Finney, who had the simple task of placing the ball into the net for his second goal that had Matthews written all over it. I saw many outstanding displays by Stanley, but nothing to top this.

CAP NO 10

Wales, Ninian Park, 18.10.47. England won 3–0
Swift   Scott   Hardwick*   Taylor   Franklin   Wright
Matthews   Mortensen¹   Lawton¹   Mannion   Finney¹

Highlights: Stanley Matthews continued where he had left off against Belgium in this first Home Championship match of the 1947–48 season. Wales brought in Arsenal's redoubtable defender Walley Barnes for his debut, and gave him the thankless task of marking Matthews. 'Stanley ran me dizzy,' admitted Barnes, who later became captain of Wales. England were 3–0 up inside the first fifteen minutes, with Matthews running riot on the right wing. Liverpool right-half Phil Taylor came in for his debut as the England selectors continued to fiddle with the line-up. *The Wright Cuttings Book* (*Daily Herald*): 'Billy Wright fits so comfortably into the No 6 shirt that it might have been tailored for him in one of those swanky hand-made places in Mayfair.'

BILLY: We might have won more convincingly but for both Laurie Scott and Stan Mortensen pulling muscles. This was in the days before substitutes, and so we had two players hobbling through the second half and we had to close the game down. Walley Barnes was a close friend of mine, and he always described that game as one of the most painful yet memorable of his career. He told me that it was almost an honour to be so humiliated by one of the greatest players ever to step foot on a pitch. Walley said that the only time he got close to Stanley was to shake his hand at the final whistle, and even then he expected a dummy!

CAP NO 11
Northern Ireland, Goodison Park, 5.11.47. Drew 2–2
Swift   Scott   Hardwick*   Taylor   Franklin   Wright
Matthews   Mortensen   Lawton[1]   Mannion[1]   Finney

Highlights: Three goals came in the last eight minutes after Northern Ireland had battled to hang on to a 54th-minute lead given to them by West Bromwich Albion centre-forward Davie Walsh. 'Peter the Great' Doherty headed a last-minute equaliser for the Irish following goals in quick succession for England by Wilf Mannion and Tommy Lawton. Mannion had a penalty saved in the 70th minute by Fulham goalkeeper Eddie Hinton. The roar that greeted the save from the predominantly Irish crowd could have been heard back in Belfast. It was the first time in thirteen meetings with England that the Irish had avoided defeat, and the game had a suitably explosive finish for Guy Fawkes Day. *The Wright Cuttings Book* (*News Chronicle*): 'Perhaps the time has come to switch Billy Wright back to the right side of the field. It is clear that Stanley Matthews is not as effective without the steady stream of simple passes that have become a Wright hallmark both for club and country. There are no Fancy Dan frills from Wright. He plays it straight, and the team benefits. The selectors should consider returning him to the right-half position to bring the best out of Matthews.'

> BILLY: It would have been an injustice had Northern Ireland not got a draw from this game. They were often the superior side, with Peter Doherty pulling the strings and playing with the skill that made him one of the world's outstanding inside-forwards. He was carried off at the end by jubilant Irish supporters, who counted this as a victory. There were 68,000 shoehorned into the Goodison ground, and most of them seemed to be shouting for the Irish who must have felt it was like a home game.

CAP NO 12
Sweden, Highbury, 19.11.47. England won 4–2
Swift   Scott   Hardwick*   Taylor   Franklin   Wright
Finney   Mortensen[3]   Lawton[1]   Mannion   Langton

Highlights: Sweden, including the famous Nordahl brothers – Gunnar, Bertil and Knut – pulled back to 3–2 after England had powered into a three-goal lead. Stan Mortensen settled it with a classic goal to complete his hat-trick, beating three defenders in a run from the halfway line before firing in an unstoppable twenty-yard shot. The game was billed as being for the unofficial championship of Europe at a time when the Swedes, coached by former Bury winger George Raynor, were rated one of the world's leading football nations. *The Wright Cuttings Book* (*Express & Star, Wolverhampton*): 'Billy Wright grows in stature with every England appearance. His performance against Sweden was, as ever, solid and reliable. He is one of the few players who always manages to produce his excellent club form at international level. He would be even more effective if the selectors would pick his Wolves clubmate Jimmy Mullen to play in front of him.'

BILLY: Stan Mortensen was in magnificent form and might have had four goals had he not been upended in the penalty area when shaping to shoot in the first half. After our bad recent record from spot-kicks, Tommy Lawton volunteered to take it and scored England's first goal from a penalty since the war. The newspapers ran a story before the match that the Swedes were on a course of pep pills. Their coach George Raynor later confided that they were just sugar-based pills, but that they had a great psychological effect on his players. I think he may have stolen the idea from Major Buckley! Most of the Swedes were amateurs, and that following summer they won the Olympic final in London with some delightful football. Gunnar Nordahl was an exceptional centre-forward, who along with Nils Liedholm later starred with AC Milan.

CAP NO 13
Scotland, Hampden Park, 10.4.48. England won 2–0
Swift   Scott   Hardwick*   Wright   Franklin   Cockburn
Matthews   Mortensen[1]   Lawton   Pearson   Finney[1]

Highlights: Tom Finney and Stan Mortensen scored a goal each in a roughhouse of a match. Goalkeeper Frank Swift insisted on playing on after being knocked out in a collision with 'Flying Scot' Billy Liddell. A crowd of 135,376 saw England clinch the Home Championship, despite having skipper George Hardwick limping on the wing with a knee injury that was to finish his international career. Finney gave England the lead a minute before half-time at the end of a four-man passing movement that started in their own goal area. Lifted by the famous Hampden Roar, Scotland dominated play early in the second half, but a 64th-minute goal from Mortensen after he had combined with Lawton knocked the fight out of the Scots. *The Wright Cuttings Book* (*Sunday Pictorial*): 'The Great Interceptor Billy Wright was at his best after being returned to his favourite No 4 shirt. There is nobody in his class for making a quick, clean tackle and then releasing the ball to a team-mate, usually Stanley Matthews. It was Wright's ability to read situations quickly and then act that gave England supremacy over the Scots in a humdinger of a midfield battle.'

BILLY: Frank Swift later collapsed on the railway platform at Manchester and was wheeled off on a porter's trolley for an examination which revealed that he had two broken ribs. The Scots kicked everything that moved, and often it wasn't the ball! Stan Pearson, the Manchester United inside-forward, was making his debut and said afterwards that he was shocked by the viciousness of the tackling because he had always thought international football was gentlemanly compared with club football. It was one of the toughest internationals in which I played. My job was to mark Billy Steel, the brilliant Derby County inside-forward. This meant I had to really be on my toes because Billy could turn a half-chance into a goal in the blink of an eye. He was a smashing player, and very difficult to keep under lock and key. I remember him getting the better of me once with a wonderful bit of skill and I was relieved to see Laurie Scott clear his shot off the line. I think we were all pleased to get off the pitch in one piece! Our dressing-room afterwards was like a casualty clearing station, and it was obvious that both our skipper George Hardwick and big Swiftie were in trouble with their injuries. For poor George, it was the end of his England career. He had been a magnificent right-back and an inspiring captain.

Two weeks later, four of the players from the England team that beat Scotland featured in one of the greatest of all FA Cup finals at Wembley. Manchester United, including Pearson and Cockburn, came from 2–1 down at half-time to beat Blackpool (Matthews and Mortensen) 4–2. United skipper John Carey gave the famous half-time instruction: 'Just keep playing football.' Morty netted for Blackpool to complete the record of scoring in every single round.

United finished runners-up in the League for a second successive year, this time seven points adrift of an Arsenal team captained by Joe Mercer. When United and Arsenal met at Maine Road on 10 January 1948 they attracted an all-time record League attendance of 83,260.

Wolves, under Billy's driving captaincy, finished fifth in the table. There was a buzz of excitement at Molineux at the end of the season when it was announced that manager Ted Vizard had resigned and that his replacement would be 31-year-old Stan Cullis. The Wolverhampton Wanderers Golden Age was about to begin.

Frank Swift recovered from his rib injury in time to become the first goalkeeper to captain England, taking over from the unfortunate George Hardwick. His first match as skipper was against the two-times world champions Italy.

CAP NO 14

Italy, Turin, 16.5.48. England won 4–0

Swift*   Scott   Howe J   Wright   Franklin   Cockburn
Matthews   Mortensen[1]   Lawton[1]   Mannion   Finney[2]

Highlights: Italy were stunned in the fourth minute when Stan Mortensen sprinted 40 yards down the right wing before cutting in and scoring with a screaming shot from an acute angle. Following a series of stunning saves by skipper Frank Swift, Morty laid on a second goal for Tommy Lawton, and two individual goals from Tom Finney finished off the Italians late in the second half. Derby County defender Jack Howe, making his debut at left-back, was the first to play for England while wearing contact lenses. There were tears among the shirt-sleeved 58,000 spectators in Turin's Stadio Communale as the Old Masters conquered the side that had won the World Cup in 1934 and again in 1938. *The Wright Cuttings Book* (*Daily Mail*): 'England function so much better with Wright playing at right-half. He links so well with Stanley Matthews, who feeds off his passes that are always so accurately and intelligently placed... At the peak of Italy's attempted revival in the first half, it was Wright and Franklin together who did most to repel the wave upon wave of Italian attacks, with Swift always alert behind them as a magnificent last line of defence.'

BILLY: That was one of the most satisfying victories in all my time with England, but I have to be honest and say we were flattered by the victory margin. For about twenty minutes in the first half Swiftie was virtually playing them on his own. I think he was so proud of being made captain that he was going to refuse to let anybody put the ball past him and spoil his big day. He saved at least half a dozen times when a goal seemed certain. The Italian team included six of the gifted Torino team that was tragically killed in an air crash a year later. Among the victims was skipper Valentino Mazzola, whose two sons later went on to play for Italy. It's chilling to think that both captains in the match against Italy, Frank Swift and Mazzola, were later to die in air crashes.

Who won what in 1947–48

First Division: Arsenal, 59pts. Runners-up: Manchester United, 52pts.

Arsenal record: P42 W23 D13 L6 F81 A32 Pts59

Arsenal squad: Swindin; Scott, Barnes; Macaulay, Compton L, Mercer*; Roper, Logie, Rooke, Lewis, McPherson, Compton D. Top scorer: Ronnie Rooke (33). Manager: Tom Whittaker.

Second Division: Birmingham City, 59pts. Runners-up: Newcastle United, 56pts.

Third Division (South): QPR, 61pts. Runners-up: Bournemouth, 57pts.

Third Division (North): Lincoln City, 60pts. Runners-up: Rotherham United, 59pts.

FA Cup final: Manchester United 4, Blackpool 2

Manchester United: Crompton, Carey*, Aston, Anderson[1], Chilton, Cockburn; Delaney, Morris, Rowley[2], Pearson[1], Mitten.

Blackpool: Robinson; Shimwell[1] (pen), Crosland; Johnston, Hayward, Kelly; Matthews, Munro, Mortensen[1], Dick, Rickett.

Top First Division marksman: Ronnie Rooke (Arsenal), 33 goals.

Footballer of the Year: Stanley Matthews (Blackpool), the winner of the inaugural award presented by the Football Writers' Association.

Scottish champions: Hibernian, 48pts. Runners-up: Rangers, 46pts.

Scottish Cup final: Rangers 1, Morton 0 (after a 1–1 draw).

SEASON 1948–49:
Captain of England

When, I wonder, did David Beckham last travel on public transport to get to and from Old Trafford? Our hero Billy Wright was sitting on the Wolverhampton to Claregate bus when he found out that he was to be the new captain of England.

It was 28 September 1948, and Billy was on his way to his digs in Tettenhall after playing for England in Denmark. He climbed on board the bus with his holdall in one hand and a huge Danish ham in the other.

BILLY: I had just settled down in my seat when the bus conductress came alongside me and said, 'Congratulations, Billy! What an honour to captain your country.' I looked at her blankly. She waved the *Wolverhampton Express & Star* at me, and there in the stop press it was reported that I had been named the England captain for the international against Northern Ireland in Belfast. I was so shocked that when I got off the bus at Tettenhall I forgot my ham. The conductress, a Helen Mearden, spotted it and called me back. You could say that I had come home with the bacon.

Frank Swift had been captain for a second time in the match against Denmark in Copenhagen, and after long discussions with Walter Winterbottom was honest enough to admit that the goal line was not the ideal position from which to lead a team. 'I had no hesitation in nominating Billy to the selectors as the man who should take over as captain,' Sir Walter told me. 'He had proved with Wolves that he was a natural leader, and he was now sufficiently experienced at international level to feel comfortable with the added responsibility. Another key factor was that he was positioned in midfield from where he could take a wide-ranging view of the match, and make decisions on the spur of the moment. I never once regretted the decision to make Billy my captain. He knew there was a lot more to the job than just carrying the ball on to the pitch, and always performed his duties both on and off the field with tremendous enthusiasm and drive.'

CAP NO 15
Denmark, Copenhagen, 26.9.48. Drew 0–0
Swift* Scott Aston Wright Franklin Cockburn
Matthews Hagan Lawton Shackleton Langton

Highlights: English hearts stopped two minutes from the end when Danish right-winger Johan Ploeger fired in a shot that went through the legs of Frank Swift and into the net, but the linesman's flag was up for offside. England's forwards were unable to make an impact against a packed Danish defence on a heavy, rain-affected pitch. The Danes were amateurs who two months earlier had finished third in the Olympics. This was their first ever match against professional opponents. John Aston, Jimmy Hagan and Len Shackleton made their international debuts in a game that brought crushing criticism for England's shot-shy performance. It marked the end of Tommy Lawton's England career after 22 games and 23 goals, not counting his 25 goals in wartime internationals. He was convinced he had scored another goal against the Danes, but the referee disallowed it because of a foul by Len Shackleton. For once Shackleton, the Clown Prince, had nothing to laugh about. *The Wright Cuttings Book (Daily Herald)*: 'Wright was one of the few England players to emerge from the match with his pride intact. He battled hard to try to lift the team, but the forwards broke their hearts against a wall-like Danish defence.'

BILLY: I recall that Shack made his debut wearing a pair of rugby boots. 'They're more comfortable,' he explained, 'and they give better grip in muddy conditions.' That certainly seemed the case when in the fifth minute he waltzed round the Danish goalkeeper and side-footed the ball towards goal. Shack turned ready to receive the congratulations of his team-mates, not realising that the ball had stuck in a mound of mud on the goal line. Of all the players I played with or against, Shack was the player with the most footballing tricks in his locker. There were often times when not only his opponents but even his own team-mates, and even perhaps Shack himself, did not know what he was going to do next. Gazza is the nearest thing I have seen to him, but Shack was quicker and even more unpredictable. The Danish game was an embarrassment to us all, because we were expected to beat them with ease. To use that old football cliché, the mud really was a great leveller. At the after-match banquet, the Danish captain said that we had given them a football lesson but had forgotten to shoot. That just about summed it up.

CAP NO 16
Northern Ireland, Windsor Park, 9.10.48. England won 6–2
Swift   Scott   Howe J   Wright*   Franklin   Cockburn
Matthews[1]   Mortensen[3]   Milburn[1]   Pearson[1]   Finney

Highlights: Billy Wright's first of ninety matches as England captain. The two Stanleys – Matthews and Mortensen – dominated the match. Matthews scored the first and helped lay on a hat-trick for his Blackpool team-mate. The Matthews goal was a freak effort. His centre from the right curled and hit an upright. The ball bounced against the head of Irish goalkeeper Willie Smyth and into the net. 'Wor Jackie' Milburn announced his debut with a neatly headed goal. Davie Walsh scored his second goal with the last kick of the match to bring a little respectability to a scoreline that flattered England. *The Wright Cuttings Book* (*The Times*): 'As expected, Wright led the team with drive and enthusiasm, bringing to the England team the same total commitment that he always exhibits with Wolves.'

BILLY: This was, without question, the proudest game of my life. I will never forget the feeling of leading my country for the first time. Big Frank Swift shook my hand just before I left the dressing-room and said, 'Good luck, Billy. Enjoy it.' I wished everybody luck, and then as I came out of the dressing-room I came face to face with my rival skipper Johnny Carey. The last time I had met him in an international he had been wearing the shirt of the Republic of Ireland. Gentleman Johnny said, 'Good luck with the captaincy, Billy, but not with today's game!' Just imagine looking behind you and seeing team-mates such as Matthews, Finney, Mortensen, Swift and Franklin! Can you wonder that I felt ten feet tall as I led them out. I was delighted to have Jackie Milburn making his debut on the same day that I was captain for the first time. He was a particular favourite of mine, and we were good mates off the pitch. Milburn's JET initials (John Edward Thompson) were suited to his electric pace. There were few faster players in the game.

CAP NO 17
Wales, Villa Park, 10.11.48. England won 1–0
Swift   Scott   Aston   Ward   Franklin   Wright*
Matthews   Mortensen   Milburn   Shackleton   Finney[1]

Highlights: A crowd of 68,750 gathered at Villa Park for this midweek Home International match. Laurie Scott limped off with a damaged knee ligament in the 25th minute and the ten men of England became disorganised as Tim Ward switched to right-back and Stan Mortensen to right-half. Tom Finney scored the only goal of a drab game on the hour after a typical sprint-speed run from Jackie Milburn had ripped open the Welsh defence. BBC television cameras were at the match and a commentator called Kenneth Wolstenholme made his debut at the microphone. Some people thought it was all beginning. It was now! *The Wright Cuttings Book* (*Empire News*): 'England were down to ten players, so skipper Billy Wright took it upon himself to play like two men. He was here there and everywhere shoring up holes in the England defence.'

BILLY: I don't think the selectors made enough allowances for the fact that the injury to Laurie threw us out of our rhythm. They tore the team apart, and Frank Swift, Tim Ward and Shack were all dropped, and poor old Laurie's international career was finished by that knee injury after a run of seventeen successive matches. Even though I was skipper, I had no say in who did and who didn't play. From the reaction of the selectors, you would have thought we had lost to Wales.

CAP NO 18

Switzerland, Highbury, 2.12.48. England won 6–0
Ditchburn   Ramsey   Aston   Wright*   Franklin   Cockburn
Matthews   Rowley J[1]   Milburn[1]   Haines[2]   Hancocks[2]

Highlights: Jack Haines and Johnny Hancocks both scored two goals on their international debuts, but the goal that had the Highbury crowd roaring came from another debutant, Manchester United's Jack Rowley. He showed why he was rated to have one of the hardest shots in the game with a left-foot drive that bulleted into the net from 35 yards. Haines, who scored both his goals in the first half, never got another chance of a cap after collecting an injury with West Bromwich Albion. There were also debuts for Tottenham team-mates Ted Ditchburn and Alf Ramsey. Both gave sound performances in an England defence that was rarely troubled by a Swiss team that lacked its usual clockwork precision and never looked like repeating their victory of 1947. The game was postponed for 24 hours because of persistent fog, and this explains why there were only 35,000 at Highbury to watch a confident performance by England. *The Wright Cuttings Book (Daily Sketch)*: 'Billy Wright gave a real captain's performance, leading by example and inspiring everybody around him with his energy and enthusiasm.'

BILLY: I was thrilled for my Wolves team-mate Johnny Hancocks that he was such a success, even though he was playing out of position on the left wing. Johnny and I had a superstition that remained with us throughout our careers together. He always tied my bootlaces for me, and did the same before the match against Switzerland. I think the familiar routine helped steady his nerves.

Johnny was a 'Tom Thumb' of a player who wore small boots, but he could hit the ball as hard as any of the big men alongside him. I will always remember this game for Jack Rowley's goal. I played the ball through to him and thought he had lost control when he slipped over. But while down on one knee he took his measure and as he got up crashed in a shot from 35 yards that had 'goal' written all over it from the moment it left his boot. That evening I had to make my first after-dinner speech as England captain. I was more nervous of that than leading England on to the pitch. I took the advice of my close friend Neil Franklin, who told me, 'Thank anybody who needs to be thanked, keep it brief and end by calling for three cheers for the opposition.' It was a routine I followed throughout my speech-making career.

CAP NO 19

Scotland, Wembley, 9.4.49. England lost 3–1
Swift   Aston   Howe J   Wright*   Franklin   Cockburn
Matthews   Mortensen   Milburn[1]   Pearson   Finney

Highlights: The selectors decided to make five changes to the team that beat Switzerland 6–0. With Derby County dynamo Billy Steel at his most potent, Scotland tore into England after Scottish goalkeeper Jimmy Cowan had almost played England on his own in the opening twenty minutes. Jimmy Mason, Steel and Lawrie Reilly put the Scots on the way to the Home Championship before Milburn snatched a consolation goal. *The Wright Cuttings Book* (*Sunday Pictorial*): 'Wright did his best as captain to rouse his team-mates, but there was a lack of cohesion and confidence. For once, the Wolves man was unable to produce his club form on the international stage.'

BILLY: In those days, the Home Championship was one of the most prized and cherished trophies of all. I had set my heart on winning it in my first season as captain, and was devastated to miss out on it at, of all places, Wembley. Scotland's goalkeeper Jimmy Cowan was rightly hailed as the hero because of a string of wonderful saves in the first twenty minutes, but the real match-winner for

Scotland was their left-back Sammy Cox. He usually played as a wing-half and everybody expected Stanley Matthews to give him a roasting. But Sammy cleverly cut Stanley out of the game by intercepting many of the passes meant for the Maestro. It was the first time I had ever seen poker-face Stanley looking so frustrated. The man was human, after all.

Two weeks later Billy was back at Wembley Stadium for one of the most important club dates of his career. Wolves had swept through to the FA Cup final in their first season under the leadership of Stan Cullis. They were scorching-hot favourites to beat Second Division opponents Leicester City after overcoming Cup holders Manchester United in a memorable semi-final saga. Wolves held on for a 1–1 draw in the first match, when reduced to nine fit men, and thanks to a Sammy Smyth goal they won a classic replay 1–0.

Stan Cullis was more aware than anybody that there was no such thing as a certainty in an FA Cup final. He had skippered Wolves on their last visit to Wembley in 1939 when nerves got the better of his young side, and they were easily beaten by unfancied Portsmouth.

BILLY: Stan went out of his way to have a quiet word with every player in the dressing-room beforehand, making sure each of us knew what was expected and also steadying the nerves. I was determined to enjoy every second of the occasion. From as long as I could remember I had listened to the singing of 'Abide with Me' on the wireless before the Cup finals, and so that I could hear it properly I went into the large bathroom and threw open the windows. It was a really moving moment to hear that wonderful tune filling our dressing-room, and it made us all realise that this was a special game that was going to require special effort.

Wolves were nearly always in command after centre-forward Jesse Pye had given them the lead with a neat header from a Johnny Hancocks cross in the thirteenth minute. The game seemed virtually wrapped up three minutes before half-time when Pye struck again following a corner. Leicester staged a rally at the start of the second half and were rewarded with a goal by right-winger Mal Griffiths, and were then unlucky to have a Ken Chisholm goal ruled offside. Seconds later Irish international Sammy Smyth restored the two-goal cushion when he corkscrewed his way through the Leicester defence before steering the ball wide of oncoming goalkeeper Gordon Bradley to clinch a memorable victory for Wolves.

Billy climbed the 39 Wembley steps to receive the FA Cup from Princess Elizabeth. His team-mates then carried him shoulder-high back to the dressing-room. 'It never ever got better than that,' said our hero. 'I had dreamed about it happening since I was a boy, and there I was climbing the steps to the Royal Box to receive the FA Cup. I was so pleased for Stan Cullis, because he had missed out on it as a player.'

CAP NO 20

Sweden, Stockholm, 13.5.49. England lost 3–1

Ditchburn Shimwell Aston Wright* Franklin Cockburn
Finney¹ Mortensen Bentley Rowley J Langton

Highlights: Even without the great Italian-based Gunnar Nordhal, Sweden were able to produce the power and precision that had brought them the 1948 Olympic gold medal. They scored their three goals in the first half, with Eddie Shimwell being given a torrid time in his only international appearance at right-back. Chelsea centre-forward Roy Bentley was unlucky not to mark his debut with a goal in the opening minutes, and both he and Tom Finney hit the woodwork in the second half as Sweden battled to hang on to their three-goal lead. It was a Bentley dribble that set up Finney for England's only goal in the 67th minute. *The Wright Cuttings Book* (*Daily Telegraph*): 'Wright needs to curb his enthusiasm. He is so determined to lead by example that his concentration on defensive duties is not all that it should be. Captaincy sits comfortably on Wright's sturdy shoulders, but he must learn to pace himself and not try to do more than his fair share.'

BILLY: I lost the toss and it proved crucial. The Swedes chose to play with a setting sun behind them and our goalkeeper Ted Ditchburn complained of being blinded for two of the three Swedish goals. But overall we could not complain about the result. The football Sweden played was a credit to English coach George Raynor. We did not need to be reminded after the match that the game was played on Friday the thirteenth!

CAP NO 21
Norway, Oslo, 18.5.49. England won 4–1
Swift   Ellerington   Aston   Wright*   Franklin   Dickinson
Finney¹   Morris¹   Mortensen   Mannion   Mullen¹ +1 own goal

Highlights: Frank Swift, one of the all-time great goalkeepers, made his farewell appearance in a comfortable canter against the amateurs of Norway. Derby inside-right Johnny Morris scored on his England debut. Much of England's play was of the exhibition variety, with Tom Finney and Wilf Mannion parading their skill. Southampton right-back Billy Ellerington won the first of his two caps, and Jimmy Dickinson – Pompey's Mr Consistent – started his run of 48 England appearances. *The Wright Cuttings Book* (*News Chronicle*): 'Wright, Franklin and Dickinson constituted as solid a looking half-back line as has appeared in England shirts since the days of Britton, Cullis and Mercer. They had an iron grip on the Norwegian forwards, and Wright found time to prompt the attack with penetrating passes.'

BILLY: It was difficult to believe that I would not play with big Swiftie any more. He was the outstanding goalkeeper of my generation, and only Gordon Banks and Peter Shilton could match him of the modern players. As well as his great goalkeeping, I will always remember him for his personality. He really was a genial giant, and he and Tommy Lawton together were as funny as any music-hall comedy double act. Jimmy Dickinson, so solid and so reliable, thoroughly deserved his England call-up. He was a key player in the Portsmouth side that was on its way to two successive League championships.

CAP NO 22:

France, Paris, 22.5.49. England won 3–1

Williams   Ellerington   Aston   Wright*[1]   Franklin   Dickinson
Finney   Morris[2]   Rowley J   Mannion   Mullen

Highlights: Making his debut in the England goal, Wolves custodian Bert 'The Cat' Williams was beaten after just 28 seconds by an instant goal from French debutant Georges Moreel. The match was played under a boiling sun and on a Colombes Stadium pitch as hard as concrete. Billy Wright made it a match to remember in the 26th minute by scoring his first international goal. It was the first goal scored for England by a non-forward since the war. Johnny Morris netted twice, including a late victory-clinching goal in the 86th minute that silenced the 61,500 shirtsleeved Parisian spectators. *The Wright Cuttings Book* (*Daily Sketch*): 'A goal by Billy Wright is as rare as snow in the Sahara, and it is always a puzzle why this excellent player does not score more often. He started off as a goal-scoring forward, but seems to have lost his appetite for goals. Perhaps this neatly taken goal against France will help him recover that goalden [sic] touch.'

BILLY: I only scored three goals in all for England, so this one has obviously got a special place in my memory. Johnny Morris, Jimmy Mullen, Wilf Mannion and Jack Rowley cut open the French defence with some brilliant passes before Rowley pushed the ball diagonally into space in the penalty area. I ran on to the ball and lashed it right-footed past the French goalkeeper from twelve yards. It was one of the sweeter moments of my career. My Wolves team-mates Bert Williams and Jimmy Mullen congratulated me, and the goal gave Bert the confidence to show his great club form after his unfortunate start of conceding a goal in the first minute of his international career. It was often said that I should have scored more goals, but I saw it as my job to win the ball in midfield and then feed it to such talented players as Stanley Matthews and Tom Finney, who were so much better at setting up goals than me.

Who won what in 1948–49

First Division: Portsmouth, 58pts. Runners-up: Manchester United, 53pts.
Portsmouth record: P42 W25 D8 L9 F84 A42 Pts 58
Portsmouth squad: Butler, Rookes, Ferrier, Scoular, Fiewin*, Dickinson, (from) Harris, Barlow, Reid, Clarke, Phillips, Froggatt. Top scorers: Harris (17), Reid (17). Manager: Bob Jackson.
Second Division: Fulham, 57pts. Runners-up: West Bromwich Albion, 56pts.
Third Division (South): Swansea, 62 pts. Runners-up: Reading, 55pts.
Third Division (North): Hull City, 65pts. Runners-up: Rotherham United, 62pts.
FA Cup final: Wolves 3, Leicester City 1
Wolves: Williams, Pritchard, Springthorpe, Crook, Shorthouse, Wright*, Hancocks, Smyth[1], Pye[2], Dunn, Mullen.
Leicester City: Bradley, Jelly, Scott, Harrison W, Plummer, King, Griffiths[1], Lee, Harrison J, Chisholm, Adam.
Top First Division marksman: Willie Moir (Bolton Wanderers), 25 goals.
Footballer of the Year: Johnny Carey (Manchester United).
Scottish champions: Rangers, 46pts. Runners-up: Dundee, 45pts.
Scottish Cup Final: Rangers 4, Clyde 1

SEASON 1949–50:
The Team Player

We have looked at Billy Wright, the person: honest, cheerful, as solid as an English oak, enthusiastic, determined, modest, dependable, clean living, a filmgoer and a rug-maker. What about Billy, the player?

Sir Walter Winterbottom summed him up like this: 'All the attributes that Billy showed off the pitch were what he showed on the pitch, and vice versa. If you were in the trenches, he would be the man you wanted alongside you. You could trust him with your life, and on the football pitch he could be trusted to do all in his power to help win a match. But he was always honest with his efforts. That's why he was never ever booked. He was essentially a team player. You never saw him trying to seek personal glory. He wanted everybody to share in any success. Billy was schooled at Wolves to do the simple things well, and he turned simplicity into an art form when playing for England.'

What about his skill as a player? 'Billy was a much better player than people have given him credit for,' said his lifelong friend Jimmy Mullen, whose death in 1987 was the catalyst for the founding of the Wolves Former Players' Association with Billy as the chairman. 'The young Billy was a fast and clever forward who could get the better of most defences, and when he dropped back into midfield he became the complete controller. He could dictate the pace of a match, and his passing was always accurate. He didn't go in for the clever stuff, but basic, simple passes that helped drive the team forward or relieve the pressure on the defence. The biggest surprise to those of us who knew him when he was a tiddler is the way he developed a powerful tackle that stopped some of the best forwards in the world.'

How about Billy the centre-half? For an assessment I went to Neil Franklin, the man who caused a crisis in the England ranks when he walked out on Stoke City in 1950 to become a rebel footballer in the then outlawed Colombian league. After a string of unsuccessful experiments with established centre-halves, the selectors finally called on Billy to become Neil's successor. 'Billy turned himself into a great centre-half,' Neil told me during his days as manager at Colchester United. 'He could have done with a couple of extra inches, but made up for his lack of height with intelligent positional play. He was robust and would never give his rival centre-forward an inch. There were better headers of the ball, but Billy could be relied on to make a challenge in the air, and when he was beaten he used to show quick recovery powers. There was no more determined centre-half in the League, and he did an exceptional job for England at a time when we seemed to have a dearth of good number fives. People always asked whether I regretted my temporary move to Colombia. All I can say is that I thought I was doing what I considered best for my wife and family at a time when professional footballers in Britain were treated appallingly. It did not work out for me because of broken promises, but I had to give it a go.'

BILLY: I was never in the same class as Neil in the number five shirt. He was one of the finest footballing centre-halves I ever saw, and it was a massive blow to us when he elected to go to South America. I was lucky to have two fine tutors in Stan Cullis and Walter Winterbottom. Both were specialist centre-halves, Stan probably the best ever to wear the England shirt. They spent hours with me helping me get the positioning right. I know I had my critics who considered me something of a workhorse, but I like to think I had skill that I could bring out if and when necessary. As a wing-half, I saw my priority as getting the ball to our brilliant forwards as quickly as possible. When I switched to centre-half, I considered my main role was to bring order and stability to the middle of the defence, working closely with my goalkeeper and encouraging the players around me by example. I was not a shouting, fist-brandishing captain. That was just not my style. Nat Lofthouse once said to me, 'Billy, you're too nice.' Well, I could only play the game the way I felt was right.

There it is again. The description 'too nice'. It will rear its ugly head again when we assess Billy Wright, the manager.

One thing I *had* to take up with our hero. *A rug-maker?* Can you imagine what the press would make of it if they discovered David Beckham was working at home with a needle and thread? 'It was a hobby that I found nice and relaxing,' Billy explained. 'I used to sit in the evenings listening to something like my collection of light-opera records or perhaps The Goons or a good *Curtain Up* play on the wireless. While sitting there I would embroider rugs. People might scoff at it, but I recommend it for anybody who wants to do something creative and restful. The finished product gives tremendous satisfaction. It was my landlady Mrs Colley who encouraged me. She said I was a natural. Nobody thought it was odd in those days because it was a time when everybody had a hobby. There was no gogglebox to stare at, and so you kept yourself occupied while listening to the wireless. Some people read, others built model planes and many played board games. I made rugs. Mrs Colley had become like a second mum to me following the death from cancer of my mother at the young age of 42. That was a very painful moment in my life, and I was grateful for the support of the Colley family.'

England had the rug pulled out from under them when they played Eire at Goodison Park in September 1949. They were beaten on English soil by a non-British team for the first time in their history.

CAP NO 23

Republic of Ireland, Goodison Park, 21.9.49. England lost 2–0
Williams   Mozley   Aston   Wright*   Franklin   Dickinson
Harris   Morris   Pye   Mannion   Finney

Highlights: Nine of the Irish players were with Football League clubs and two from Shamrock Rovers but all of them were born in Ireland.

Johnny Carey was a magnificent captain, and Con Martin (penalty) and Peter Farrell scored in each half to produce a stunning result. Derby defender Bert Mozley made his England debut at right-back on his 26th birthday. It was an unhappy debut, too, for Wolves centre-forward Jesse Pye and Pompey's John Harris, who struck a shot against the bar with the score at 1–0. It sounded as if the majority of the 52,000 fans packed into Goodison were supporting the Irish as they battled their way to an amazing victory. *The Wright Cuttings Book* (*Daily Mirror*): 'Even big-hearted Billy Wright could not turn back the green tide that swept across the Goodison pitch. The defeat brought shame to English football, but if anybody could be absolved it was Wright, who strove manfully to stop the ship from sinking. In the end, like all good captains, he went down with the ship.'

BILLY: It was one of those days when nothing would go right for us. We had a strong wind at our backs in the second half, but still could not break down the Irish defence in which Johnny Carey was a colossus. We might have had three or four goals, but the ball just would not go into the net. When it was all over, I shook Johnny's hand and told him, 'Well done, you deserved it.' I am not sure who was more shocked by our defeat, me or the winning skipper.

The four home countries had agreed to take part in the World Cup for the first time, and FIFA dictated that the Home Championship should be the qualifying stage for the finals in Brazil in the summer of 1950. The first two teams were to qualify, but Scotland announced that they would only go if they won the Home Championship.

CAP NO 24
Wales, Ninian Park, 15.10.49. England won 4–1
Williams   Mozley   Aston   Wright*   Franklin   Dickinson
Finney   Mortensen[1]   Milburn[3]   Shackleton   Hancocks

Highlights: This was the first ever World Cup qualifying match in which England or Wales had taken part. Jackie Milburn scored a spectacular hat-trick, and England won comfortably despite having Billy Wright as a limping passenger on the wing for most of the second half. The game was virtually settled during an England blitz midway through the first half when they scored three goals in twelve minutes. Milburn made it 4–0 when he completed his hat-trick to puncture an attempted revival by Wales, who had to be content with a late goal by Mal Griffiths after goalkeeper Bert Williams had saved brilliantly from Trevor Ford. *The Wright Cuttings Book* (*London Evening Star*): 'Even though he was a virtual passenger for much of the second half, Wright continued to have an influence on the match with his quiet words of encouragement. He has become an inspirational player just by his presence in an England team.'

> BILLY: It was a miserable game for me because I severely strained a thigh muscle, and it forced a two week lay-off. By the time I came back the edge had gone off my game and for the first time in my career I started to get some bad press write-ups, many of them deserved. I discussed the crisis with Stan Cullis, and he advised me to just keep playing my natural game and that my form would soon return. Thankfully it did, but it gave me a taste of how quickly the press could turn if you fell below the standards you had set. I desperately wanted to be involved in the World Cup and was relieved to find the selectors had kept faith with me when the team was announced for the next qualifying match against Northern Ireland.

CAP NO 25

Northern Ireland, Maine Road, 16.11.49. England won 9–2

Streten   Mozley   Aston   Watson   Franklin   Wright*
Finney   Mortensen[2]   Rowley J[4]   Pearson[2]   Froggatt J[1]

Highlights: Jack Rowley, deputising for injured Jackie Milburn, hammered four goals against an Irish team that had gone down 8–2 against Scotland in their previous match. Pompey's Jack Froggatt scored on his debut. England Test cricketer Willie Watson won the first of four caps at right-half, and former amateur international Bernard

Streten got his only full England call while playing in the Second Division with Luton. Fulham's Irish goalkeeper Hugh Kelly had to pick the ball out of his net 28 times in five successive international matches. *The Wright Cuttings Book* (*Manchester Guardian*): 'It was comforting to find Wright back to form after a spell when many were questioning what appears to be his automatic selection for England. On the evidence of this performance, he must remain a key figure in Walter Winterbottom's World Cup plans.'

> BILLY: The only surprise is that we did not reach double figures. That's how commanding we were against an Irish team that was disjointed and disorganised. Ireland had the great Celtic character Charlie Tully in their team. He was famous for scoring direct from corner-kicks, but we gave him little chance to show off his party trick. I was just happy to get through the game without giving the press anything to criticise. For some reason, a couple of the London writers had decided I was not the man to captain England and had started knocking me at any opportunity. But with a 9–2 scoreline they could find little fault in my performance.

CAP NO 26
Italy, White Hart Lane, 30.11.49. England won 2–0
Williams   Ramsey   Aston   Watson   Franklin   Wright*[1]
Finney   Mortensen   Rowley J[1]   Pearson   Froggatt J

Highlights: England were outplayed for long periods by an over-elaborate Italian team, and only a series of fine saves by Bert 'The Cat' Williams kept them in the game in a goalless first half. England snatched an undeserved lead fourteen minutes from the end when Jack Rowley scored with one of his typical thunderbolt left-foot shots that the Italian goalkeeper could only wave to on its way into the net. The match was settled by a goal in a million from Billy Wright. *The Wright Cuttings Book* (*Daily Sketch*): 'Despite his freak goal, Wright cannot be satisfied with his performance. There were times in the game when he was too far upfield, leaving Alf Ramsey exposed to the thrusting counter attacks by the quick and clever Italian forwards.'

BILLY: My second goal for England was a complete freak. I lobbed the ball forward from a position just over the halfway line. It was intended for the far post. The Italian goalkeeper, unchallenged, came out to collect it just as a gust of wind made the ball change direction. He grasped at thin air as it curled over his head and into the net. I think I must have been the first England goalscorer who blushed as his team-mates congratulated him! The press were unmerciful with their knocking of our performance, even though we had beaten the reigning world champions. I was really concerned about my form, and after a long talk with Stan Cullis, the club sent me to see a medical specialist. He examined what I thought was my recovering thigh-strain injury, and discovered a blood clot which had been upsetting my balance. An operation cleared the problem, and after a break at Blackpool I came back raring to get into the action and to help Wolves with their challenge for the championship. With my balance back to normal, my game improved and I got the critics off my back.

Wolves, unbeaten in their first twelve matches, made the pace in what was a neck-and-neck race for the championship. They were then overhauled by Liverpool who went nineteen games without defeat. Manchester United celebrated their return to rebuilt Old Trafford by catching up with Liverpool in the spring, but their challenge faded as Sunderland came through to take the lead during the Easter programme.

The vital Scotland–England match was played on a Saturday, depriving several of the challenging teams of key players. Defending champions Portsmouth took the opportunity to climb into top spot for the first time, with only one point separating the top four clubs. Coming into the final Saturday Pompey were a nose ahead of Wolves on goal average, with Sunderland one point behind.

Portsmouth (5–1), Wolves (6–1) and Sunderland (4–1) all had emphatic victories, and supporters held their breath while the mathematicians did their sums. At the final count, Pompey had retained their title by 0.4 goals ahead of Wolves. It was the first time for a quarter of a century that the championship had been decided on goal average.

England, meantime, had qualified for the World Cup finals.

CAP NO 27

Scotland, Hampden Park, 15.4.50. England won 1–0

Williams   Ramsey   Aston   Wright*   Franklin   Dickinson
Finney   Mannion   Mortensen   Bentley[1]   Langton

Highlights: Chelsea centre-forward Roy Bentley, playing a twin spearhead role with Stan Mortensen, scored the winning goal midway through the second half. It was a goal that confirmed England's entry into the World Cup finals. The 133,250 Hampden Park spectators were left screaming their frustration because the Scottish Football Association had surrendered their chances of a World Cup finals place by electing to go only if they won the Home Championship. *The Wright Cuttings Book* (*Wolverhampton Express & Star*): 'How those critics who have been calling for Billy Wright to be axed were forced to eat their words! He was the driving force behind this England victory that sends them flying all the way down to Rio. Magnificent in defence alongside the immaculate Franklin, he also found time to torment the Scots with a procession of passes that kept the top-form Tom Finney supplied.'

BILLY: I have rarely known so much tension on a football field as in that match at Hampden. The Scottish officials had put ridiculous pressure on their players. They *had* to win to qualify for the trip to Brazil, and they played like men possessed. But the pressure got to them and Roy Bentley's beautifully taken goal just knocked the wind out of them. I would have hated to be in their situation. Soon afterwards came the bombshell news that Neil Franklin did not want to be considered for the World Cup because he was joining an outlawed club in Bogota. It was a complete shock, because Neil was a close friend, but he had kept everything secret even from me. Like me, he had played in all 27 England matches since the war and we had a terrific understanding on the pitch. Now we had lost our linchpin with the World Cup just weeks away. I was fond of Neil and understood his motives for taking the offer to go to Bogota. We were so poorly paid in England, and he wanted to put his wife and children first. But I could have kicked him for his timing.

The selectors were now in a dither as to who to play in the vital centre-half role, this in an era before the two central backs system. Everything at the back revolved around the pivotal position of the man in the number five shirt, and Neil Franklin was the best by a country mile. England had lost their anchor, and would soon be all at sea.

CAP NO 28

Portugal, Lisbon, 14.5.50. England won 5–3
Williams Ramsey Aston Wright* Jones Dickinson
Milburn Mortensen[1] Bentley Mannion Finney[4] [(2 pen)]

Highlights: Four goals from Tom Finney, including two from the penalty spot, and a spectacular effort from Stan Mortensen lifted England to victory. But there were worrying signs that the defence was creaking without the steadying influence of Neil Franklin. Laurie Hughes was the original choice to fill the centre-half vacancy, but he pulled out at the last minute because of injury and the job went to his Liverpool team-mate Bill Jones. Portugal, after trailing 3–0 at half-time, had battled back and England were struggling to hold on at 4–3 when Finney settled it with his second penalty. *The Wright Cuttings Book (Daily Mirror)*: 'Time will tell, but there was disturbing evidence that Billy Wright was missing that all-important understanding that he had with Neil Franklin. We cannot possibly begin to consider going to Rio with a defence that leaks goals like this.'

BILLY: Just like the Scots in our previous match, the Portuguese had been promised a trip to the World Cup finals if they beat us. They played their hearts out, and we had to battle hard to hold them in the second half. Their African-born centre-forward Ben David scored two of their goals, and as well as Bill Jones played it was obvious that we had lost a lot of stability in the middle of our defence. We had major problems, and the World Cup finals were just a few weeks away.

CAP NO 29
Belgium, Brussels, 18.5.50. England won 4–1
Williams   Ramsey   Aston   Wright*   Jones   Dickinson
Milburn (Mullen¹)   Mortensen¹   Bentley¹   Mannion¹   Finney

Highlights: Wolves winger Jimmy Mullen became England's first ever substitute when he replaced injured Jackie Milburn, and he scored one of the goals as England staged a second-half recovery after trailing 1–0 at half-time. Roy Bentley had a foot in three of the goals and scored the last one himself in this final warm-up before the World Cup. The Belgians, trained by former Blackburn and Northampton goalkeeper Bill Gormlie, scored their goal through centre-forward Joe Mermans. It exposed the fact that England were still struggling at the heart of their defence. *The Wright Cuttings Book (The Times)*: 'As good a result as this looks on paper, seasoned witnesses of England abroad are distinctly concerned over the way Billy Wright is suddenly having to worry about covering at the centre of the defence as well as carrying out his duties as a wing-half.'

BILLY: The match was virtually won for us by a half-time tactical talk from Walter Winterbottom. He was often accused of being too long-winded and technical with his instructions, but he got straight to the point and made it clear how we should tighten at the back and push forward in midfield. We followed his orders and comfortably outplayed the Belgians in the second half. Poor Bill Jones had failed to impress the selectors, and was not even in the squad named the following week for the trip to Brazil. I felt sorry for Bill, because to be thrown into the team at the last minute was hardly the proper preparation for his debut in international football.

For the record, the squad selected was: Williams (Wolves), Ditchburn (Spurs), Ramsey (Spurs), Scott (Arsenal), Aston (Man United), Eckersley (Blackburn), Wright (Wolves, captain), Hughes (Liverpool), Dickinson (Portsmouth), Watson (Sunderland), Nicholson (Spurs), Taylor (Fulham), Cockburn (Man United), Milburn (Newcastle),

Mortensen (Blackpool), Bentley (Chelsea), Mannion (Middlesbrough), Finney (Preston), Mullen (Wolves), Baily (Spurs), Matthews (Blackpool).

A dream trip to Rio? The nightmare was about to start.

Who won what in 1949–50

First Division: Portsmouth, 53pts. Runners-up: Wolves, 53pts.

Portsmouth record: P42 W22 D9 L11 F74 A38 Pts53

Portsmouth squad: Butler, Hindmarsh, Ferrier, (from) Spence, Scoular, Flewin*, Dickinson, Pickett, Harris, Reid, Clarke, Phillips, Froggatt. Top scorer: Clarke (17). Manager: Bob Jackson.

Second Division: Tottenham, 61pts. Runners-up: Sheffield Wednesday, 52pts.

Third Division (South): Notts County, 58pts. Runners-up: Northampton Town, 51pts.

Third Division (North): Doncaster Rovers, 55pts. Runners-up: Gateshead, 53pts.

FA Cup final: Arsenal 2, Liverpool 0

Arsenal: Swindin, Scott, Barnes, Forbes, Compton L, Mercer*, Cox, Logie, Goring, Lewis², Compton D.

Liverpool: Sidlow, Lambert, Spicer; Taylor, Jones, Hughes, Payne, Baron, Stubbins, Fagan, Liddell.

Top First Division marksman: Dick Davis (Sunderland), 25 goals.

Footballer of the Year: Joe Mercer (Arsenal).

Scottish champions: Rangers, 50pts. Runners-up: Hibernian, 49pts.

Scottish Cup final: Rangers 3, East Fife 0

SEASON 1950–51:
Horizontal in Horizonte

England, captained by Billy Wright, had the players with the ability to win the World Cup when they first entered the tournament in 1950, but the Football Association made a complete hash of it. Let me lay out the evidence, and see what you think.

The FA saw fit to organise a goodwill tour of Canada at the same time as the World Cup finals in Brazil, and then ummed and ahhed when Manchester United requested that none of their players should be considered because they had arranged a trip to the United States.

Walter Winterbottom, battling against this blinkered club-before-country attitude, almost had to get on his knees to have first choice for the World Cup. As it was, he had to go to Brazil without England's most famous player, Stanley Matthews, who was sent on the totally meaningless Canadian trip as a footballing ambassador. Special arrangements had to be made to fly him down to Rio for the World Cup, and he arrived after England had won their opening match 2–0 against Chile. Stanley had crossed through so many time zones that he quite literally did not know what day it was.

Winterbottom wanted to play Matthews in the second game against the United States, and Sir Stanley Rous argued the case for him with the chairman of the selectors, a Grimsby fish merchant called Arthur Drewry, who had been appointed the sole selector for the World Cup. 'My policy is that I never change a winning team,' the dogmatic Drewry said dismissively.

On one of the blackest days in English football history, England

75

were beaten 1–0 by the United States with Stanley Matthews among the spectators. It was like leaving Wellington on the bench at Waterloo.

Billy told me a story from that 1950 World Cup tournament which captures the amateurish way in which we approached international football. Nobody had bothered to check what food the hotel would serve in Brazil, and the players complained that they could not eat it because it was too spicy. Winterbottom decided the only way round the problem was to go into the hotel kitchen and do the cooking himself. Talk about head cook and bottle washer!

England's humiliation by the United States in Belo Horizonte was not, as reported at the time, against a team imported from overseas by the Americans. The football writers failed to do their homework, and wrote inaccurate stories that England had been beaten by a team that had come from Ellis Island, with only a couple of true Americans among them. Research has since proved this to be false information. All but three of the team were born in the United States. They were boosted by immigrants Joe Maca from Belgium, Ed McIllveney from Scotland, and the goalscorer, Larry Gaetjens from Haiti.

England had made a far from impressive start to their World Cup campaign against Chile but got away with a victory. The vast Maracana Stadium, with workmen still putting the finishing touches, held 200,000 spectators and it looked and sounded deserted with fewer than 30,000 watching the game.

CAP NO 30

Chile, World Cup, Rio de Janeiro, 25.6.50. England won 2–0
Williams   Ramsey   Aston   Wright*   Hughes   Dickinson
Finney   Mannion   Bentley   Mortensen[1]   Mullen[1]

Highlights: Laurie Hughes replaced his Liverpool clubmate Bill Jones at centre-half. He won three England caps, all in this World Cup tournament. Stan Mortensen gave England a 38th minute lead against the run of play when he headed in a Jimmy Mullen cross. Mullen turned goalscorer just after the hour when he drove the ball into the net following neat approach work by Mortensen and Tom Finney. George Robledo, the Newcastle forward playing for his home country of Chile,

The Billy Wright Photo Album 1

Many of the following photographs and documents have been taken from Billy's personal effects, and are the copyright of the Billy Wright Estate. The action pictures have been kindly provided by the *Wolverhampton Express & Star*.

This is Billy (*left*) at the age of ten when he was growing up in Ironbridge, Shropshire. He was born there on 6 February 1924.

Billy's first team picture (*right*). Billy is with his mother (*far right*) as his father, Tommy, (*front row, extreme left*) poses with the Coalbrookdale Works Welfare XI at the end of the 1926–27 season when they won the Bridgnorth Infirmary Cup.

The 1937 Madeley Senior School side for which Billy scored ten goals on his debut. Team captain Billy holds the leather ball and Norman Simpson, the schoolmaster who first spotted his talent and recommended him to Wolves, is in the back row.

Wolverhampton Wanderers Football Club (1923) Ltd.

REGISTERED OFFICE:
MOLINEUX GROUNDS,
WOLVERHAMPTON.

WINNERS OF F.A. CUP, 1892-3 AND 1907-8.
FINALISTS, 1888-9, 1895-6, 1920-1.
CHAMPIONS—DIV. 2, 1931-2.
DIV. 3 (NORTHERN SECTION) 1923-4.
CENTRAL LEAGUE, 1931-2.

FRANK C. BUCKLEY.

Molineux Grounds,
Wolverhampton.

JTH/FJ.

30th June, 1938.

N.D. Simpson, Esq.,
Senior School,
Madeley,
Salop.

Dear Mr. Simpson,

Thank you very much for your letter of the 28th inst. Will you please arrange for the lad Wright to be at the above address on the morning of Monday July the 11th ready to start on the ground.

Again thanking you for the interest you have taken in this matter.

Yours faithfully,

Secretary-Manager

The start of the great adventure. This letter to Billy's school teacher, Norman Simpson, from legendary Wolves manager, Major Frank Buckley, launched one of the all-time great playing careers. The 'lad Wright' was now on his way into the football history books.

Billy's first international call-up was as a reserve for England against Wales in the 1945 Victory International. In this letter from Billy's personal papers, FA secretary Stanley Rous addresses him coldly as 'Wright' in an era when footballers were treated like servants by their masters. It has been carelessly typed on a clapped-out typewriter, and Corporal Billy learns that he has been 'selceted' [sic]. This was in the days long before spell checkers! The match fee was £20 for – another typing error – 'professio players'. Billy was paid £10 as a reserve.

THE FOOTBALL ASSOCIATION.

PATRON:
HIS MAJESTY THE KING.
PRESIDENT:
THE RT. HON. THE EARL OF ATHLONE, K.G.

SECRETARY:
S. F. ROUS, C.B.E.

22, LANCASTER GATE.

TELEGRAPHIC ADDRESS:
"FOOTBALL ASSOCIATION
PADD. LONDON."

LONDON, W. 2.

F/CB/JC

October 1, 1945

Our reference

Dear Wright,

Victory International
England v. Wales

You have been selceted to travel as reserve in the above match at West Bromwich on Saturday 20th October kick-off 3 p.m. Will you please let me know by return of post whether or not you are able to do so.

An application for the necessary leave of absence has been sent to your Commending Officer.

Travelling expenses will be refunded and professio players will be allowed a fee.

You will be notified in due course of the Headquarters and the time at which you will be required to report on Friday October 19, .. programme of arrangements will follow.

Yours faithfully,

S.J.Rous.
Secretary

Cpl. W. Wright.

Stanley Matthews Denis Compton G Hagan Frank Swift

Bill Elliott

THE FOOTBALL ASSOCIATION

VICTORY INTERNATIONAL

SCOTLAND v. ENGLAND

Neil Franklin

To be played at Hampden Park, Glasgow, on Saturday April

13, 1946, Kick-off 3.p.m.

Laurie Scott

PROGRAMME OF ARRANGEMENTS.

Len Shackleton

Bill Wright

Friday, April 12

    Players will make their own travelling arrangements and
report at the Central Hotel, Glasgow, not later than 8.p.m.
Friday evening. Dinner will be served in the Hotel on arrival.
    Service players should travel on a concession voucher, if
possible.
    For those travelling via London the train leaves Euston at
10.a.m. arriving Glasgow 6.55.p.m. Luncheon and Tea will be
served on the train.
    Bedrooms have been reserved for the party at the Central
Hotel.

Saturday, April 13. *Frank Soo J Mercer George Hardwick*

    Luncheon at the Grosvenor Restaurant, 74, Gordon Street,
Glasgow, at 12 o'clock noon.
    Depart for the ground at 1.40.p.m. Kick-off 3.p.m.
    After the match (5.10.p.m.) a conveyance will leave the
ground for the Central Hotel. *A. Stubbins*

Return Journey. *T Lawton*

    Players may leave for home or unit on Saturday night or stay
until Sunday morning. Sleeping compartments (3rd class) have been
reserved on the 9.30.p.m. train from Glasgow Central (non-stop,
due at Euston 6.35.a.m. Sunday) for those who wish to return to
London on Saturday night.
    On Sunday a   train leaves Glasgow Central at 10.a.m. and is
due at Euston 7.40.p.m.

Billy was an avid autograph hunter and used to get his team-mates to sign his match programmes.
The prized signatures collected by Billy on this travel itinerary for the 1946 Scotland–England Victory
International at Hampden Park are: Frank Swift, George Hardwick, Laurie Scott, Neil Franklin, Joe
Mercer (captain), Bill Elliott, Jimmy Hagan, Tommy Lawton, Albert Stubbins, Denis Compton, and
Billy himself (who at this early stage in his career was signing himself 'Bill Wright'). Stanley
Matthews, Len Shackleton and Frank Soo were travelling reserves. The match drew 135,000
spectators. The players were paid a £20 match fee and had to travel third-class. Scotland won 1–0
with a last-minute goal by Manchester United's Jimmy 'Old Bones' Delaney. It was the only time Billy
was ever on a losing side at Hampden.

Action man Billy, throwing, heading and tackling for Wolves. Billy was never booked throughout his career, but in today's football this tackle from behind (*left*) against club-mate Barry Stobart in his very last match in 1959 would have earned him an instant red card. It has been outlawed since Billy hung up his boots.

One of Billy's proudest moments, receiving the FA Cup from Princess Elizabeth after the 3–1 FA Cup final victory over Leicester City at Wembley in 1949, and then (*left*) taking the shoulder-high victory parade around Wembley with his team-mates.

A rare photograph (*above*) in which Billy is seen with a glass of champagne in his hand as he toasts a Wolves League championship victory with team-mate Ron Flowers. He was teetotal throughout his playing career.

A picture of hero-worship (*left*). Billy thought he was seeing treble when the Haden triplets of Lower Gornal queued for his autograph in the early 1950s. Derek Haden, centre, said: 'Billy was the hero of the century as far as we lads were concerned. There was a massive queue for his autograph, and he did not disappoint a single one of us.'

BEFORE AND AFTER: Billy Wright and Ferenc Puskas lead out the teams for the 1953 England–Hungary match at Wembley that was to change the face of English football. 40 years later Billy and Ferenc were reunited at Molineux. A fan shouted from the new Billy Wright Stand: 'That's the closest you ever got to him, Bill.' Billy laughed louder than anybody.

The England team for the 1959 match against Scotland at Wembley in which Billy became the first footballer in the world to win 100 caps. *Back row left to right*: Ronnie Clayton, Don Howe, Eddie Hopkinson, Ron Flowers, Billy, Graham Shaw; *front row*: Bryan Douglas, Peter Broadbent, Bobby Charlton, Johnny Haynes, Doug Holden. At the end of the game Billy was chaired back to the dressing-room by Ronnie Clayton and Don Howe (*below*).

rattled the England woodwork with a 30-yard free-kick, and neutral observers thought the Chileans unlucky not to get at least a draw. But an easier match against the USA was to follow! *The Wright Cuttings Book (Sunday Chronicle)*: 'It was reassuring to see Wright back to his best at wing-half, but a question mark remains as to whether Hughes is the right man for the England No 5 shirt.'

BILLY: There was no elation in our dressing-room after this victory. We knew we were flattered by the scoreline, and it was going to take a big improvement if we were going to make a telling challenge for the World Cup. Many of us had come out of a punishing season in which we had played as many as fifty-five games, and after taking thirty-one hours to get to Brazil we were very sluggish when it came to playing against Chile. What was worrying was that we found the conditions really humid, and the oxygen laid on in the dressing-room did little to help. This all sounds like excuses, but the fact was we went into that tournament feeling jaded. After our poor start, we were determined to show the United States just how well we could play.

CAP NO 31
USA, World Cup, Belo Horizonte, 29.6.50. England lost 1–0
Williams   Ramsey   Aston   Wright*   Hughes   Dickinson
Finney   Mannion   Bentley   Mortensen   Mullen

Highlights: A freakish headed goal from Haitian-born centre-forward Larry Gaetjens eight minutes before half-time gave the United States a victory that caused a shock that could have been measured on the Richter scale. England hit the woodwork three times, and what seemed a certain face-saving goal from a Ramsey free-kick in the closing minutes was miraculously saved by the diving goalkeeper Borghi, a professional baseball catcher. Another Ramsey free-kick had earlier found the back of the net, but the referee whistled for an infringement. England spent 85 per cent of the game in the American half but finished up the losers. Nobody could have felt more frustrated than Stanley Matthews, who sat watching impassively from the sidelines. The goalscoring hero Gaetjens was later reported to have died in a Haitian jail after helping to organise a guerrilla movement against the island's dictator, 'Papa Doc' Duvalier. His name will live on in football history. *The Wright Cuttings Book* (*Daily Sketch*): 'Captain Billy Wright must take his share of the blame for this humiliating defeat. Along with his team-mates, he was running round like a headless chicken in the second half as the England dream of World Cup glory started to turn into the worst sort of nightmare.'

BILLY: It was the biggest freak result I ever experienced throughout my playing career. I promise you that 99 times out of a hundred we would have won the match. I always remember Wilf Mannion saying as we came off at the end, 'Can't we play it again? We could never lose to this lot a second time.' The game was played on a cramped, narrow pitch that meant we were unable to make full use of our strength down the wings. The stadium was still being built and I recall that the dressing-rooms were so dirty that Walter Winterbottom ordered us on to the coach, and we changed in a sports club a ten-minute drive away. This was easily the most frustrating and one-sided international in which I ever played. We must have had twenty shots to their one. Even their goal was a freakish affair. Bert Williams had a high centre covered, but Gaetjens ducked and the ball glanced off the back of his head and into the net. Even Alf Ramsey, who used to be expressionless throughout a game, threw his arms up and looked to the sky when his perfect free-kick was somehow saved by their unorthodox goalkeeper. I had never felt worse on a football pitch than at the final whistle. Walter took it all in his stride, but inside I am sure he was hurting just as much as the rest of us. He did not deserve the scathing criticism that was poured on him after our defeat. I was particularly sorry for a group of British supporters who worked in a mining township at Morro Velho. They had gone out of their way to give us hospitality, and we felt as though we had let them down. We consoled ourselves with the fact that a victory over Spain in our next match would still take us through to the second round.

CAP NO 32

Spain, World Cup, Rio de Janeiro, 2.7.50. England lost 1–0

Williams Ramsey Eckersley Wright* Hughes Dickinson
Matthews Mortensen Milburn Baily Finney

Highlights: Spain took the lead through centre-forward Zarra in the 47th minute and then dropped back into deep defence. Even with Matthews and Finney operating, England could not make the breakthrough and their World Cup challenge was over. Jackie Milburn had a legitimate-looking equaliser ruled offside. Alf Ramsey and Bill Eckersley started a fifteen-match full-back partnership, and Tottenham pass master Eddie Baily got a long overdue cap. Tom Finney was tripped twice in the penalty area, but each time the referee waved play on. It was one of those games, one of those tournaments. *The Wright Cuttings Book* (*Reynolds News*): 'In the inquests that follow this shambles of a World Cup challenge, questions must be asked as to whether Billy Wright is the right man to lead England. His captaincy lacks the fire and brimstone element that just might have sparked some sort of reaction in his tame, tired-looking team-mates. The big debate is now certain to start: "Is Wright right for England?"'

BILLY: We played our best football of the finals against Spain, but our finishing left a lot to be desired. Eddie Baily had a cracking debut, and his passing cut huge holes in the Spanish defence. Stan Mortensen and Jackie Milburn might have had a couple of goals each but for some brilliant saves by Barcelona goalkeeper Ramallets. Tom Finney was the most mild-mannered of men, but even he got heated when the referee ignored our claims for penalties after Tom had twice been fouled. Let's be honest, we made a mess of it. We should have beaten both the United States and Spain, and failed. So we got what we deserved. The criticism was poured on us like burning oil. Ouch! I still think that if Neil Franklin had been in the team we would have done much better. Losing him robbed our defence of the composure we had built up over the previous four years.

While England took the long haul home, Uruguay went on to win the World Cup. They beat hosts Brazil in front of a world record crowd of 199,854 in a deciding match refereed by England's George Reader, who later became chairman of Southampton. Brazil needed only a draw to take the trophy, but the Uruguayans came from a goal down to win 2–1 and so lift the Cup for a second time. Sweden beat Spain 3–1 to clinch third place.

Billy returned to a First Division season which was dominated by Tottenham's push-and-run side in which Alf Ramsey, Bill Nicholson, Ronnie Burgess and Eddie Baily were key players. Wolves had one of their least effective seasons of the decade, finishing down in fourteenth position and there was a sudden slump in the form of Billy 'Mr Reliable' Wright.

CAP NO 33
Northern Ireland, Windsor Park, 7.10.50. England won 4–1
Williams   Ramsey   Aston   Wright*[1]   Chilton   Dickinson
Matthews   Mannion   Lee[1]   Baily[2]   Langton

Highlights: Eddie Baily, more noted for his skilful scheming, scored two goals and big Jackie Lee, a Leicestershire cricketer, marked his only international with a goal. Northern Ireland were chasing an equaliser with the score at 2–1 when England scored twice in the last five minutes. Billy Wright netted his third and final goal for England with a shot that went into the net through a forest of legs, and Baily finished the Irish off with a superbly executed hook shot. Manchester United centre-half Allenby Chilton had to wait until he was 32 for this first cap as the selectors continued to hunt for a successor to Neil Franklin. *The Wright Cuttings Book* (*Sunday Graphic*): 'Despite his goal, Billy Wright can feel far from happy with his contribution to what was not as comfortable a victory as it appears in the scoreline.'

BILLY: I was just a shadow of myself in those first few months after the World Cup, and it came almost as a relief when an injury put me out of the running for a place in the next two internationals. It broke a run of 33 successive matches for England, and the club sent me off to Blackpool again for some sea air and a rest. Johnny Hancocks came with me, and we used to run together along Blackpool sands to maintain our fitness. Staying at the seaside did not really do me a lot of good because I had too much time on my hands to fret about my loss of form.

For the record, these were the two matches that Billy missed – with Alf Ramsey taking his place as skipper:

Wales, Roker Park, 15.11.50. England won 4–2
Williams   Ramsey*   Smith L   Watson   Compton   Dickinson
Finney   Mannion¹   Milburn¹   Baily²   Medley

Highlights: Eddie Baily, nicknamed the 'Cheeky Chappie' because of his impersonation of comedian Max Miller, repeated his two-goal act. Arsenal centre-half Leslie Compton made his England debut at the age of 38 alongside county cricketing colleague Willie Watson. Les Medley partnered his Tottenham team-mate Baily on the left wing. Lionel Smith, converted from centre-half by Arsenal, came in at left-back. Goalkeeper Bert Williams kept his place in goal to maintain the Wolves record of having at least one player in the England team in every international match since the war. Trevor Ford, playing for Wales in front of his Sunderland fans, scored twice in the second half to give the Welsh the hope of a championship point. It was not until Jackie Milburn scored in the final seconds that England could feel confident that they had the match won.

Yugoslavia, Highbury, 22.11.50. Drew 2–2
Williams   Ramsey*   Eckersley   Watson   Compton   Dickinson
Hancocks   Mannion   Lofthouse²   Baily   Medley

Highlights: Bolton centre-forward Nat Lofthouse announced his arrival on the international stage with two goals. It was the first time in post-war football that England had gone into action without either Matthews or Finney. Leslie Compton deflected the ball into his own net, and Yugoslavia forced a late equaliser to become the first Continental side to avoid defeat in England in a full international.

For the crucial Home Championship match against Scotland, the selectors recalled fit-again Billy. It was an unhappy comeback.

CAP NO 34

Scotland, Wembley, 14.4.51. England lost 3–2

Williams   Ramsey   Eckersley   Johnston   Froggatt J   Wright*
Matthews   Mannion   Mortensen   Hassall¹   Finney¹

Highlights: Wilf Mannion was carried off with a fractured cheekbone in the eleventh minute. With Walter Winterbottom accompanying Mannion to hospital, skipper Billy Wright took the decision to switch Finney to the right to partner Matthews and the two wing wizards often made the Scottish defenders think they were seeing double. The ten men of England made the Scots battle all the way after debutant Harold Hassall had given them a 25th minute lead. Hibs partners Bobby Johnstone and Lawrie Reilly netted for Scotland and then the barnstorming Billy Liddell made it 3–1. England, who had briefly been down to nine men after Stan Mortensen had been knocked out, refused to give in and Tom Finney conjured a goal. But the Scots held on for a deserved victory against the Auld Enemy. *The Wright Cuttings Book* (*Daily Mirror*): 'This was a horror match for Billy Wright. His tackles were mistimed, his passes inaccurate and his concentration not what it should have been.'

BILLY: I would have to describe this as my worst performance in an England shirt. My passing was poor, and my marking nowhere near as tight as it needed to be. I held myself responsible for two of Scotland's goals and I fully expected to be dropped for the first time for the next international against Argentina the following month. Amazingly, the selectors stuck with me even though I was still clearly way off form. I was carried through the season by my Wolves team-mates, and my confidence was at rock bottom.

CAP NO 35

Argentina, Wembley, 9.5.51. England won 2–1

Williams   Ramsey   Eckersley   Wright*   Taylor J   Cockburn
Finney   Mortensen¹   Milburn¹   Hassall   Metcalfe

Highlights: Goals in the last ten minutes from Stan Mortensen and Jackie Milburn (following the two he had scored for Newcastle on the same pitch in the FA Cup final four days earlier) gave England a scrambled victory. Eccentric Argentinian goalkeeper Rugilo, nicknamed 'Tarzan', had the crowd roaring with laughter as he swung on the crossbar and clowned his way through the match, which was staged as part of the Festival of Britain celebrations. Fulham centre-half Jim Taylor won the first of two caps at the age of 33. Argentina were only the second country other than Scotland to play England at Wembley. *The Wright Cuttings Book* (*Sunday Express*): 'For his own sake, the time has come for the selectors to give Billy Wright a rest from the pressures of international football.'

BILLY: This time the selectors spotted that I was below par, and as I had anticipated the axe fell. My old friend Bill Nicholson was called up in my place against Portugal. Walter Winterbottom wanted to soften the blow by telling the press that I had been released to join Wolves on their club tour to South Africa. But I preferred the truth to come out. I deserved to be dropped, and I needed to face up to it. Now I had something to motivate me. I was determined to win back my place and the England captaincy.

For the record, this was the third match that Billy missed:

Portugal, Goodison Park, 19.5.51. England won 5–2
Williams Ramsey* Eckersley Nicholson¹ Taylor J Cockburn
Finney¹ Pearson Milburn² Hassall¹ Metcalfe

Highlights: Bill Nicholson scored with his first kick in international football in what was to prove his only match for England. Portugal were a goal down in twenty seconds and level a minute later in a blistering start to the match. Jackie Milburn restored England's lead in the eleventh minute. Alf Ramsey, skippering the side for a third time, mishit a back pass that let Portugal in for a second equaliser soon after half-time. Tom Finney then took over and ran the Portuguese into such disarray that at the after-match banquet their entire team stood and toasted 'Mr Finney, the Master'. He scored a magnificent solo goal, and then laid on goals for Milburn and Harold Hassall.

Meantime, Billy Wright was sunning himself in South Africa and preparing for his comeback.

Who won what in 1950–51

First Division: Tottenham, 60pts. Runners-up: Manchester United, 56pts.

Tottenham's record: P42 W25 D10 L7 F82 A44 Pts60

Tottenham squad: Ditchburn, Ramsey, Willis, Nicholson, Clarke, Burgess*, (from) Walters, Murphy, Bennett, Duquemin, Baily, Medley. Top scorers: Duquemin (15), Walters (15). Manager: Arthur Rowe.

Second Division: Preston, 57pts. Runners-up: Manchester City, 52pts.

Third Division (South): Nottingham Forest, 70pts. Runners-up: Norwich City, 64pts.

Third Division (North): Rotherham, 71pts, Runners-up: Mansfield Town, 64pts.

FA Cup final: Newcastle United 2, Blackpool 0

Newcastle United: Fairbrother, Cowell, Corbett, Harvey, Brennan, Crowe, Walker, Taylor, Milburn[2], Robledo, Mitchell.

Blackpool: Farm, Shimwell, Garrett, Johnston, Hayward, Kelly, Matthews, Mudie, Mortensen, Slater, Perry.

Top First Division marksman: Stan Mortensen (Blackpool), 30 goals.

Footballer of the Year: Harry Johnston (Blackpool).

Scottish champions: Hibernian, 48pts. Runners-up: Rangers, 38pts.

Scottish Cup final: Celtic 1, Motherwell 0

1950 World Cup final at the Maracana Stadium, Rio, 16 July 1950: Uruguay 2, Brazil 1

Uruguay: Maspoli, Gonzales M, Tejera, Gambetta, Varela, Andrade, Ghiggia[1], Perez, Miguez, Schiaffino[1], Moran.

Brazil: Barbosa, Augusto, Juvenal, Bauer, Danilo, Bigode, Friaca¹, Zizinho, Ademir, Jair, Chico.

Stats: Top scorer: Ademir (Brazil), 9. Total goals: 88 (4 per game). Attendance (22 matches): 1,337,000 (average 60,773); 199,854 (deciding match). Referee: George Reader (England).

SEASON 1951–52:
The Comeback

What a difference a year makes! From being convinced that he was washed up as an international player, Billy found himself standing at the top table in a posh London hotel on the eve of the 1952 FA Cup final making an acceptance speech as the Footballer of the Year.

This was the prestigious Football Writers' Association award, the first of its kind in the world and introduced as an annual prize in 1947–48. Stanley Matthews was the first recipient, and Billy was number five after Johnny Carey, Joe Mercer and Harry Johnston. I wrote a history of the award, *The Golden Heroes*, in collaboration with distinguished colleagues Dennis Signy and Michael Parkinson and we interviewed every surviving winner. All of them made the point that this was the number one award because it was the first; all other awards are imitations.

The fact that Billy was elected is proof that he had won back the support of not only the England selectors but also those football writers who had used poison pens in describing his nightmare season following the World Cup debacle.

BILLY: It came as a pleasant shock to be told that I had won the award because at club level Wolves had a very poor year, finishing sixteenth in the First Division and going out of the FA Cup in the fourth round. There were much better candidates, I thought, in the Manchester United, Arsenal and Tottenham teams that dominated the League title race, and Newcastle, who won the cup for a second successive year. I like to think it was my performances with England that took the eye, and shrewd judges among the football writers realised that Wolves were laying the foundations for some great years ahead. Over the next eight or so seasons we rivalled and often surpassed [Manchester] United as the best side in the country. I saw my award as recognition of what was being achieved at Molineux, and it belonged as much to the team and manager Stan Cullis as to me. If anybody had told me twelve months earlier that I would have been collecting the trophy I would have told them they were mad. My confidence and self-belief had been shattered, and I honestly thought my international career was finished.

Billy's recall to the England team after being dropped for just one match started one of the most extraordinary sequences in the history of international football. It began a run of a record seventy consecutive England appearances that was only to end with his retirement in 1959. If I can invent a word: it was consistency on a Bradmanesque scale.

CAP NO 36
France, Highbury, 3.10.51. Drew 2–2
Williams   Ramsey   Willis   Wright*   Chilton   Cockburn
Finney   Mannion   Milburn   Hassall   Medley[1] +1 own goal

Highlights: Les Medley's first goal for England and an own goal saved a mediocre England team from a first home defeat by a foreign side. France were robbed of a deserved victory when Bert Williams made a desperate late save from French centre-forward Jacques Grumellon, who gave centre-half Allenby Chilton a nightmare afternoon. Arthur Willis, partnering his Spurs team-mate Alf Ramsey, was one of four players – along with Chilton, Henry Cockburn and Wilf Mannion – who never played for England again. *The Wright Cuttings Book* (*Daily Herald*): 'It was like welcoming back an old friend to see Billy Wright leading with enthusiasm and drive. What a pity so many of his colleagues were unable to match his energy and passion.'

BILLY: 'I almost cried when the selection card arrived in the post telling me that I had been recalled to the England team. Walter Winterbottom took me on one side before the match against France and told me that he had never lost faith in me. He advised me to just play my natural game, just as Stan Cullis had when I started out as Wolves captain. It did wonders for my confidence to know that the England manager still believed in me. I was happy with my personal contribution against France, but it was a scrappy team performance and our problems continued in the middle of the defence. France could count themselves unlucky not to have won by a convincing margin, and it was my Wolves team-mate Bert Williams who saved us from defeat. 'The Cat' was almost in Frank Swift's class. I could give him no higher praise.'

CAP NO 37

Wales, Ninian Park, 20.10.51. Drew 1–1

Williams   Ramsey   Smith L   Wright*   Barrass   Dickinson
Finney   Thompson   Lofthouse   Baily¹   Medley

Highlights: Eddie Baily saved England from defeat against a Welsh team in which Ivor Allchurch and Trevor Ford were constantly putting England's defence under pressure. Newcastle right-winger Billy Foulkes scored in the third minute with his first shot for Wales in international football. Baily, a master with the ball at his feet, equalised with a rare header following a counter attack generated by a perfect pass from Billy Wright. Ford, the idol of Sunderland, missed two easy chances late in the game to give Wales their first victory over England since the war. Malcolm Barrass was the seventh centre-half tried by the selectors since the defection of Neil Franklin. Tommy Thompson, Aston Villa's diminutive ball-playing inside-right, won the first of two caps. *The Wright Cuttings Book (Daily Mirror)*: 'It was a frustrating afternoon for Billy Wright. You could see his anxiety to help out in attack, but he was too often drawn back into defence to cover for the less than comfortable Malcolm Barrass, who should be renamed "Embarrass" after the chasing he was given by Trevor Ford.'

BILLY: Trevor Ford let us off the hook, which was rare for him. He was one of the finest centre-forwards of my generation, mixing good ball control with physical strength. We had many great duels during our careers and always finished up hugging each other at the end of games in which we had tried to knock the hell out of each other. He and Len Shackleton had a legendary partnership at Sunderland, and it was no secret that they didn't always get on with each other. There was a famous incident when Trevor complained that Shack never passed to him. Shack responded by dribbling the ball around four defenders and the goalkeeper and then stopping the ball dead on the goal line before pushing it back into the path of Trevor twenty yards behind him. 'Now don't say I never blankety-blank pass to you,' shouted Shack as Trevor steered the ball into an empty net. The linesman flagged Shack offside and the goal did not count!

CAP NO 38

Northern Ireland, Villa Park, 14.11.51. England won 2–0
Merrick   Ramsey   Smith L   Wright*   Barrass   Dickinson
Finney   Sewell   Lofthouse²   Phillips   Medley

Highlights: The selectors experimented by giving inside-forwards Jackie Sewell and Len Phillips their first caps either side of Nat Lofthouse, who scored a goal in each half. Birmingham City goalkeeper Gil Merrick made the short journey to Villa Park for his first of 23 caps. He kept a clean sheet, but was lucky in the second half when a screaming 25-yard shot from Barnsley forward Eddie McMorran crashed against the crossbar. *The Wright Cuttings Book* (*Daily Express*): 'This was a vintage performance from Billy Wright, who was the boss both of the defence and the midfield. His tackles were panther-like in their speed, and then he always found a team-mate with a well judged pass.'

BILLY: My memory of that match is of being frightened out of my life. Somebody threw a firework on to the pitch in the second half, and it sounded just like a gunshot. It was the sort of thing you expect when playing in South America, but this was pretty near unheard of in an English ground. Like the rest of the players, I jumped out of my skin. There was the hilarious sight of all the photographers behind the goal throwing themselves to the ground.

CAP NO 39

Austria, Wembley, 28.11.51. Drew 2–2

Merrick   Ramsey[1] [(pen)]   Eckersley   Wright*   Froggatt J   Dickinson
Milton   Broadis   Lofthouse[1]   Baily   Medley

Highlights: An injury to Tom Finney forced yet another permutation by the selectors, with Gloucester cricketer and Arsenal forward Arthur Milton partnering Ivor Broadis on the right wing. Austria, under the baton of the remarkable Ernst 'Clockwork' Ocwirk, took the lead in the 47th minute after a first half of cut-and-thrust football of the highest quality. Ocwirk sent a precision free-kick into the penalty area where Melchior forced it wide of goalkeeper Gil Merrick. England equalised in the 70th minute when the ice-cool Alf Ramsey scored from the penalty spot after his Spurs team-mate Eddie Baily had been sent sprawling. Six minutes later Ramsey made a goal for Nat Lofthouse with a pinpoint free-kick, which the Bolton centre-forward steered high into the net with a powerful header. Austria, rated the best side in Europe and fresh from becoming the first overseas team to beat Scotland at home, saved the match two minutes from the end with a penalty by Stojaspal. There were some breathtaking attacking movements by both teams, yet all the goals came from set-piece play. Milton was the last player capped by England at cricket and football. *The Wright Cuttings Book* (*The Times*): 'We tend to take Billy Wright for granted. While it was the magnificent Ocwirk who took the eye, we should not forget that the reason he did not function as well as he might is because the energetic Wright was there to foil him almost at every turn.'

BILLY: Our pre-match plans were thrown into confusion by the late withdrawal of the injured Tom Finney. I was going to play wearing the number ten shirt, with the job of shadowing Ernst Ocwirk. He went down into the programme as their centre-half, but had a roving role and was as much a schemer as a defender. Bill Nicholson was all set to play at right-half, releasing me for my marking job. But then Bill reported that he was not one hundred per cent fit, and so we reverted to our usual formation. Walter's instructions were that the nearest man to Ocwirk should 'sit on him', and try to cut out his ball supply. He was in the Alex James class as a passer and organiser, and we felt pleased that we managed to keep him relatively quiet. When Eddie Baily was fouled for the penalty, he picked himself up and said to his Spurs team-mate Alf Ramsey, 'I've done all the hard work winning the blankety-blank penalty, now make sure you score.' Alf appeared to tuck the penalty away as coolly as if in a training session, but he told me later that his knees were knocking as he placed the ball on the spot.

CAP NO 40

Scotland, Hampden Park, 5.4.52. England won 2–1
Merrick   Ramsey   Garrett   Wright*   Froggatt J   Dickinson
Finney   Broadis   Lofthouse   Pearson²   Rowley J

Highlights: Two neatly taken goals by Stan Pearson stretched England's unbeaten run in full internationals at Hampden Park to fifteen years. His first after eight minutes was a superb hooked shot, and his second just before half-time followed a mix-up in Scotland's defence. The Scots screamed that they were robbed of a penalty when Gil Merrick pulled down Lawrie Reilly, and the 134,504 crowd roared with rage when the referee waved play on. Reilly managed to score in the last minute, Scotland's first home goal against England since the war. But it was too late to stop an England victory that gave them a share of the Home Championship with Wales. Blackpool's Tom Garrett made a sound debut at left-back in place of injured Bill Eckersley. *The Wright Cuttings Book (Daily Mail)*: 'Billy Wright stands just 5ft 8in in his stockinged feet, yet when he pulls on the England shirt he suddenly seems seven feet tall. He was a tower of strength against the Scots, continually breaking up their attacks with smart interceptions and then releasing the ball to start an England offensive.'

BILLY: Hampden matches were always memorable. I rarely played there with fewer than 130,000 spectators inside and the noise of the Hampden Roar was deafening. It was pointless trying to shout out any instructions to team-mates, and we had to rely on sign language. Playing in Glasgow always seemed to bring the best out in me, and I was never a losing captain at Hampden. I had a love-hate relationship with the Scottish spectators. They gave me terrible abuse in a bid to unsettle me, but they were always fair and sporting after each game was over.

CAP NO 41:

Italy, Florence, 18.5.52. Drew 1–1

Merrick   Ramsey   Garrett   Wright*   Froggatt J   Dickinson
Finney   Broadis¹   Lofthouse   Pearson   Elliott

Highlights: Only Billy Wright and Tom Finney remained of the England team that had conquered Italy 4–0 in Turin in 1948. Ivor Broadis gave England a fourth minute lead that was cancelled out by a spectacular solo effort from Amadei in the 63rd minute. The idolised centre-forward Piola, who had helped Italy retain the World Cup in 1938, was recalled for a swansong appearance at the age of 39. It ended on a sad note for him when he missed an easy chance for a winner in front of an empty net. *The Wright Cuttings Book* (*Daily Telegraph*): 'It was the cool heads of Wright and Ramsey that brought England safely through to a draw when the Italians were threatening to run riot in the second half.'

BILLY: It was incidents off the pitch that have stayed in my memory. As we walked off at the end of the first half we heard a low-flying aircraft. It swooped right overhead and looked ready to bomb the stadium. Suddenly miniature parachutes appeared and down on to the pitch dropped 22 watches for we players as a present from the match sponsors. Things turned nasty in the second half when Nat Lofthouse was pelted with coins and bottles after one of his typical shoulder charges on the goalkeeper. I admired the bravery of half a dozen of the Italian players who faced the crowd from close range and appealed for them to show sportsmanship. It worked, and as the Italian fans applauded us off at the end Nat said with typical Lancashire humour: 'I'd have been happier if they'd thrown watches at me.'

CAP NO 42
Austria, Vienna, 25.5.52. England won 3–2
Merrick   Ramsey   Eckersley   Wright*   Froggatt J   Dickinson
Finney   Sewell[1]   Lofthouse[2]   Baily   Elliott

Highlights: The match that earned Nat Lofthouse the nickname 'The Lion of Vienna'. Eight minutes from the end, with the game deadlocked at 2–2, Tom Finney collected a long throw from Gil Merrick and released a pass that sent Lofty clear just inside the Austrian half. He galloped 45 yards with a pack of defenders snapping at his heels, and collided with oncoming goalkeeper Musil as he released a shot. He was flat out unconscious and did not see the ball roll over the goal line for the winning goal. The Bolton hero was carried off on a stretcher, but, still dazed, returned for the final five minutes. He struck a shot against a post in the closing moments. England's counterattacking tactics had worked to perfection. They took the lead in the 21st minute after soaking up nonstop pressure from the Austrians, who were rated the number one team in Europe. A penetrating pass by Eddie Baily opened the heart of the Austrian defence and Lofthouse finished off the move with a left-foot volley deep into the net. The cheers of the squads of British soldiers in the 65,500 crowd were still filling the Prater Stadium when Jack Froggatt conceded a penalty from which Huber side-footed an equaliser. The Portsmouth centre-half quickly made amends with a pass that put Jackie Sewell through to score after he had wrong-footed the Austrian defenders with two exaggerated dummies. Austria pulled level again just before half-time through centre-forward Diego, who shrugged off Billy Wright's challenge before powering the ball past goalkeeper Gil Merrick. Then came the storybook climax from Lofthouse. *The Wright Cuttings Book* (*The People*): 'While praising the incredible heroism of Lofthouse, let us not lose sight of the fact that it was the captain Billy Wright who drove England on to greater efforts when the Austrians looked set to dominate the match. The glory belongs to Lofthouse, but there were ten other England heroes in support led by a stirring performance from their skipper.'

BILLY: The courage Nat showed in this match was typical of him as a man and as a player. The way he insisted on coming back into the match although out on his feet lifted the heart of every Englishman in the stadium. It made us redouble our efforts to keep the Austrians out. If ever you were in trouble, Nat was the sort of iron man you wanted alongside you. We could only stand and watch his long, lonely run into the Austrian half and as the goalkeeper came out it was obvious there was going to be a collision. But Nat didn't check his stride. He just kept going. It was unbelievable bravery. We were so pleased to have given the British Army boys something to cheer them up. The only person who knew little about it was Nat, who was still giddy at the end of the game. We were carried back to our dressing-room on the shoulders of cheering Tommies, who had come from their posts in Germany in their thousands.

CAP NO 43
Switzerland, Zurich, 28.5.52. England won 3–0
Merrick   Ramsey   Eckersley   Wright*   Froggatt J   Dickinson
Allen R   Sewell[1]   Lofthouse[2]   Baily   Finney

Highlights: Billy Wright was credited with taking over the England caps record from Bob Crompton with this 43rd international appearance (although most record books give Crompton's old record as 41 caps). The Swiss were beaten by the same scoring combination that had won the match in Vienna three days earlier: Jackie Sewell one, Nat Lofthouse two. West Bromwich Albion's versatile forward Ronnie Allen won the first of his five caps, and gave a lively performance on the right wing. *The Wright Cuttings Book* (*Sunday Express*): 'Record-breaker Billy Wright gave yet another outstanding performance, and his 43rd cap fits on the same size head as his first.'

BILLY: I was presented with a beautiful framed illuminated address to mark my taking over from Bob Crompton as the most-capped

England player. Little did I know then that I had not even reached the halfway mark in my collection of caps. To say I was proud would be an enormous understatement, particularly as just a year earlier I was convinced my international career was over. It's all about confidence. Once you lose self-belief, you are in trouble. It took the support and friendly advice of Stan Cullis and Walter Winterbottom to get me back on track, and for that I will always be grateful.

Who won what in 1951–52

First Division: Manchester United, 57pts. Runners-up: Tottenham, 53pts.

Man United record: P42 W23 D11 L8 F95 A52 Pts57

Man United squad: Allen, McNulty, Byrne (Aston), Carey*, Chilton, Cockburn, Berry, Downie, Rowley, Pearson, Bond. Top scorer: Rowley (30). Manager: Matt Busby.

Second Division: Sheffield Wednesday, 53pts. Runners-up: Cardiff City, 51pts.

Third Division (South): Plymouth, 66pts. Runners-up: Reading, 61pts.

Third Division (North): Lincoln City, 69pts, Runners-up: Grimsby, 66pts.

FA Cup final: Newcastle United 1, Arsenal 0

Newcastle: Simpson, Cowell, McMichael, Harvey*, Brennan, Robledo E, Walker, Foulkes, Milburn, Robledo G¹, Mitchell.

Arsenal: Swindin, Barnes, Smith, Forbes, Daniel, Mercer*, Cox, Logie, Holton, Lishman, Roper.

Top First Division marksman: George Robledo (Newcastle), 33 goals.

Footballer of the Year: Billy Wright (Wolves).

Scottish champions: Hibernian, 45pts. Runners-up: Rangers, 41pts.

Scottish Cup final: Motherwell 4, Dundee 0

SEASON 1952–53:
Golden Wolves

This was the season in which Wolves first indicated that something extra special was developing at Molineux. It gives me the opportunity to take a temporary step aside from Billy's international career and to put the focus on his club record, which was every bit as impressive as his achievements with England.

All that glistered on the English soccer scene during the 1950s were the old gold shirts of Wolves as they powered through a startling sequence of success. In nine years from 1952–53 they won the League crown three times including successive championships, finished out of the first three only once and missed a hat-trick of First Division titles and the FA Cup and League double by just one precious point in 1959–60.

After two team-building seasons when they flirted with life in the bottom half of the table, Wolves made a spirited challenge for the 1952–53 championship. They finally finished third behind Joe Mercer's Arsenal and Tom Finney's Preston, a race won on goal average by the North London giants. For Wolves, it was just a beginning. The next seven seasons were truly golden years.

Billy was the chief motivator on the pitch for all but the final year of the decade, by which time he had voluntarily climbed off at the top of the mountain. While he was the heart of the team, master tactician Stan Cullis was the brains. Billy provided the drive, Cullis the direction.

Cullis famously put a heavy emphasis on fitness and strength, and their overall impression was of muscularity and raw power. Yet there was also a thread of artistry running through the side, and they provided a procession of players for the England team.

The Wolves method of pumping long balls out of defence for their forwards to chase might appear a crude tactic on paper but on the pitch it was mightily effective. There was sneering criticism of their method from so-called purists in the game who dismissed it as 'kick-and-rush'. It was more like a goal rush. In their peak-success years they scored 878 goals and, astonishingly, topped the century mark in the First Division in four consecutive seasons.

The Cullis theory was a simple one. He argued that one long ball, accurately placed in the path of fast-moving attacking players, could do the work of three or four short passes and in half the time. The modern name for it would be route one. It was not particularly pretty, but it was extremely potent.

Cullis himself had been schooled by Major Frank Buckley, his famous predecessor as Wolves manager who, as we have learned, was a tough disciplinarian and a firm believer in the doctrine of quick and simple attacking football; also of discovering and developing young talent rather than raiding the transfer market. Cullis did not buy his teams – he built them; and many outstanding Wolves players came off the conveyor belt at Wath Wanderers, the Wolves nursery club in South Yorkshire which was run for them on professional lines by former Molineux winger Mark Crook. Every Wolves team – from the 'cubs' through to the first team – was fashioned around the controversial but successful 'long ball' game.

With Billy Wright as their shining role model, the Wolves youngsters were encouraged to battle for every ball as if their lives depended on it and then to move it into the opposition penalty area as quickly as possible. The biggest sin any Wolves player could commit was to shirk a challenge, and to dwell on the ball instead of releasing it was rated nearly as serious. A player pulling out of a tackle knew he faced the even more unnerving experience of having to explain his action to the awesome Cullis, who considered football to be first and foremost a physical game. He was, remember, out of the 1930s school where barging and charging were a vital and integral part of the game.

To support his 'long ball' theories Cullis made use of the computer-like mind of a statistician called Charles Reep, a football-loving wing commander who was stationed at RAF Bridgnorth close to Wolverhampton. Reep had a system of plotting and recording in detail every move of a football match, and he fed Cullis with facts and figures that strengthened his argument that long, direct passes provided the most efficient and successful method of breaking down a defence. Cullis claimed that if too much time was spent in building up an attack with a series of short passes it gave the opposition time to cover, and allowed fewer opportunities for his forwards to shoot at goal.

Stamina and strength were as valued as skill in Cullis-influenced teams, and pre-season training used to be so punishing that the players ached to play football as a release from the torture of training. They faced the daily challenge of having to tackle a commando-like assault course, culminating in an exhausting sprint up a steep hill in the tangled heathland of Cannock Chase. 'We used to call it Heartbreak Hill,' Billy revealed. 'It was used as a barometer of our fitness.'

This was all designed to get the players fit enough to last a season of physically demanding football. Opponents were quite literally run into the ground by Wolves players whom they could sometimes match for skill but never for energy, drive, and determination.

For all the criticism of the Wolves style – or rather the alleged lack of it – nobody could argue that the Cullis system did not bring startling results. As well as being dominant on the domestic front, the whirlwind Wolves side of the 1950s had some memorable triumphs in unofficial floodlit international thrillers that hastened the inauguration of organised European competition.

The goalkeeping was in the safe hands of the graceful England international Bert 'The Cat' Williams, and later of Malcolm Finlayson, a flying Scot bought from Millwall. Both had bravery to go with their great talent, and could withstand physical challenges from shoulder-charging forwards in an era when goalkeepers had little of the protection given to them by today's 'thou-shalt-not-touch' laws.

Wolves were wall solid at full-back with Eddie Stuart and Bill Shorthouse and then George Showell and Gerry Harris as resolute partners. All were dependable defenders who were strong in the tackle and well drilled in the art (if art is the right word) of hammering huge clearances deep into opposition territory.

These were the days when all teams played two orthodox wingers, so full-backs were detailed to full-time defensive duties and 'overlap' had not found a way into the football vocabulary. Wingers did not relish facing Wolves because they had a tradition for producing full-backs who tackled like a clap of thunder and took no prisoners.

The real match-winning power emanated from a magnificent half-back line that featured a combination of skipper Billy Wright, Bill Slater, Eddie Clamp and Ron Flowers, all England internationals, gifted footballers, and with the right mixture of skill and strength; each of them was capable of putting the emphasis on defence or attack as the situation demanded.

Billy was the kingpin. He made a successful switch to the middle of the defence after winning 59 of his 105 England caps as a robust wing-half. As an indication of their reliability as the backbone of the Wolves team, there were four international matches when the England half-back line read Clamp–Wright–Slater.

With the calculating Cullis insisting on quick release, the ball rarely stayed long in midfield. The chief architect of the attacking movements was Peter Broadbent, a master of ball control and precise passing. He was one of the few players allowed the luxury of dwelling on the ball while he looked for the best place to deposit it with passes that were both accurate and incisive.

Wright, Slater and Ron Flowers shared midfield duties with Broadbent, the intelligent and versatile Slater later replacing Billy as captain and centre-half. Eddie Clamp brought discipline and a competitive edge to the midfield as a powerful right-half who epitomised the Wolves style of play with his driving enthusiasm and vigorous challenges that struck terror into the hearts of opposing inside-forwards.

A feature of the Wolves format was the flying wing play of the tiny Johnny Hancocks and the clever Jimmy Mullen. Both were deadly accurate crossers of the ball and Hancocks packed a rocket shot in his schoolboy-size right boot (legend has it that it was a size two, but I am assured that it was nearer a five). Norman Deeley later carried on the winger tradition and scored two goals in the 1960 FA Cup final. Waiting in the middle to convert the crosses of the Wolves wingers into goals were powerful forwards of the calibre of Roy Swinbourne,

Dennis Wilshaw, Colin Booth, Jim Murray and Bobby Mason. They followed in the footsteps of the idolised Jesse Pye, an enterprising centre-forward in the immediate post-war years at Molineux, who plundered 90 goals in 188 League games.

All the forwards who wore the gold shirts during the 1950s followed the Cullis creed of putting industry before invention. They were skilled workers of great heart who were prepared to take knocks in the penalty area in the cause of the team effort. While their chief priority was to get the ball into the net they were also expected to hassle and harass any opposing defender in possession so that he was unable to make a comfortable clearance. If any Wolves forward came off at the final whistle feeling less than exhausted, the demanding Cullis would want to know the reason why. Wolves worked for their success.

Under the Cullis–Wright axis, Wolves were FA Cup winners in 1949, League Champions in 1953–54, 1957–58 and 1958–59, FA Cup winners again in 1960 (the season after Billy's retirement), and out of the first three in the First Division only three times between 1950 and 1961. In the same period the reserves won the Central League title seven times and the youth team reached three FA Youth Cup Finals. They narrowly missed a hat-trick of championships in 1959–60 when Burnley overhauled them with victory in their final match of the season. By beating Wolves to the title by a point, Burnley stopped them becoming the first team in the twentieth century to pull off the League and FA Cup double. Tottenham did it the following season.

In the first fifteen post-war seasons their final positions in the First Division were 3, 5, 6, 2, 14, 16, 3, 1, 2, 3, 6, 1, 1, 2 and 3, and in each of the last four seasons they scored over a hundred League goals, which remains a unique feat. They had one of the most successful seasons ever undertaken by an English club in 1957–58 when they won the League Championship with a near-record 64 points, the reserves topped the Central League, the third team won the Birmingham and District League, the fourths carried off the Worcester Combination League and Cup, and the youth team won the FA Youth Cup.

Wolves started their successful run under Cullis with a 3–1 FA Cup final victory over Second Division Leicester City at Wembley in 1949. Wolves took eventual cup winners Newcastle to a semi-final replay in

1951, and won the Cup again in 1960 with a comfortable 3–0 victory over Blackburn Rovers at Wembley.

For those of us of a certain age, this golden Wolves era will be best remembered for their pioneering of European club football under floodlights. They mastered the mightiest teams in Europe in a series of unofficial world club championship matches at Molineux. Honved of Budapest – virtually the Hungarian national side that had ripped the heart out of the England team – Moscow Spartak, Moscow Dynamo and Real Madrid were conquered in so-called 'friendlies' that were played at full throttle because of the enormous international prestige and pride involved.

These midweek evening games were screened live on television – a rarity in those days – and the exciting exploits of Wolves captured the nation's interest and imagination. They triumphed against all-comers in what proved a trailblazer for European inter-club competitions. The influential French sports newspaper, *L'Equipe*, noticed that English newspapers were calling Wolves the kings of Europe, and they proposed a proper competition to decide just who were the champions of Europe. Typical of our blinkered, insular football hierarchy, the European Cup kicked off in 1955–56 without English involvement. The Football League and FA Cup competitions were seen as the be-all-and-end-all, and European football was considered a bridge too far. After all the visionary ground work of Wolves, English clubs were banned from competing in Europe. It was the 'Euro' controversy of the 1950s. Wolves concentrated on their domestic world where they battled with Manchester United for the unofficial mantle of England's greatest club side – the Cullis Cubs versus the Busby Babes.

BILLY: It was the easiest job in the world to captain the Wolves teams of the 1950s. Everybody knew exactly what he had to do. Our success was due to our team understanding and the willingness of everyone to work for each other. Off the pitch, Stan Cullis was an inspiration and demanded and got one hundred per cent effort and enthusiasm from everybody who pulled on a Wolves shirt. He set the highest standards of discipline and responsible behaviour, and made every player aware that it was an honour to wear the old gold of Wolves. Pride and loyalty were important in football in those days, and all the Wolves players and fans of that era were proud to be associated with the club. Stan could be hard and sometimes strict to the point of harsh, but his heart was in the right place and you were only in trouble with him if you gave less than your best. You could almost warm your hands on the club spirit, and it used to be a joy to meet up with the lads for matches and training. We were on first-name terms with many fans, and used to drink tea and chat to them in a local café called the Copper Kettle. There was no 'them' and 'us'. We were one big, happy family, and I felt honoured to be the captain.

Sir Matt Busby, who was creating his own miracles with Manchester United, went on record near the close of his career with this assessment of the team that provided his greatest opposition: 'Wolves in those days stood for everything that was good about British football. They played with great power, spirit and style. Their performances against top-class continental teams gave everybody in the game over here a lift. Stan Cullis moulded his teams in his own image. They were honest, straightforward, uncomplicated, and full of zest and determination.'

This is how mastermind Stan Cullis summed up his team and his triumphs: 'The whole style of play in my time as manager was geared towards keeping the ball in the opponents' penalty area for as long as possible. We had the players to make our plan work. It was really exhilarating. There were critics of the way we played, but I have not the slightest doubt that the entertainment value of our matches was higher than at any time in my long experience of the game. We gave the spectators goals and excitement, and we managed to win all the trophies that mattered. My one regret is that the directors saw fit to dismiss me when I still had much to give to the club. I had given them a yardstick by which they could measure my achievements, and when we had the dip in fortunes that happens to all teams at some time they quickly removed me. They took away my job, but they could never take away my memories. They were unforgettable years.'

While helping Wolves monopolise the domestic scene, Billy was continuing to build one of the greatest of all individual international records.

CAP NO 44

Northern Ireland, Windsor Park, 4.10.52. Drew 2–2

Merrick   Ramsey   Eckersley   Wright*   Froggatt J   Dickinson
Finney   Sewell   Lofthouse¹   Baily   Elliott¹

Highlights: Nat Lofthouse scored in the first minute and Billy Elliott in the last minute of a dramatic match. Sandwiched in between was the magic of Celtic ball artist Charlie Tully, who scored twice for Ireland. He beat Merrick from 25 yards and then with his specialist inswinging corner-kick after the Irish team had been reduced by injury to ten men. (In a game for Celtic against Falkirk, Tully netted direct from a corner and was ordered to retake it because the referee was not ready. He immediately repeated the trick and put the ball in the exact same spot in the net!) Northern Ireland, urged on by a record 60,000 Windsor Park crowd, had two young midfield partners called Danny Blanchflower and Jimmy McIlroy dictating the pace and the pattern of the match. They were on the verge of their first victory over England since 1927 when Elliott silenced the celebrating fans with an equalising header in the desperate closing moments. *The Wright Cuttings Book* (*Daily Herald*): 'Billy Wright and Jimmy Dickinson were the match stars for England, steadying the ship with their cool defensive work when the Irish threatened to take a stranglehold on the game.'

BILLY: I recall Walter Winterbottom being furious over the goal that Charlie Tully scored direct from a corner-kick. Charlie was famous for his inswinging corners, and we had worked at cutting them out in training by placing Alf Ramsey on the near post and then our centre-half Jack Froggatt directly behind goalkeeper Gil Merrick. The corner from which he scored was curling towards Alf, who suddenly ducked under the ball. Gil reached out but only caught thin air as the ball swung into the net. Alf said later that he thought Gil had shouted 'mine', but it had apparently been one of the Irish forwards. The crowd went berserk when the ball hit the net. And no wonder – it was Northern Ireland's first international goal for eighteen months!

CAP NO 45
Wales, Wembley, 12.11.52. England won 5–2
Merrick   Ramsey   Smith L   Wright*   Froggatt J[1]   Dickinson
Finney[1]   Froggatt R   Lofthouse[2]   Bentley[1]   Elliott

Highlights: This was the first time Wales had ever played at Wembley, and a Wednesday afternoon crowd of 93,500 paid record gate receipts of £43,000. England were two goals up in the first ten minutes through Tom Finney and Nat Lofthouse. Five minutes later Trevor Ford pulled a goal back for Wales, and was then involved in a collision with Jack Froggatt that led to the England centre-half being carried off. Billy Wright switched to the middle of the defence, with Billy Elliott dropping back from the wing to left-half. Jack Froggatt, whose cousin, Redfern, was making his debut at inside-right, came back on as a passenger on the left wing. Remarkably, it was Jack who scored England's third goal just before half-time with a brave diving header. Roy Bentley made it 4–1 in England's first attack after half-time, with Ford instantly replying for Wales. Nat Lofthouse rounded off the scoring with a shot from 25 yards that goalkeeper Bill Short could only help into the net. *The Wright Cuttings Book (The Times)*: 'It will surely not have escaped the attention of Walter Winterbottom that Billy Wright looked comfortable and assured at the heart of the English defence.'

BILLY: The significant thing about this match was that it was the first time that I played at centre-half for England. I could not have asked for a tougher test than to have to mark the one and only Trevor Ford. Walter Winterbottom congratulated me on my performance, and I think he made a mental note that I was worth considering for the number five shirt.

CAP NO 46
Belgium, Wembley, 26.11.52. England won 5–0
Merrick   Ramsey   Smith L   Wright*   Froggatt J   Dickinson
Finney   Bentley   Lofthouse[2]   Froggatt R[1]   Elliott[2]

Highlights: Nat Lofthouse kept up his one-man bombardment with a double strike that took his haul to nine goals in five games. Redfern Froggatt scored his first goal for England, and Burnley winger Billy Elliott netted twice against the outplayed Belgians. The game was played in a driving sleet, and ice patches formed on the famous Wembley turf, making it difficult for defenders to keep their feet. England led 2–0 at the end of a first-half in which they might have had half a dozen goals against a completely outplayed Belgian team. *The Wright Cuttings Book* (*Wolverhampton Express & Star*): 'It is widely accepted that Billy Wright is now the complete captain. He leads by example, and against Belgium he was always in the thick of things. He seemed to attract the ball like a magnet, continually breaking from defence in possession and then starting a fresh England raid with a neat pass, usually to the feet of Tom Finney.'

BILLY: That outstanding Dutch referee Leo Horn was in charge of the match. A large, impressive and friendly man, he came into our dressing-room afterwards, congratulated us on our performance and said, 'You are still the number one football nation. I expect you to do very well in the 1954 World Cup.' We shared that view because we had now lost only one out of sixteen matches since the 1950 World Cup, and our one defeat by Scotland came when we were reduced to ten men.

CAP NO 47

Scotland, Wembley, 18.4.53. Drew 2–2

Merrick Ramsey Smith L Wright* Barrass Dickinson
Finney Broadis² Lofthouse Froggatt R Froggatt J

Highlights: Lawrie 'Last Minute' Reilly equalised for Scotland with the final kick of the match. It was Reilly's second goal in reply to two from Ivor Broadis. The Scots, driven from midfield by Preston's Tommy Docherty and Dundee's Doug Cowie, dominated play for long spells and thoroughly deserved their late equaliser. They played for much of the second half with only ten men after Rangers left-back Sammy Cox had been injured trying to stop a thrusting run by Tom Finney. Utility player Jack Froggatt, capped by England at centre-half and as an outside-left, partnered his cousin Redfern on the left wing. Each of the cousins missed simple chances to give England the lead before Broadis scored what looked like being a winning second goal. *The Wright Cuttings Book (Daily Sketch)*: 'Wearing the number four shirt with his usual pride, Billy Wright was one of the few England players to match the passion and industry of the Scots. It might easily have been a defeat by the Auld Enemy but for Wright's steadying influence under heavy pressure.'

BILLY: It was odd how we could always beat or hold the Scots at Hampden Park, yet struggled against them at Wembley. This draw meant that it was nineteen years since we had last beaten them on our home ground. There were just thirty seconds left when Lawrie Reilly popped up with one of his typical late goals that so often saved Scotland. We could not complain because they had been on top for so long, despite the injury to Sammy Cox.

CAP NO 48

Argentina, Buenos Aires, 17.5.53.
Abandoned at 0–0 after 23 minutes following a rain storm
Merrick   Ramsey   Eckersley   Wright*   Johnston   Dickinson
Finney   Broadis   Lofthouse   Taylor T   Berry

Highlights: The pitch became waterlogged following a cloudburst and British referee Arthur Ellis, up to his ankles in water, had no alternative but to abandon the game. Three days earlier an Argentinian XI had beaten an FA XI 3–1 in an unofficial international watched by a crowd of 120,000 including Juan Peron and his wife, Eva. The selectors had to wait to see if the new left-wing partnership of Manchester United team-mates Tommy Taylor and Johnny Berry would work at international level.

BILLY: I had never seen rain like it. Referee Arthur Ellis, later to make a name for himself in television's *It's A Knockout*, was quite a joker. As he signalled for us to return to our dressing-room, he said to me, 'If we stay out any longer we'll need lifeboats!' The pitch just disappeared under a lake of water, and our kit was so wet that we needed help from the training staff to strip off. We tried to get the game replayed, but the pitches were underwater for days and we had to move on to Chile for our next match. We were really angry that the Argentinian press had reported the first game as being an official international match, while we regarded it as a practice game to get acclimatised. The Football Association quite rightly insisted that the game should not be included in the records as an official international.

CAP NO 49

Chile, Santiago, 24.5.53. England won 2–1

Merrick   Ramsey   Eckersley   Wright*   Johnston   Dickinson
Finney   Broadis   Lofthouse¹   Taylor T¹   Berry

Highlights: Tommy Taylor's first goal for England in the 48th minute was a freak. His intended cross was turned into the net by Chilean goalkeeper Livingstone-Eves, who was the son of a Scot. Nat Lofthouse scored the second decisive goal after one of a dozen thrusting runs by Finney, and three minutes later he headed another Finney cross against the bar. The Chileans scored their only goal seven minutes from the end when a Rojas shot was deflected wide of the diving Gil Merrick. *The Wright Cuttings Book* (*Sunday Express*): 'The contribution from Billy Wright to this victory was, as ever, enormous. He is not one of those players you can marvel at because of any skill factor, but there are few players in the world who can match him for endeavour and alertness. Quietly and efficiently, he is the man who makes England tick.'

BILLY: Earlier that month Blackpool skipper Harry Johnston had been carried off shoulder high along with Stanley Matthews at the end of the unbelievable 1953 FA Cup final at Wembley. Nat Lofthouse had been in the Bolton team beaten 4–3 in what will always be remembered as the Matthews final, and he had a no-holds-barred duel with Harry. Now here they were as team-mates and playing their hearts out in a victory that was much more convincing than the scoreline shows. We had got the club spirit at international level, and that made for a happy tour party.

CAP NO 50

Uruguay, Montevideo, 31.5.53. England lost 2–1
Merrick   Ramsey   Eckersley   Wright*   Johnston   Dickinson
Finney   Broadis   Lofthouse   Taylor T¹   Berry

Highlights: World champions Uruguay turned on an exhibition against the old masters, and might have trebled their score but for being over-elaborate with dazzling approach play. Abbadie gave Uruguay the lead in the 27th minute, and clever centre-forward Miguez made it 2–0 on the hour. Nat Lofthouse and Ivor Broadis struck the woodwork and Tommy Taylor scored in the closing moments after an Alf Ramsey shot had been blocked. It was a spirited fightback by England after they had struggled to hold the world champions in a one-sided first half. *The Wright Cuttings Book (Daily Mail)*: 'Miguez, a master of ball control and as crafty as a monkey, led the entire England defence a dance. Billy Wright played him as well as any defender could do, but several times was left tackling his shadow. The England captain came off at the end knowing that there is a mountain for him and his team-mates to climb if they are to succeed Uruguay as world champions next year.'

BILLY: Their floating centre-forward Miguez was a real box of tricks, and in one run he whipped the ball over the top of me, ran round me and caught it on his head. It was incredible skill, but he was too clever by half and I thought he let his team down by being too selfish. I think we might have given them a much tighter game if five or six of our players had not been suffering the after-effects of a stomach bug picked up in Chile. I would have liked to have had a victory with which to mark my half-century of caps.

CAP 51

USA, New York City, 8.6.53. England won 6–3
Ditchburn   Ramsey   Eckersley   Wright*   Johnston   Dickinson
Finney²   Broadis¹   Lofthouse²   Froggatt R¹   Froggatt J

Highlights: This first full soccer international staged in New York was arranged to mark the Queen's Coronation six days earlier. The freak rain followed England from South America and a storm forced a 24-hour postponement. Then, under the floodlights at the Yankee Stadium, England – with Tom Finney running riot – avenged the 1–0 World Cup defeat with a comfortable victory in front of a 7,271 crowd. England missed a shoal of chances before Ivor Broadis gave them the lead two minutes before half-time. They quickly went 3–0 clear with goals early in the second half from Finney and Lofthouse. The Americans battled back with the help of a dubious penalty, but another goal each from Lofthouse and Finney followed by a sixth goal from Redfern Froggatt underlined England's supremacy in a match in which they could and should have reached double figures. *The Wright Cuttings Book* (*Sunday People*): 'At last, Billy Wright exorcised the ghosts that have haunted him ever since England's humiliating 1–0 World Cup defeat by the USA in Brazil in 1950. He played like a man possessed, determined not to suffer the same embarrassment. This time England outshone the Yankee Stadium floodlights, and Billy's beam at the final whistle signalled his great satisfaction.'

BILLY: This was the first international match that England had ever played under floodlights. It was a new experience, and a glimpse at what the future of our game would be like when our clubs got floodlights installed. The press described us as avenging our World Cup defeat by the United States, but it was empty revenge because it was a pretty meaningless match that attracted very little interest in New York. There was a ghostly atmosphere in the Yankee Stadium with the seven thousand fans 'lost' in that vast arena. It was enjoyable but odd to come up against my old Wolves team-mate Terry Springthorpe in the American defence. He had shared digs with me and he had played in the 1949 FA Cup winning team.

Who won what in 1952–53

First Division: Arsenal, 54pts. Runners-up: Preston, 54pts.

Arsenal record: P42 W21 D12 L9 F97 A64 Pts54

Arsenal squad: Kelsey, Wade, Lionel Smith; (from) Shaw, Forbes, Daniel, Mercer*; (from) Milton, Logie, Goring, Holton, Lishman, Roper. Top scorer: Lishman (22). Manager: Tom Whittaker.

Second Division: Sheffield United, 60pts. Runners-up: Huddersfield, 58pts.

Third Division (South): Bristol Rovers, 64pts. Runners-up: Millwall, 62pts.

Third Division (North): Oldham Athletic, 59pts. Runners-up: Port Vale, 58pts.

FA Cup final: Blackpool 4, Bolton Wanderers 3

Blackpool: Farm, Shimwell, Garrett, Fenton, Johnston, Robinson, Matthews, Taylor, Mortensen[3], Mudie, Perry[1].

Bolton: Hanson, Ball, Banks, Wheeler, Barrass, Bell[1], Holden, Moir[1], Lofthouse[1], Hassall, Langton.

Top First Division marksman: Charlie Wayman (Preston), 24 goals.

Footballer of the Year: Nat Lofthouse (Bolton).

Scottish champions: Rangers, 43pts. Runners-up: Hibernian, 43pts.

Scottish Cup final: Rangers 1, Aberdeen 0 (after a 1–1 draw).

SEASON 1953–54:
The Revolution

A devastating thing happened to English football on the way to the 1954 World Cup finals in Switzerland. The Hungarians – the Magical Magyars – trounced England 6–3 at Wembley and 7–1 in Budapest. The defeat at Wembley was the first ever suffered on home territory by a foreign team (not counting the 2–0 setback against the Republic of Ireland at Goodison in 1949), and the seven-goal tanking in Budapest remains the heaviest defeat ever suffered by an England team.

For the rest of his life, Billy remained haunted by a classic goal scored by the one and only Ferenc Puskas during the first match at Wembley on 25 November 1953.

BILLY: It was as if the Hungarians had stepped off another planet. I will never be allowed to forget how Puskas controlled the ball with the sole of his left boot on the right side of the penalty area. As I made a challenge he pulled the ball back like a man loading a rifle, and fired it into the net all in one sweet movement while I was tackling thin air. It was their third of four goals scored in the first half. Geoffrey Green, one of the finest of all football writers, described it beautifully in *The Times*. He wrote that I went flying into the tackle like a fire engine going in the wrong direction for the blaze. I doubt if there has ever been a better-executed goal at Wembley. I became good friends with Ferenc over the years, and we always laugh when discussing that goal. He said it was the most memorable of his career because it was at Wembley where he had always dreamed of playing. His dream was my nightmare. To this day I have never seen football to match that played by Hungary. They were a phenomenal side, and the result had enormous repercussions for our game.

It was the moment of truth. England could no longer claim to be the masters of world football. Walter Winterbottom led the inquests into the defeats, and it was accepted that England had fallen behind the times with their tactics and their technique. They were still playing the old-fashioned WM formation, with two full-backs, three half-backs and five forwards. The Hungarians played their number nine Nandor Hidegkuti as a deep-lying centre-forward and Blackpool centre-half Harry Johnston had no idea how to mark him. Hidegkuti played hide-and-seek, and nipped in unseen for a hat-trick. Even the old men who ran our football were forced to pull their heads out of the sand, and leading club managers were called together for their opinions.

Winterbottom took careful note of their views, and it all led to a gradual change in training methods, playing tactics and style of kit. Out went the heavy boots, bulky shinpads, baggy shorts and shirts and the thick socks. The lapping of football pitches as the main part of training sessions was dropped in favour of more concentrated work with the football. Appearance money for international players was increased from £30 to £50 (the equivalent of more than three weeks' wages), and the FA selectors accepted at last that they had to start listening to professional opinion, although they were not willing to go so far as to give up the job of picking the team.

There had been no hint of the debacle to come in England's first three international matches of the 1953–54 season.

CAP NO 52
Wales, Ninian Park, 10.10.53. England won 4–1
Merrick   Garrett   Eckersley   Wright*   Johnston   Dickinson
Finney   Quixall   Lofthouse[2]   Wilshaw[2]   Mullen

Highlights: Dennis Wilshaw celebrated his first England cap with two goals, and Nat Lofthouse netted twice for the second successive match.

All of England's goals came in the ten minutes either side of the half-time interval after Wales had taken a deserved 23rd minute lead through Ivor Allchurch. Wales played for much of the game with left-back Alf Sherwood a passenger on the wing after he had been concussed in the 32nd minute. Giant Leeds centre-forward John Charles might have had a hat-trick but for a succession of superb saves by England goalkeeper Gil Merrick. Albert Quixall, literally worth his weight in gold when sold by Sheffield Wednesday to Manchester United for £45,000 in 1958, made his England debut at inside-right at the age of twenty. *The Wright Cuttings Book* (*Daily Express*): 'Wales were unlucky not to have salvaged a draw from a game they often dominated. Time and again they were stopped in their tracks by the magnificent defensive work of Billy Wright. So much of Wright's work goes unnoticed by the average fan, who does not appreciate the amount of ground he covers and his impeccable timing in the tackle that makes it all look so easy.'

BILLY: As in 1949–50, the Home Championship was used to determine Great Britain's qualifiers for the World Cup finals. There were more than 60,000 fans packed into Ninian Park, and the atmosphere was just like the Welsh stoke up for their rugby internationals. We were very flattered with the size of our victory. This was the beginning of the rise of the greatest Welsh football team in their history, with John Charles and Ivor Allchurch laying the foundations to their memorable careers. If there has been a more gifted all-round British footballer than Big John, then I have not seen him. He was equally effective at centre-forward or centre-half, and once he had moved to Juventus from Leeds he developed into the perfect player. He not only had great technique, but also the ideal temperament. His nickname, the Gentle Giant, was misleading because he could be as physical as Nat Lofthouse one minute and then as beautifully balanced as Tom Finney the next. He was commanding in the air and could head with the force of a Tommy Lawton. When the conversation gets around to who has been the greatest British footballer of all time John tends to get left out of the argument because he spent so much time in Italy, but he should be in anybody's top six players.

CAP NO 53

Rest of Europe, Wembley, 21.10.53. Drew 4–4

Merrick Ramsey[1] (pen) Eckersley Wright* Ufton Dickinson
Matthews Mortensen[1] Lofthouse Quixall Mullen[2]
Rest of Europe: Zeman (Spain), Navarro (Spain), Hanappi
(Austria), Cajkovski (Yugoslavia), Posipal (West Germany),
Ocwirk (Austria), Boniperti (Italy)[2], Kubala (Spain)[2 (1 pen)], Nordahl G
(Sweden), Vukas (Yugoslavia), Zebec (Yugoslavia).

Highlights: An Alf Ramsey penalty in the last minute gave England a
draw in a showpiece match to mark the Football Association's 90th
birthday. England trailed three times against the European all-stars in a
Wednesday afternoon match that provided a feast of football for the
97,000 spectators. Some 46 years later FIFA saw fit to downgrade the
game to non-international status, but the Football Association awarded
Billy a cap and it stays in English records as a full international. That
is good news for talented Charlton defender Derek Ufton, a solid
batsman and understudy at Kent to wicket keeper Godfrey Evans, who
won his only cap in the game. *The Wright Cuttings Book* (*London
Evening Standard*): 'Despite all the glittering overseas talent on the
show, it was home-grown Billy Wright who stood out as the finest
defender on the pitch. His covering work for newcomer Derek Ufton
was support play of the highest order.'

BILLY: We took the game very seriously because there was a lot
of pride and prestige at stake. Considering they had only been
together for a couple of days, the Rest of Europe side played
some magnificent football. The pick of the players was Ladislav
Kubala, who had been the first of the outstanding Hungarians to
switch his football allegiance to Spain. Ask anybody from
Barcelona or Budapest and they will tell you that he was in the
class of Puskas. He had wonderful ball control and the ability to
make space for himself with clever changes of pace. Many years
later I gave his son a trial at Arsenal, but the lad had not inherited his father's skill. Kubala was a one-off. A naturally gifted
genius, he left Hungary just before the rise of their greatest of

all teams. Just imagine how good they would have been had he still been available for selection! Kubala *and* Puskas to mark. The mind boggles!

CAP NO 54

Northern Ireland, Goodison Park, 11.11.53. England won 3–1
Merrick   Rickaby   Eckersley   Wright*   Johnston   Dickinson
Matthews   Quixall   Lofthouse[1]   Hassall[2]   Mullen

Highlights: Harold Hassall, playing alongside his Bolton team-mate Nat Lofthouse, scored the first of his two goals in just thirty seconds to mark his international recall after two years. It was Hassall's fifth and last cap. Eddie McMorran equalised for the Irish nine minutes after half-time, and they were the superior side for long periods. Stanley Matthews turned the game England's way with a typical mazy run on the hour before passing to Billy Wright, who set up a simple second goal for Hassall. It was Nat Lofthouse who wrapped up victory for England fifteen minutes later when he headed in a Jimmy Mullen cross, colliding with goalkeeper Smyth as he powered the ball into the net. Lofthouse limped off and Smyth was carried off with a broken nose. West Bromwich right-back Stan Rickaby played in his one and only England match in place of the injured Alf Ramsey. *The Wright Cuttings Book* (*Daily Telegraph*): 'Wright had his work cut out in defence, and was not able to support the attack in his usual fashion. There were occasions when both Wright and Dickinson came second in midfield battles against Blanchflower and McIlroy, a tandem team that will make the Irish a team to fear over the next few years.'

BILLY: We were relieved at the end to get away with a victory that put us on our way into the 1954 World Cup finals in Switzerland. Northern Ireland had become difficult opposition now that Danny Blanchflower, Jimmy McIlroy and Billy Bingham were established in the team. Nat Lofthouse came off with an injury that was obviously going to keep him out of our match against Hungary two weeks later. Lucky man!

CAP NO 55
Hungary, Wembley, 25.11.53. England lost 6–3
Merrick   Ramsey[1] (pen)   Eckersley   Wright*   Johnston   Dickinson
Matthews   Taylor E   Mortensen[1]   Sewell[1]   Robb

Highlights: This was England's first defeat by foreign opponents on home territory, and the match that changed the face of English football. The Hungarians, Olympic champions and on a run of 29 successive matches without defeat, played to a flexible 4–2–4 formation and made England's 2–3–5 pattern seem about as outdated as a hansom cab on a motorway. Nandor Hidegkuti, a deep-lying centre-forward, nipped in for a hat-trick as two-goal Ferenc Puskas pulled the defence inside out. England were flattered by the 6–3 scoreline. Alf Ramsey, Bill Eckersley, Harry Johnston, Ernie Taylor, Stan Mortensen and George Robb never played for England again. Taylor and Robb were making their debuts. Hungary had given just a taste of what was to come in the first minute when Hidegkuti collected a through ball from Puskas, deceived centre-half Johnston with a distracting dummy and then fired the ball high into the net from twenty yards. Gil Merrick was left flapping at thin-air. Moments after Sewell had equalised in the fifteenth minute England were flattened by a thirteen-minute burst of Magyar magic. Two goals from the purist Puskas and another from the elusive Hidegkuti made it England 1, Hungary 4. The 100,000 Wembley spectators could not believe their eyes. Stan Mortensen pulled it back to 4–2 by half-time. But any hope England had of getting back into the game died within ten minutes of the second half. First the cultured Jozef Bozsik scored with a rising drive, and then Hidegkuti completed his hurricane hat-trick when he put the finishing touch to a dazzling succession of passes that ripped the England defence apart. Alf Ramsey scored a late penalty after his Tottenham team-mate George Robb, a schoolmaster, was pulled down by goalkeeper Grosics. The final scoreline could easily have read 10–3 to the Hungarians. *The Wright Cuttings Book* (*Daily Mirror*): 'Billy Wright has never been given such a chasing in all his life as the one he got from Ferenc Puskas. We all know Wright is a world-class defender, so what does that make Puskas? Collect all your money from your piggybank and put it on Hungary now to win the World Cup in Switzerland next summer. They made England look second-class citizens.'

> BILLY: I remember that when I was called to the middle for the toss of the coin their captain Puskas was standing in the centre-circle all on his own juggling the match ball on his left foot. As I approached him he flicked the ball in the air, caught it on his thigh and then let it run down his shin and back on to the centre spot. That was my first sight of Ferenc Puskas. He gave me a big grin as much as to say, 'Just wait until you see the rest of my tricks.' He did not disappoint me! There was a mist over Wembley that afternoon and I think we felt as if we were lost in a fog as the Hungarians completely outplayed us. It was not that England played badly. Hungary were just in a different class, and playing a style of football that was, well, foreign to us. I was convinced I was watching the team that would collect the World Cup the following summer. It was a defeat that started a revolution in our game. We knew from that day on that we needed to get into the modern world. They were playing a different game to us.

CAP NO 56
Scotland, Hampden Park, 3.4.54. England won 4–2
Merrick   Staniforth   Byrne R   Wright*   Clarke H   Dickinson
Finney   Broadis¹   Allen R¹   Nicholls¹   Mullen¹

Highlights: The England selectors made eight changes to the team taken apart by Hungary. Johnny Nicholls had good reason to remember his debut. It was his 23rd birthday and he celebrated with England's second goal, a flying header from a Tom Finney cross. Playing alongside his West Bromwich Albion team-mate Ronnie Allen, he was one of four debutants, along with Ron Staniforth, Harry Clarke and Manchester United left-back Roger Byrne, who was to prove himself one of the finest players ever to wear the number three shirt. Clarke, the 31-year-old centre-half, followed Ditchburn, Ramsey, Willis, Nicholson and Medley as members of the Spurs 'push-and-run' team who were capped after the age of thirty-plus.

Roared on by a vast crowd of 134,554, Scotland took the lead in the seventh minute through Blackpool's Allan Brown. Ivor Broadis equalised eight minutes later after penetrating approach work by Wright and Finney. It was the same combination of Wright and Finney that set up England's second goal by birthday boy Nicholls five minutes into the second half. Headed goals by Allen and Jimmy Mullen wrapped the game up for England and guaranteed them going to the World Cup finals as Home Champions. Scotland scored a strange second goal in the last minute when a cross from Willie Ormond suddenly swirled into the net. *The Wright Cuttings Book* (*Sunday Pictorial*): 'Back to his best, Billy Wright was prominent in attack and defence for England. He was obviously so relieved that the Scots did not have anybody in the class of Puskas to torment him.'

> BILLY: It was good to get back to winning ways after the mauling we got against Hungary, but even though we beat Scotland it was clear we were not a settled side. The problems persisted in the middle of our defence, and the selectors did not seem to know which way to turn next. We had still not found a suitable replacement for Neil Franklin, and the World Cup was just a couple of months away.

Billy was enjoying much better times on the domestic scene. He led Wolves to their first League championship under Stan Cullis. They took the title by four points from nearest rivals West Bromwich Albion, scoring more goals (96) and conceding fewer (56) than any other team in the table. It was a tremendous triumph for the tactical planning of Cullis, who insisted that the Wolves style was similar to that adopted by the Hungarians but with fewer frills. 'They ping the ball around in defence,' said the Master of Molineux, 'but then suddenly unleash the sort of long ball that is our speciality and which seems to drive our critics to distraction. But look at the damage it does to opposition defences! They can criticise all they like, but I don't think you will hear our supporters complaining. They get more entertainment from watching Wolves than any other two teams put together.'

There was no time for Billy to put his feet up at the end of the season.

It was straight off on a two-match warm-up tour before the World Cup finals. Another Hungarian nightmare was waiting round the bend.

CAP NO 57
Yugoslavia, Belgrade, 16.5.54. England lost 1–0
Merrick   Staniforth   Byrne R   Wright*   Owen   Dickinson
Finney   Broadis   Allen R   Nicholls   Mullen

Highlights: Syd Owen, of Luton Town, was the eleventh centre-half tried since the defection of Neil Franklin to the outlawed Colombian league. England concentrated on a deep defence and a counterattacking policy, and almost got away with a draw. Jimmy Mullen, Ronnie Allen and Johnny Nicholls had shots saved during breakaway raids, but the Yugoslavs were generally in control. They were always the sharper side and deserved their winning goal three minutes from the end when a 35-yard free-kick was deflected by Owen into the path of Mitic, who scored from six yards. *The Wright Cuttings Book*: (*News of the World*): 'It is going to take all Billy Wright's powers of captaincy to make the players around him raise their game for the World Cup. This performance was lamentable.'

BILLY: This was Tom Finney's fiftieth international for England, and we wanted so much to get at least a draw to mark the occasion. Tom was arguably the finest player to wear the England shirt in my time in international football. Stanley Matthews was the people's favourite, but most of the professionals would have given Tom the nod just ahead of Stanley because there was so much to his game. He was comfortable in any forward position, could dribble almost as well as Stanley and was as brave as a lion. I felt fortunate that my career coincided with the Matthews and Finney era, and had I been picking the team they would have both appeared in the same forward line on many more occasions. The defeat in Yugoslavia did little to help our confidence as we went on to Budapest for the return match with Hungary.

CAP NO 58
Hungary, Budapest, 23.5.54. England lost 7–1
Merrick   Staniforth   Byrne R   Wright*   Owen   Dickinson
Harris P   Sewell   Jezzard   Broadis¹   Finney

Highlights: This was the biggest defeat in England's 90-year football history. Just four of the England team had survived from the 6–3 slaughter at Wembley in November: Merrick, Wright, Dickinson and Finney. Fulham centre-forward Bedford Jezzard made a best-forgotten debut, while the unfortunate Peter Harris was winning his second and last cap after a gap of five years. His first cap came in the 2–0 home defeat by the Republic of Ireland in 1949. Puskas and Kocsis scored two goals each. The Hungarians, leading 3–0 at half-time, were six goals clear and cantering before Ivor Broadis opened the scoring for England. Hungary immediately replied with their seventh goal, scored by Puskas from a pass by Hidegkuti. Hungary's scorers were Puskas (2), Kocsis (2), Lantos, Tóth and Hidegkuti. *The Wright Cuttings Book (Daily Express)*: 'Billy Wright came off with his face as white as his shirt, and looking like a man who has seen a ghost come back to haunt him. As hard as this giant-hearted man tried, he could not get near to suppressing the irrepressible Puskas.'

BILLY: Hungary were even more devastating than they'd been at Wembley. They were unstoppable, and we were just happy to get off the pitch without the score going into double figures. What it confirmed was that we needed to go back to the drawing board. I felt sorry for our goalkeeper Gil Merrick, who had picked the ball out of his net thirteen times in his two matches against the Hungarians. Only a couple of them were down to Gil, and he saved at least another half-a-dozen certain goals over the course of the two games. You could say that we were not the most confident of teams going into the World Cup finals. Hungary, on the other hand, looked certain to add the World Cup to their Olympic crown in the days when they were allegedly amateurs. But take it from me, these were among the wealthiest sportsmen in Hungary. Many of them were serving in the Hungarian Army and playing for the services side, Honved. Ferenc Puskas had the rank of major, and was known as the Galloping Major. But he never ever galloped. He was always smooth and almost glided over the turf.

Who won what in 1953–54

First Division: Wolves, 57pts. Runners-up: West Bromwich Albion, 53pts.
Wolves record: P42 W25 D7 L10 F96 A56 Pts57
Wolves squad: Williams, Short, Pritchard, Slater, Shorthouse, Wright*, Hancocks, Broadbent, Swinbourne, Wilshaw, Mullen. Top scorer: Hancocks (25). Manager: Stan Cullis.
Second Division: Leicester City, 56pts. Runners-up: Everton, 56pts.
Third Division (South): Ipswich Town, 64pts. Runners-up: Brighton, 61pts.
Third Division (North): Port Vale, 69pts, Runners-up: Barnsley, 58pts.
FA Cup final: West Bromwich Albion 3, Preston North End 2
West Brom: Sanders, Kennedy, Millard, Dudley, Dugdale, Barlow, Griffin[1], Ryan, Allen[2 (1 pen)], Nicholls, Lee.
Preston: Thompson, Cunningham, Walton, Docherty, Marston, Forbes, Finney, Foster, Wayman[1], Baxter, Morrison[1].
Top First Division marksmen: Jimmy Glazzard (Huddersfield) and Johnny Nicholls (West Brom), 29 goals.
Footballer of the Year: Tom Finney (Preston).
Scottish champions: Celtic, 43pts. Runners-up: Hearts, 38pts.
Scottish Cup final: Celtic 2, Aberdeen 1

SEASON 1954–55:
The Big Switch

It was by accident rather than design that England at last found their ideal centre-half after more than four years of searching for a successor to Neil Franklin. The accident was to first-choice centre-half Syd Owen. The man the selectors turned to was our hero for all seasons, Billy Wright, who had played half a dozen games in the number five shirt for Wolves in the previous season.

Owen was injured during the opening World Cup match against Belgium, and Billy switched to the middle of defence in emergency. He remained there until retiring five years and 45 caps later.

BILLY: It seemed fate was determined that I should become a specialist centre-half. First of all Syd Owen's injury in the World Cup prompted Walter Winterbottom to ask me to play there. When I got back into club football, manager Stan Cullis told me he still needed me to play at wing-half, even though he had for some time felt centre-half was my best position. Then, in the third match of the season, our regular centre-half Bill Shorthouse was injured and I took his place in the number five shirt. It was to be my shirt number for the rest of my career. I was lucky to have one of the greatest centre-halves of all time as my manager. Stan gave me invaluable advice on how to master the role. He told me to note which way centre-forwards like to turn, the foot with which they preferred to control the ball, to get my tackle in when they were on the half-turn, and to always try to force them out towards the flanks. I spent hours in training learning how to make proper challenges in the air, and how to perfect my positional play. You know the hurdles that are used in athletics? Well I used to spring over them with my knees tucked up. It helped strengthen my thighs and I developed a leap that helped make up for my lack of inches. My short hamstrings gave me the explosive power I needed at takeoff. I was never going to be the complete centre-half because of my lack of real height, but I was determined to be as tough an obstacle as possible to all centre-forwards. They were the new enemy! When I first started to establish myself as a centre-half dear old Nat Lofthouse said with a straight face, 'I'm not sure I can talk to you any more, skipper. You've joined *them*. I hate centre-halves.' He waited to see my reaction before bursting out laughing. He and I had some great tussles over the years, but we were never ever enemies.

England's World Cup challenge in Switzerland was just about satisfactory, considering the depths to which they had sunk in their build-up to the finals. They managed to survive to the quarter-finals before going out to the reigning world champions.

CAP NO 59
Belgium, World Cup, Basle, 17.6.54. Drew 4–4 after extra-time
Merrick   Staniforth   Byrne R   Wright*   Owen   Dickinson
Matthews   Broadis²   Lofthouse²   Taylor T   Finney

Highlights: A Jimmy Dickinson own goal during extra-time gave Belgium a draw in a helter-skelter match full of defensive blunders as England made an eventful start to their challenge for the World Cup. A goal down in five minutes, England produced some enterprising and energetic football and deserved their 2–1 half-time lead from goals by Ivor Broadis and Nat Lofthouse. The Lofthouse goal was a cracker, a spectacular diving header to send a Tom Finney cross powering into the net. When Broadis added a third goal early in the second half it looked odds-on an England victory. Then defensive lapses let the Belgians in for two soft goals that took the game into extra-time. Nat Lofthouse made it 4–3 in the opening moments of extra-time, and England seemed destined for full points when Jimmy Dickinson turned an intended headed clearance into his own net. Billy Wright took over at centre-half in the closing stages as Syd Owen limped to a passenger's role on the wing. It was to prove the most significant positional switch of Billy's career. *The Wright Cuttings Book (Daily Mail)*: 'It has to be said that the England defence looked more composed when Billy Wright moved to centre-half in place of the limping Syd Owen. Could it be that at long last England have found the pivot they have been seeking ever since the defection of Neil Franklin? How ironic if it turns out that Wright proves the right man for the No 5 shirt. He has been on Walter Winterbottom's doorstep for years!'

BILLY: We felt so frustrated when we came off at the end. There was no question that we had been the better team, but three of their four goals were carelessly conceded. Walter Winterbottom pulled me on one side as we prepared to leave the ground. 'I don't want to risk Syd against Switzerland on Sunday,' he said. 'How do you feel about playing at centre-half?' The selectors had tried eleven players in the number five shirt since Neil Franklin walked out on the job. I suppose it was only a question of time before they got round to me! I told Walter I was ready to give it a go.

CAP NO 60
Switzerland, World Cup, Berne, 20.6.54. England won 2–0
Merrick   Staniforth   Byrne R   McGarry   Wright*   Dickinson
Finney   Broadis   Taylor T   Wilshaw[1]   Mullen[1]

Highlights: Wolves left-wing partners Dennis Wilshaw and Jimmy Mullen scored the goals, and their club captain Billy Wright started his first match as England's centre-half. Bill McGarry (who later became the manager of Wolves following the dismissal of Stan Cullis) gave a solid debut performance in Wright's old position at right-half against the host nation and in searing-hot conditions that sapped the energy of the players. Mullen scored the first goal three minutes before half-time to silence a capacity 60,000 crowd. Wilshaw clinched the victory with a superb individual goal midway through the second-half, cleverly evading three Swiss defenders before steering a firm shot into the net. *The Wright Cuttings Book* (*Reynolds News*): 'Syd Owen's injury has accidentally solved England's on-going centre-half crisis. Billy Wright slotted into the position as naturally as if born to the job, and the Swiss centre-forward was not allowed a sniff at goal.'

> BILLY: My memory of that match is feeling as if I was playing in an oven. It was so scorching that we were in danger of getting sunburned tongues! We all lost several pounds, and were so wet with sweat that it looked as if we had stepped out of the shower. When I wished Bill McGarry luck before the kick-off, he told me: 'I'm fully expecting your shirt to run around on its own!' I wondered what I had let myself in for as the centre-half. Already I realised that playing at the centre of the defence was, mentally, much more draining. You dare not lose your concentration, and you are aware of responsibilities all around you. There's the goalkeeper behind you who is relying on your call for whether to come for crosses, a charging centre-forward in front of you and wing-halves who you link with both in defence and attack. The experience made me even more appreciative of just what an exceptional player Neil Franklin had been. He made it all look so easy.

CAP NO 61
Uruguay, World Cup, Basle, 26.6.54. England lost 4–2
Merrick   Staniforth   Byrne R   McGarry   Wright*   Dickinson
Matthews   Broadis   Lofthouse[1]   Wilshaw   Finney[1]

Highlights: Two mistakes by goalkeeper Gil Merrick let defending world champions Uruguay in for goals that turned this quarter-final match in their favour after Nat Lofthouse and Tom Finney had each scored to give England hope of causing an upset. Shuffling Stanley Matthews, the undisputed man of the match, hit a post and had a shot pushed off target before Uruguay clinched victory with their fourth goal in the 84th minute when Merrick failed to save a speculative shot from Ambrois. It was shell-shocked Merrick's final match for England. He had let in thirty goals in his last ten games after conceding only fifteen in his first thirteen internationals. The Uruguayans had beaten Scotland 7–0 in a qualifying-round match, but were never allowed to show that sort of superiority by an England team that performed with pride and purpose. *The Wright Cuttings Book*: (*The Times*): 'One of the few positive things to come out of this World Cup campaign is that England have unearthed a genuinely solid centre-half in Billy Wright. He looks tailor-made for the role.'

> BILLY: All my sympathy was with Gil Merrick. You can get it wrong out in the middle of the pitch and get away with it, but there's no hiding place when a goalkeeper makes a mistake. It was such a vital game for us, and for the first time the World Cup was being shown live on television at home. The spotlight was on every move we made. Poor old Gil carried the can. With a little luck, we might have reached the semi-finals, because there were long spells when we had Uruguay on the back foot. Stanley Matthews was at his tantalising best and he ran their left-back silly. I came home feeling pretty pleased with my personal performances. I had proved that I could play in the middle of the defence without making a fool of myself. While I was disappointed that we failed to go any further in the World Cup finals, I was astonished that Hungary had not managed to win the tournament.

The Hungarians went into the finals as the hottest favourites of all time. They had gone four years without a single defeat, including crushing defeats of both England and Scotland in home and away matches on their way to Switzerland. In their opening matches they beat Korea 9–0 and then a deliberately under-strength West Germany 8–3. Ferenc Puskas was wickedly fouled in the match against the Germans, and was limping heavily with an ankle injury at the end of the game. He later claimed that the tackle that damaged him had been a deliberate attempt to put him out of the tournament.

The concentration of the Hungarians was interrupted by an ugly dressing-room brawl with the Brazilians after an ill-tempered quarter-final that they won 4–2. Minus the injured Puskas, Hungary had a scare in the semi-final against Cup-holders Uruguay. They led 2–0 at half-time but the Uruguayans pulled back in the second half to force extra-time. Juan Hohberg was a coat of paint away from completing a hat-trick for Uruguay before Josef 'Golden Head' Kocsis scored two of his typical headers to clinch a place for Hungary in the final against a now full-strength West Germany.

Hungary's long unbeaten record finally crashed at the heartbreak hurdle of the World Cup final. A gamble of playing Puskas when half-fit blew up in their faces and the unheralded West Germans, splendidly marshalled by Fritz Walter, became the new champions. But that Hungarian team of the early 1950s will always be remembered as one of the greatest combinations ever to operate on a football pitch.

Just six months after the World Cup final, Billy Wright had another memorable meeting with Ferenc Puskas. This time they came face to face as club captains, Billy skippering Wolves and Puskas leading Honved of Budapest, which was virtually the Hungarian national team.

There were 54,998 fans packed into the Molineux ground and millions more watched their black-and-white television screens at the peak of an era when Wolves were pioneering midweek floodlit matches against invited overseas clubs.

Wolves spectacularly came from being two goals down at half-time to win 3–2, with a second-half penalty from Johnny Hancocks followed by two goals from Roy Swinbourne in the final frantic fifteen minutes.

'It was without any question the most exciting match I ever saw,' said ecstatic manager Stan Cullis, echoing the view of many witnesses. 'Even when we were two goals down at half-time I was convinced we could win. I just told the lads to keep plugging away. It was a magnificent team performance.'

BILLY: It was the greatest moment in my club football career. There have been few nights to match it for atmosphere and excitement. To give a team of Honved's calibre a two-goal start and then beat them 3–2 was like something out of a fairy story. It helped restore pride and self-confidence after those nightmare matches against Hungary. The newspapers dubbed us the Kings of Europe, and that triggered the idea for a European club competition.

With Billy as captain and centre-half, the England selectors decided on a new look for the international season.

CAP NO 62

Northern Ireland, Windsor Park, 2.10.54. England won 2–0
Wood   Foulkes   Byrne R   Wheeler   Wright*   Barlow
Matthews   Revie¹   Lofthouse   Haynes¹   Pilkington

Highlights: Don Revie and Johnny Haynes got their first taste of international football together and scored a goal each. There were five other new caps in a team that had been completely remodelled following the quarter-final exit from the World Cup finals: Ray Wood, Bill Foulkes, Johnny Wheeler, Ray Barlow and Brian Pilkington, who played in place of the injured Tom Finney. Foulkes, Wheeler, Barlow and Pilkington were not capped again after this victory. The Irish worked desperately hard in a bid for their first victory over England since 1927, but the wind was knocked out of them by two goals inside two minutes late in the second half. Haynes exchanged a one-two pass with Revie before shooting wide of Portsmouth goalkeeper Norman Uprichard. Within a minute it was 2–0, Revie running on to a pass from Haynes and steering the ball low into the net. *The Wright Cuttings Book* (*Daily Express*): 'Billy Wright was magnificent in the number five shirt. Why oh why has it taken the selectors so long to realise that the answer to their centre-half problem was under their nose?'

BILLY: I was impressed by the debut performance of Johnny Haynes. He was just nineteen, and he already looked an assured and confident player who could hit accurate 40-yard passes with either foot. But the powers-that-be decided he was too young to trust with the role of midfield general, and he was dropped along with Don Revie and six other players. This was at a time when the selectors seemed to be acting like headless chickens, and it was difficult to get any continuity or rhythm. It was a particularly frustrating period for our manager Walter Winterbottom, whose plans were being continually sabotaged by the juggling of the selectors.

CAP NO 63
Wales, Wembley, 10.11.54. England won 3–2
Wood   Staniforth   Byrne R   Phillips   Wright*   Slater
Matthews   Bentley³   Allen R   Shackleton   Blunstone

Highlights: Roy Bentley, at last forgiven for his part in the 1950 World Cup humiliation against the United States, celebrated his recall by sinking Wales with a hat-trick. Two of his goals came from headers at the far post after he had exchanged passes with Matthews. John Charles, leading the Welsh attack with fire and flair, scored twice to bring the scores level at 2–2 before Bentley completed his hat-trick two minutes from the end of a thrilling match played on a rain-saturated Wembley surface. Bentley's Chelsea team-mate Frank Blunstone made his England debut on the left wing and Bill Slater played alongside his Wolves skipper Billy Wright in his first international match. *The Wright Cuttings Book* (*News Chronicle*): 'The duel between John Charles and Billy Wright was worth the admission money on its own. Two great and talented competitors locked in a struggle for supremacy. Charles won on points, but it would have been a knockout against any other England centre-half that the selectors have tried since the Neil Franklin fiasco.'

> BILLY: This was a massive test for me in my new role . It could not have been tougher than having to mark the great John Charles. I managed to shut the big man out for most of the match, but he took the two chances that came his way in dynamic style. What a player! John shook my hand at the end and paid me the compliment of saying, 'The sooner you go back to right-half the happier I shall be!' That was music to my ears. It meant I was making my presence felt.

CAP NO 64
West Germany, Wembley, 1.12.54. England won 3–1
Williams   Staniforth   Byrne R   Phillips   Wright*   Slater
Matthews   Bentley¹   Allen R¹   Shackleton¹   Finney

Highlights: The 100,000 crowd for this Wednesday afternoon match against the world champions broke the Wembley receipts record by paying £51,716 to watch a classic encounter. With Stanley Matthews running the German defenders into dizzy disarray, England took the lead in the 27th minute when Roy Bentley headed in a pinpoint centre from the Maestro. Ronnie Allen made it 2–0 three minutes after half-time following neat combination work between Finney and Len Shackleton. The Germans pulled back to 2–1 through Beck before Shackleton, the Clown Prince, clinched a memorable victory in the 80th minute with an impudent chip shot as the goalkeeper came racing towards him. Shack had thrilled the crowd throughout the match with his tricks, but he was too much an individualist for the taste of the selectors and never played for England again after a paltry five caps. *The Wright Cuttings Book* (*Daily Telegraph*): 'There was a quite majestic display at centre-half by Wright, who plays with the assurance and composure of a man who has worn the No 5 shirt all his life.'

BILLY: It is a mystery to many people why Len Shackleton did not win a cupboardful of caps. He just refused to conform. Shack upset the selectors with a book published in 1955 in which a chapter headed 'The Average Director's Knowledge of Football' was left completely blank. Most of the England selectors were club directors. With his ability, he should have won dozens of caps but he just could not bring himself to toe the line. At least he could say he went out at the very top, because his brilliant goal made sure that we toppled the new world champions. I have to confess that they picked only three of the players who helped them win the World Cup as they started rebuilding for their 1958 defence. But that did not stop some of the newspapers declaring that we were the new world champions!

Len Shackleton became a respected football writer after his retirement, and reminiscing in the press box one day he regaled us with this story that captures the times in which he played: 'After scoring what I considered one of my finest ever goals to help England beat world champions Germany at Wembley, I was handed a third-class rail ticket for the overnight sleeper back to Sunderland. I said to the Bowler Hat handing me the ticket, "Couldn't you raise enough money for a first-class ticket?" The FA official said that all the first-class tickets had been sold. When I got to Kings Cross I had no trouble transferring to first-class because there was plenty of space, and I was happy to pay the five pounds difference out of my own pocket. By the time I'd paid tax and expenses, I was left with just £20 out of my £50 match fee. The Wembley receipts for the match were over £50,000, but we footballers who had drawn the crowd and the money were considered third-class citizens by those blinkered fools who ran the Football Association.'

CAP NO 65

Scotland, Wembley, 2.4.55. England won 7–2
Williams   Meadows   Byrne R   Armstrong   Wright*   Edwards
Matthews   Revie[1]   Lofthouse[2]   Wilshaw[4]   Blunstone

Highlights: Stanley Matthews was the engineer and Dennis Wilshaw the executioner in this annihilation of the Scots. Wilshaw's four goals included the first hat-trick by an England player against Scotland. Duncan Edwards, the human powerhouse from Manchester United, was, at eighteen years and 183 days, the youngest England player of the twentieth century. Chelsea right-half Ken Armstrong collected his only cap, and later emigrated to New Zealand for whom he won thirteen caps. This was England's first victory over Scotland at Wembley since 1934. Wilshaw started his goal rush in the first minute, and two goals from Nat Lofthouse and one from Don Revie gave England a commanding 4–1 lead at half-time. Scotland caved in as Wilshaw snatched three goals in thirteen minutes in the last third of the match. Tommy Docherty, who ran himself into the ground for the Scots, got a little reward for all his work when he scored with a late free-kick. *The Wright Cuttings Book* (*London Evening Star*): 'The goals of Wilshaw, the promise of Edwards and the class and authority of Wright made this a match to remember for a lifetime.'

BILLY: Two things stick in my memory from this match – the four goals from my clubmate Dennis Wilshaw, and the storming debut performance of young Duncan Edwards. Dennis was a versatile forward who could score goals from virtually any position. He was an intelligent man who was a schoolteacher when not playing football, and he later became a respected psychologist who helped many players come to terms with the pressures of modern big-time football. Duncan was the most exciting prospect I had ever seen. He had immense strength in the tackle, and was dynamic on the ball. Duncan played with such assurance and confidence, that you would have thought he was a veteran rather than a young man just starting out on his international career. Walter Winterbottom summed it up when he said quietly to me after the match, 'I think we've uncovered a gem.' As Duncan was born and raised in Dudley in the West Midlands, Stan Cullis kept scratching his head while trying to work out how he had let him escape from on his doorstep to Old Trafford.

CAP NO 66
France, Paris, 15.5.55. England lost 1–0
Williams   Sillett P   Byrne R   Flowers   Wright*   Edwards
Matthews   Revie   Lofthouse   Wilshaw   Blunstone

Highlights: Peter Sillett, making his debut at right-back, conceded the 36th minute penalty from which the great Raymond Kopa scored the winning goal for France. Just a month earlier Sillett's penalty goal against Wolves had virtually clinched the League championship for Chelsea, and forced Wolves into settling for runners-up place. Ron Flowers, making his debut alongside his Wolves skipper Billy Wright, had to wait three years for his second cap and then won forty in a row – an unbroken sequence beaten only by Billy's seventy consecutive appearances. The nearest England came to scoring was when Frank Blunstone was unceremoniously pulled down as he shaped to shoot. England appeals for a penalty were turned down, while the German referee had no hesitation in awarding the penalty to France for a less obvious foul by Sillett. *The Wright Cuttings Book* (*Sunday Express*): 'Billy Wright is finding out the hard way that the job of centre-half is the toughest on the pitch. He had his hands full with the clever and cunning Kopa, and it is to his credit that the French master did not score a hatful of goals.'

> BILLY: Nobody could say I was having an easy introduction to the world of centre-halves. If there was a better centre-forward in Europe than John Charles then it was probably Raymond Kopa. He was a totally different player to John, who was muscular as well as skilful and a major threat in the air. Kopa was a comparatively small but beautifully balanced player, who relied on quick acceleration and good ball control to make an impact. He was a difficult man to mark because he liked to make sudden bursts from deep positions, and by the time our game with France was over I felt as if I'd been on a marathon run keeping up with him. But at least he only managed to score from the penalty spot. I felt comfortable having my Wolves team-mate Ron Flowers alongside me, but the selectors with weird logic ignored him for the next three years.

CAP NO 67
Spain, Madrid, 18.5.55. Drew 1–1
Williams   Sillett P   Byrne R   Dickinson   Wright*   Edwards
Matthews   Bentley¹   Lofthouse   Quixall   Wilshaw

Highlights: In a bad-tempered match Nat Lofthouse had his shirt ripped off his back in the first half, and played throughout the second half with a numberless shirt. Even Stanley Matthews was drawn into the roughhouse, and conceded a free-kick with a tackle, the first time anybody could recall him committing a foul. Roy Bentley scored from a Lofthouse pass in the 38th minute and Spain equalised in the 65th minute following a mistake by Duncan Edwards that was as rare as a foul by Matthews. The trouble flared after Lofthouse had been rugby-tackled to the ground when on a run towards the penalty area. There were so many personal feuds going on after this that the game lost all of its rhythm, and the Italian referee had little or no control. *The Wright Cuttings Book (Daily Herald)*: 'Gentleman Billy Wright refused to get drawn into the ugly battles going on around him, and he gave a true captain's performance as he concentrated on stopping the

Spaniards with superbly timed tackles that were skilful rather than spiteful.'

BILLY: It was on that trip that I saw my first bullfights at the Plaza de Toros in Madrid. When we played a couple of days later in the Chamartin Stadium I can honestly say that the 125,000 crowd sounded as if they were at a bullfight as they cheered on the Spaniards and booed the English. We were furious over the foul against Lofthouse, and we could not believe it when the player who had rugby-tackled him was allowed to stay on the pitch. Tempers were on a short fuse, and when Stanley Matthews is moved to foul somebody then something has to be seriously wrong. The referee completely lost it, and the wonder is that there were no legs broken. It was one of the roughest and most bad-spirited games in which I ever played overseas. I am flattered to think that anybody considered me a gentleman in this match because I was going in as hard as anybody on the pitch!

CAP NO 68

Portugal, Oporto, 22.5.55. England lost 3–1

Williams   Sillett P   Byrne R   Dickinson   Wright*   Edwards
Matthews   Bentley¹   Lofthouse (Quixall)   Wilshaw   Blunstone

Highlights: England were disjointed from the moment Nat Lofthouse went off injured with the score at 1–1. Albert Quixall came on as substitute in what was his final England appearance. It was also Roy Bentley's last match for England after twelve appearances in three different shirts over a period of six years. His 19th-minute goal could not save England from their first defeat by Portugal. Defensive errors let the Portuguese in for two late goals and a famous victory. Stanley Matthews and Billy Wright were the only players on the pitch who had featured in the 10–0 slaughter of Portugal in Lisbon eight years earlier. *The Wright Cuttings Book (Daily Mail)*: 'You can count Billy Wright's bad games for England on the fingers of one hand, and this was one of them. He looked stale after his hard season, and the summer break is much needed so that he can recharge his batteries. He remains one of the discoveries of the season, developing into the finest centre-half in the First Division since the days of Neil Franklin at his best.'

> BILLY: I have to hold my hands up to being responsible for Portugal's third goal. Trying to find our goalkeeper Bert Williams with a back-header, I misdirected the ball and it opened the way for an easy goal. You would have thought Portugal had won the World Cup when the final whistle went. Thousands of spectators poured on to the pitch, and mobbed their players. It just went to show that beating England was still counted as the big prize. The annoying thing is that if we had taken our chances we could easily have been three goals in the lead before Lofty limped off.

For Billy, the domestic season had ended in disappointment when Wolves were beaten to the championship by the Chelsea team managed by Ted Drake. But all memories at Molineux were warmed by the victory over Honved. For the record, these were the two teams that lined up under the Wolverhampton floodlights on the evening of 13 December 1954:

Wolves: Williams,   Stuart,   Shorthouse,   Slater,   Wright, Flowers,   Hancocks,   Broadbent,   Swinbourne,   Wilshaw,   Smith.
Honved: Farago,   Sarosi,   Kovaks,   Bozsik,   Lorant,   Banyai, Budai,   Kocsis,   Machos (Tichy 84),   Puskas,   Czibor.

Highlights: After throwing bouquets to the crowd, the Hungarians started to deflower the Wolves defence masterminded by Billy Wright. Honved might easily have scored three goals in the opening ten minutes as they skipped lightly over the muddy Molineux turf to test goalkeeper Bert 'The Cat' Williams. A goal seemed inevitable and it came in the eleventh minute when Puskas floated over a free-kick for 'Golden Head' Kocsis to send a bullet header past Williams to add to the belief that he was the most powerful header of a ball in the world.

Three minutes later goal-taker Kocsis turned goal-maker with a defence-splitting pass to Machos, who drove the ball firmly past the oncoming Williams. These two knife thrusts would have been enough to kill off most sides, but Wolves – characterising the iron will of their demanding manager Stan Cullis – were never a team of quitters. The match settled into a fascinating duel between two worlds: the short-passing game of the Hungarians against the thumping long-ball tactics of Wolves. With the pitch becoming heavier and muddier by the minute, it was the Wolves strategy that began to pay dividends, and despite going off at half-time two goals in arrears there were definite signs of the game beginning to swing in favour of the Midlanders.

With the huge Black Country roar of the capacity crowd urging them on, Wolves started a second-half revival movement that had Honved stretched to breaking point. Tiny England winger Johnny Hancocks used his favourite right boot to hammer a 49th-minute penalty into the net after he had been bundled off the ball by Kovaks. Captain Wright, with nightmare memories of Hungary's thirteen goals against England as his motivation for revenge, was giving a Herculean performance in the middle of the defence, and he drove his forwards to new peaks of effort as Wolves set up camp in the Honved half.

After half-a-dozen chances had been made and missed, Wolves finally snatched an equaliser in the 76th minute when Bill Slater and Denis Wilshaw combined to create an opening for centre-forward Roy Swinbourne, who nodded the ball wide of Farago's despairing dive.

Honved were suddenly almost visibly drained of spirit and energy, and all resistance was knocked out of them two minutes later when Wilshaw neatly pushed the ball into the path of Swinbourne, who ran on to score the dramatic winning goal.

Ferenc Puskas said after this match in a million for Molineux supporters: 'Billy Wright is a good friend of mine as well as a respected opponent. I told him after the match that he should be proud to be captain of such an outstanding team. We have not come up against a better club side. Wolves do not have a single weakness.'

Not a soul at Molineux on that never-to-be-forgotten night would have argued with his assessment. Billy Wright considered it one of the most glorious chapters in his career.

Who won what in 1954–55

First Division: Chelsea, 52pts. Runners-up: Wolves, 48pts.

Chelsea record: P42 W20 D12 L10 F81 A57 Pts52

Chelsea squad: Robertson (Thomson), Harris (Peter Sillett), Willemse, Armstrong, Greenwood (Wicks), Saunders; (from) Parsons, McNichol, Bentley*, Stubbs, Blunstone, Lewis, O'Connell (Peter Brabrook made three appearances). Top scorer: Bentley (21). Manager: Ted Drake.

Second Division: Birmingham City, 54pts. Runners-up: Luton Town, 54pts.

Third Division (South): Bristol City, 70pts. Runners-up: Leyton Orient, 61pts.

Third Division (North): Barnsley, 65pts. Runners-up: Accrington Stanley, 61pts.

FA Cup final: Newcastle United 3, Manchester City 1

Newcastle United: Simpson, Cowell, Batty, Scoular, Stokoe, Casey, White, Milburn[1], Keeble, Hannah[1], Mitchell[1].

Manchester City: Trautmann, Meadows, Little, Barnes, Ewing, Paul, Spurdle, Hayes, Revie, Johnstone[1], Fagan.

Top First Division marksman: Ronnie Allen (West Bromwich Albion), 27 goals.

Footballer of the Year: Don Revie (Manchester City).

Scottish champions: Aberdeen, 49pts. Runners-up: Celtic, 46pts.

Scottish Cup final: Clyde 1, Celtic 0 (after a 1–1 draw).

1954 World Cup final at the Wankdorf Stadium, Berne, 4 July 1954: West Germany 3, Hungary 2

West Germany: Turek, Posipal, Kohlmeyer, Eckel, Liebrich, Mai, Rahn[2], Morlock[1], Walter O, Walter F, Shäfer.

Hungary: Grosics, Buzanszky, Lantas, Bozsik, Lorant, Zakarias, Puskas[1], Kocsis, Hidegkuti, Czibor[1], Toth J.

Stats: Top scorer: Sandor Kocsis (Hungary) 11. Total goals: 140 (5.38 per game). Attendance (26 matches): 943,000 (average 36,269); 60,000 (final). Referee: Bill Ling (England).

SEASON 1955–56:
A Born Leader

There were mixed views and verdicts on Billy Wright the captain. Some hard-bitten professionals in the game thought that he was too soft, too undemanding and not demonstrative enough with his leadership. They would have liked to have seen him show more passion. Others considered him the ideal skipper, earning the respect of his team-mates by leading from the front; by example rather than exhortation.

For the expert opinion I went to one of his successors as England skipper, Johnny Haynes. Famous for being the first footballer to earn £100 a week in 1961, the Fulham favourite had made his international debut under Billy's captaincy at the age of nineteen in 1954, and led England himself in the final 22 of his 56 appearances.

For anybody not lucky enough to have seen Johnny in action, let me tell you that he could pass the ball as well as David Beckham. But here's the difference – he could do it with either foot. Becks is a magnificent player and one of the few around who could look the old masters in the eye, but he relies heavily on his golden right boot.

Johnny was two-footed, and could dictate the pace and pattern of a match from a central-midfield position that gave him a field marshal's view of the pitch.

'When I first joined the England squad for the match against Northern Ireland in 1954,' Johnny recalled, 'Billy went out of his way to make me feel comfortable and relaxed with my new team-mates. He was keen that there should be a club-style spirit in the England camp. That was an important part of his captaincy that the public never saw.'

What about the charge that he was too soft as a leader on the pitch? 'If that was the case,' Johnny said with a laugh, 'it doesn't say much for the judgement of Stan Cullis and Walter Winterbottom. Cullis had him leading Wolves to a succession of trophies over more than twelve years, and Walter picked him as skipper the little matter of 90 times.

'Billy was one of those captains who inspired by example. He would never give less than one hundred per cent, and none of his team-mates could slacken while their skipper was running himself into the ground. He almost shamed you into producing that little bit extra just when you were ready to drop.

'If there were any problems, he would sort them out quietly. He did not flourish his fist like a Dave Mackay, or keep talking like a Danny Blanchflower. His way was to give quiet encouragement, and he was always the first to shout 'bad luck...keep going lads' if things were going against us. Everybody who played with Billy learned a lot about humility. He was an outstanding man, and such a good bloke that you wanted to play your heart out for him.'

Stan Cullis summed up Billy's captaincy succinctly. 'He was a born leader,' he said. 'Where Billy led his team-mates followed. It's an old-fashioned word, but his clubmates were *loyal* to him. Loyalty and Billy Wright went together like eggs and bacon.'

Billy had captained England 53 times by the kick-off to the 1955–56 international season.

CAP NO 69

Denmark, Copenhagen, 2.10.55. England won 5–1

Baynham   Hall   Byrne R   McGarry   Wright*   Dickinson
Milburn   Revie$^{3\,(1\,pen)}$ Lofthouse^1 Bradford^1 Finney

Highlights: Luton goalkeeper Ron Baynham, Birmingham City right-back Jeff Hall and Bristol Rovers inside-left Geoff Bradford all made debuts. Bradford, a consistent force with Rovers in the Second Division and winning his only cap, scored the fifth and final goal eight minutes from the end after a hat-trick from Don Revie (including a penalty) and the usual goal from Lofthouse had floored the Danes. Hall and Byrne were to partner each other at full-back for seventeen successive matches, with only one defeat. This match was played on a Sunday in front of the King and Queen of Denmark to coincide with a British Trades Fair. So as not to weaken club sides for the previous day's League programme, the squad was chosen on a one club, one man basis. In eight instances the players were paired off from the Saturday games so that their clubs were equally weakened. *The Wright Cuttings Book* (*Daily Mirror*): 'So settled in the No 5 England shirt is Billy Wright that it is easy to take for granted the fact that he is a manufactured centre-half. He looked the perfect pivot against a Danish centre-forward who was simply swallowed up.'

BILLY: I get very sad when I think of that wonderful full-back partnership of Jeff Hall and Roger Byrne. They died within a few months of each other, Roger in the Munich air crash and Jeff from polio. There were few better full-back pairings in English football history. They were smashing lads, and extremely talented footballers. Both were comfortable in possession, firm tacklers and always looked to use the ball intelligently out of defence. Don Revie had just started experimenting with his Hidegkuti-style deep-lying centre-forward role with Manchester City, but he played as an orthodox inside-right alongside Nat Lofthouse in this match and the pair of them together were always too much of a handful for the Danish defenders.

CAP NO 70

Wales, Ninian Park, 22.10.55. England lost 2–1
Williams   Hall   Byrne R   McGarry   Wright*   Dickinson
Matthews   Revie   Lofthouse   Wilshaw   Finney 1 own goal

Highlights: Wales conquered England for the first time since 1938 thanks to a headed winning goal from young Swansea winger Cliff Jones, whose Uncle Bryn had scored one of the four goals that beat England seventeen years earlier. England's high-powered attack floundered against a Welsh defence in which the Charles brothers, John and Mel, played side by side. The game was virtually settled in a two-minute spell just before half-time. Derek Tapscott took advantage of hesitancy in the England defence to shoot Wales into the lead, and then Cliff Jones made it 2–0 with a stunning header from a Roy Paul cross. The only time England got the ball into the net was when John Charles, trying to clear his lines in the 51st minute, turned the ball past brilliant Arsenal goalkeeper Jack Kelsey for a spectacular own goal. *The Wright Cuttings Book (Daily Herald)*: 'For once, Billy Wright looked less than assured at centre-half and was never comfortable against the thrusting Derek Tapscott.'

BILLY: Wales were coming into that period when they could not be considered pushovers for any team. Young Cliff Jones was quick enough to catch pigeons and had the drive of a rugby wing three-quarter, and they also had the Allchurch brothers joining the Charles brothers in their impressive squad. It made me feel quite ancient seeing Cliffie Jones in a Welsh shirt. I had joined Wolves the summer that his Uncle Bryn was sold to Arsenal for a then world record £14,000. The critics said that it was a crazy fee and that the game had gone mad. John Charles showed his all-round ability by playing brilliantly in the middle of the defence. With his brother Mel alongside him, they were like a couple of Welsh mountains. It meant I really had my work cut out at corner-kicks because Big John and Big Mel would come up into our penalty area. It was times like that I wished I had been two or three inches taller. I tried to make up for my lack of height by making sure that I got to the ball first.

CAP NO 71
Northern Ireland, Wembley, 2.11.55. England won 3–0
Baynham   Hall   Byrne R   Clayton   Wright*   Dickinson
Finney[1]   Haynes   Jezzard   Wilshaw[2]   Perry

Highlights: Fulham clubmates Johnny Haynes and Bedford Jezzard played alongside each other for the only time in an England international. Haynes, partnering Tom Finney on the right wing, played farther upfield than usual to confuse his marker, Danny Blanchflower, and it was mainly because of his probing passes that England won comfortably with two goals from Dennis Wilshaw and another from Finney. Jezzard's career was ended a year later by an ankle injury. South

African-born Bill Perry came into the attack in place of his Blackpool team-mate Stanley Matthews, and Ronnie Clayton won the first of his 35 caps. This was Northern Ireland's first appearance at Wembley, and the only time they threatened to mark the occasion with a goal was when Charlie Tully had a point-blank shot superbly saved by goalkeeper Ron Baynham in the second half. *The Wright Cuttings Book (Daily Express)*: 'Hard as they tried, the Irish could make little impact against an England defence in which Billy Wright reigned supreme. What a revelation Billy is as a centre-half. The switch to the middle of the defence has added several years to his international career.'

BILLY: I was delighted to see Johnny Haynes recalled, even though it was out of position at inside-right. There was no question that he was the most accurate passer of the ball in the League. Walter Winterbottom instructed Johnny to push up, which meant Danny Blanchflower was unable to play his usual attacking role because he had to keep an eye on Johnny. I almost used to purr when watching Johnny play his beautifully disguised reverse passes with either foot, and he used to be able to land his crossfield pass on a handkerchief for distances up to fifty yards. There used to be something of a provincial bias against Johnny, and a lot of fans considered him big headed because of the petulant way he put his hands on his hips and glared when a team-mate failed to collect his pass cleanly. But this was just a perfectionist unable to understand why somebody was not meeting his sky-high standards. I had retired by the time Johnny became British football's first £100-a-week player with Fulham in 1961. If anybody was worth that money, it was Haynsie. He was a footballing master.

CAP NO 72
Spain, Wembley, 30.11.55. England won 4–1
Baynham   Hall   Byrne R   Clayton   Wright*   Dickinson
Finney[1]   Atyeo[1]   Lofthouse   Haynes   Perry[2]

Highlights: The Wembley floodlights were switched on for the first time in an international match fifteen minutes from the end of a game in which Spain were always in the dark. Finney missed from the penalty spot in the fifth minute, but then made amends by laying on one goal and scoring another. John Atyeo, the schoolteacher from Bristol City, put the finishing touch to a magnificent seven-man passing movement in the fifteenth minute, and sixty seconds later South African-born Bill Perry scored the first of his two goals. Finney and Perry made it 4–0 in the second half before the Spaniards snatched a consolation goal ten minutes from the end. *The Wright Cuttings Book* (*Daily Sketch*): 'The Spanish Armada sank against the rock that is Billy Wright.'

> BILLY: There had been scorching sunshine and a cloudless blue sky when we played Spain in Madrid in the May. For this match, it was perishing cold and murky. Floodlit football was just beginning to become accepted by clubs and the public, and we had pioneered it at Molineux. I have to say the Wembley lights were hopeless when switched on for the first time. There was a fog swirling around and we could hardly see the ball.

CAP NO 73
Scotland, Hampden Park, 14.4.56. Drew 1–1
Matthews R   Hall   Byrne R   Dickinson   Wright*   Edwards
Finney   Taylor T   Lofthouse   Haynes[1]   Perry

Highlights: Johnny Haynes silenced the Hampden Roar with a last-minute equaliser, shooting the ball past goalkeeper Tommy Younger after Manchester United team-mates Roger Byrne and Tommy Taylor had created the opening. Reg Matthews, making his debut in front of a 134,000 crowd while a Third Division goalkeeper with Coventry City, pulled off a string of magnificent saves and was only beaten on the hour by a mis-hit shot from Aberdeen's Graham Leggat. The last-gasp equaliser from man-of-the-match Haynes stopped Scotland from registering their first victory over the Auld Enemy at Hampden Park since 1937. *The Wright Cuttings Book* (*The Times*): 'Hampden as usual brought out the best in Wright, and he hardly put a foot wrong all afternoon.'

BILLY: The incredible thing about this match was that we had to call the trainer on to treat our goalkeeper Reg Matthews before a ball was kicked. Reg, used to playing in front of fewer than ten thousand spectators in the Third Division, was shaking with nerves as we left the dressing-room, and when he heard the roar from the 134,000 Scottish fans he almost passed out. Our trainer came on and gave Reg a whiff of smelling salts, and he quickly pulled himself together and gave an excellent debut performance. Reg, who later played for Chelsea, was nervy at the best of times and smoked like a trooper in the dressing-room. If he'd had more self-belief, he could have developed into a goalkeeper in the Frank Swift class. As it was he was a very, very good player and likeable. I enjoyed playing with him.

CAP NO 74

Brazil, Wembley, 9.5.56. England won 4–2

Matthews R   Hall   Byrne R   Clayton   Wright*   Edwards
Matthews S   Atyeo   Taylor T²   Haynes   Grainger²

Highlights: It was billed as the 'Old World meets the New' and Brazil arrived with many of the players who two years later were to win the World Cup in such dazzling fashion. England got off to a flying start under the Wembley Stadium floodlights with Tommy Taylor and Colin Grainger scoring inside the first five minutes. The Brazilians fought back to 2–2, and then John Atyeo and Roger Byrne each had a penalty saved by goalkeeper Gylmar. The penalty misses sandwiched a second goal by Taylor, made for him by a Stanley Matthews at his magical best against one of the all-time great left-backs, Nilton Santos. Matthews had been recalled by England at the age of 41, and he played like a 21-year-old. There was a farcical second-half hold-up following a dispute over a quickly taken free-kick by Johnny Haynes. The ball was caught by Nilton Santos and the Brazilians staged a walk-off protest when the referee awarded a penalty. By the time peace was restored it was no wonder that Atyeo failed with the spot-kick. Colin Grainger crowned a memorable debut with a second goal five minutes from the end of an extraordinary match. *The Wright Cuttings Book* (*Daily Mail*): 'Cool and commanding at all times, Billy Wright kept his head when all about were losing theirs. He acted as a peacemaker when the talented but temperamental Brazilians threatened to walk off. It was a real captain's performance, a mix of diplomacy and sportsmanship.'

BILLY: It was not only newcomers who were affected by nerves. I remember Johnny Haynes asking Stanley Matthews for his autograph in the dressing-room before this match against Brazil. The Maestro's hands were shaking so much that he could not hold the pen properly, and he asked Johnny to wait until after the game! Stanley was really wound up for this one because the Brazilians had stressed in the pre-match build-up that there was not a player in the world who could get the better of the great Nilton Santos. But as good a player as Santos was, he could not get near Stanley who was in untouchable form. At the end of the game Nilton was sporting enough to say, 'Mister Matthews, you are the king.'

CAP NO 75
Sweden, Solna, 16.5.56. Drew 0–0
Matthews R Hall Byrne R Clayton Wright* Edwards
Berry Atyeo Taylor T Haynes Grainger

Highlights: England were lucky to escape with a draw in a match ruined by a near-gale force wind. Goalkeeper Reg Matthews made three stunning saves to stop the Swedes from getting the victory their superior approach play deserved. It was the first goalless draw in which England had been involved since the game in Denmark in 1948. *The Wright Cuttings Book* (*Daily Telegraph*): 'In conditions that would have sent a yachtsman racing for the shelter of any port, Wright managed to stop England from sinking with a cultured performance in the middle of the defence.'

BILLY: The wind was so strong that it was almost impossible to measure a pass. I can't remember a game when the ball was out of play so often. You would push a pass upfield for the forwards and invariably it would get caught by the wind and be taken for a goal-kick. It was a frustrating and fruitless game for everybody.

CAP NO 76
Finland, Helsinki, 20.5.56. England won 5–1
Wood   Hall   Byrne R   Clayton   Wright*   Edwards
Astall[1]   Haynes[1]   Taylor T   (Lofthouse[2])   Wilshaw[1]   Grainger

Highlights: Nat Lofthouse came on as a substitute for the injured Tommy Taylor a minute before half-time, and for the twelfth time in an England shirt he scored two goals. It lifted his haul to 29 goals, one more than the previous England record set by the great Steve Bloomer before the First World War. Gordon Astall, playing in place of the unavailable Stanley Matthews, scored on his debut. England were leading 3–0 when Taylor limped off following a collision with the Finnish goalkeeper. The record-breaking goal by Lofthouse in the 82nd minute was a freak effort, the ball rolling gently over the goal line between two defenders who left the clearance duties to each other. *The Wright Cuttings Book* (*News Chronicle*): 'Wright and Edwards together is as strong a half-back combination as England have had in many a year. It promises much for the future.'

> BILLY: We celebrated Lofty's new record at a marvellous after-match banquet where we were treated royally. We sang along with Colin Grainger who did a great Al Jolson impression. Colin, a regular nightclub singer, was accompanied on the piano by the Finnish centre-forward, who played professionally with a danceband. Great memories.

CAP NO 77
West Germany, Berlin, 26.5.56. England won 3–1
Matthews R   Hall   Byrne R   Clayton   Wright*   Edwards[1]
Astall   Haynes[1]   Taylor T   Wilshaw   Grainger[1]

Highlights: This match is remembered as the finest ever played on the international stage by Duncan Edwards, who was fresh from helping Manchester United win the League championship. He strode the pitch like a colossus, scoring a scorcher of a goal from twenty yards in the twentieth minute and dominating the entire game both in defence and midfield. Nearly half the 100,000 crowd in the stadium designed by Adolf Hitler were soldiers from the British-occupied zone of Berlin. They staged a delighted pitch invasion when second-half goals from Johnny Haynes and Colin Grainger clinched victory. Fritz Walter, the outstanding German skipper, scored a fine individual goal for the team he had led to the World Cup two years earlier. *The Wright Cuttings Book* (*Empire News*): 'It is rewarding to watch the developing partnership between Billy Wright and Duncan Edwards. They were solid defensively against the Germans, and the Busby Babe had the confidence to push forward as an extra attacker, knowing that his skipper would cover for him.'

BILLY: The name of Duncan Edwards was on the lips of everybody who saw this match. He was phenomenal. There have been few individual performances to match what he produced in Germany that day. He tackled like a lion, attacked at every opportunity and topped it all off with a cracker of a goal. He was still only twenty, and was already a world-class player. Many of the thousands of British soldiers in the crowd surrounded him at the final whistle and carried him off. It was fantastic to be part of it. We had beaten the world champions in their own back yard.

Who won what in 1955–56

First Division: Manchester United, 60pts. Runners-up: Blackpool, 49pts.

Manchester United record: P42 W25 D10 L7 F83 A51 Pts60

Man United squad: Wood, Foulkes, Byrne*, Colman, Jones, Edwards, (from) Berry, Whelan, Taylor, Viollet, Pegg, Doherty, Blanchflower J. Top scorer: Taylor (25). Manager: Matt Busby.

Second Division: Sheffield Wednesday, 55pts. Runners-up Leeds United, 52pts.

Third Division (South): Leyton Orient, 66pts. Runners-up: Brighton, 65pts.

Third Division (North): Grimsby Town, 68pts, Runners-up: Derby County, 63pts.

FA Cup final: Manchester City 3, Birmingham City 1

Manchester City: Trautmann, Leivers, Little, Barnes, Ewing, Paul Johnstone[1], Hayes[1], Revie, Dyson[1], Clarke.

Birmingham City: Merrick, Hall, Green, Newman, Smith, Boyd, Astall, Kinsey[1], Brown, Murphy, Govan.

Top First Division marksman: Nat Lofthouse (Bolton), 33 goals.

Footballer of the Year: Bert Trautmann (Manchester City).

Scottish champions: Rangers, 52pts. Runners-up: Aberdeen, 46pts.

Scottish Cup final: Hearts 3, Celtic 1.

First European Cup final: Real Madrid 4, Stade de Reims 3 (Paris).

First European Footballer of the Year: Stanley Matthews (Blackpool).

SEASON 1956–57:
A World Cup Plan

For the first time, England had to qualify for the World Cup finals in a group away from the Home Championship. Walter Winterbottom revealed to Billy a plan that even met with the approval of the venerable selectors, who had been continually suffocating him.

Walter drew up a list of thirty players from which he wanted the selectors to pick the team, so that for the first time there would be some continuity on the way to the finals. The A-squad included six players from the Manchester United Busby Babes team that was on its way to two successive League championships: Goalkeeper Ray Wood, left-back Roger Byrne, wingers Johnny Berry and David Pegg, centre-forward Tommy Taylor, and the play-anywhere, do-anything Duncan Edwards. Walter also made a note that a close watch should be kept on the progress of a young utility forward called Bobby Charlton.

'Billy Wright was the first name on the list,' Winterbottom confided. 'His leadership was a vital ingredient. We had often discussed getting a club spirit running through the England team, and the warmth of Billy's personality helped enormously towards this end. He was also in on footballing merit, having developed very quickly into a world-class centre-half.'

The long-playing Stanley Matthews' England career came to an end during this 1956–57 season. Sadly, it ended with the Maestro having a dig at Walter's style of management. Matthews went on record with this sweeping criticism: 'A will to win was sadly lacking in the England team...I blame this on the pre-match talks on playing tactics that had

153

been introduced for the first time by our team manager. You just cannot tell star players how they must play and what they must do on the field in an international match. You must let them play their natural game, which has paid big dividends in the past. I have noticed that in recent years these pre-match instructions have become more and more long-winded while the playing ability of the players on the field has dwindled. So I say scrap the talks and instruct the players to play their natural game.'

Winterbottom took this savage swipe on his dimpled chin, and put up just a muted defence as he replied in that professorial way of his: 'In principle I can state quite firmly that it is grossly untrue that I have encouraged this trend of team instruction before an international match. In fact, I have repeatedly insisted on our players having every opportunity to play as a team before an important match to enable us to cut down on these instructions. Indeed, I can state quite categorically that players are always encouraged to play their own game.'

BILLY: Walter was hurt by the criticism but did not let on to the media. Yes, he could be long-winded but there was sense in everything he said. It was understandable that a player with Stanley's unique ability would want to do his own thing, but that was not always in the interest of the team. Walter was glowing with excitement when the selectors agreed to his plan for a World Cup squad. He even got them to agree to let us get together a couple of days before each match and for the occasional training session. At last, we were acting like real professionals. This was, of course, all part of the outcome of the inquests that followed our defeats by Hungary and the early exit from the 1954 World Cup finals. From the day that the selectors gave the go-ahead for Walter's squad plan we went sixteen matches with only one defeat and qualified for the finals. We were being widely talked of as possible World Cup winners. Then came Munich …

The terrible impact of the Munich air crash, that left such a scar on English soccer, will be a sad feature of the next chapter. Meantime, in the international arena, the emphasis was on World Cup qualification.

CAP NO 78

Northern Ireland, Windsor Park, 6.10.56. Drew 1–1

Matthews R   Hall   Byrne R   Clayton   Wright*   Edwards
Matthews S[1]   Revie   Taylor T   Wilshaw   Grainger

Highlights: A rare goal from Stanley Matthews (his eleventh and last in international football) after just two minutes gave England a dream start, but they were hustled out of their stride by a Northern Ireland team motivated by a dazzling performance from skipper Danny Blanchflower. Jimmy McIlroy equalised after ten minutes when goalkeeper Reg Matthews palmed a long throw from Peter McParland into his path. McIlroy was faced with an open goal five minutes from the end but hit a post. If he had found the net, it would have given Northern Ireland their first home win over England since 1927. *The Wright Cuttings Book (News Chronicle)*: 'Ireland cleverly played twin centre-forwards to weaken the influence of Wright, who was never quite sure which one to mark. This left holes that the mercurial Blanchflower exposed with relish. With Wright caught in two minds, Edwards should have been detailed to purely defensive duties but he has such an appetite for going forward that he could not curb his desire to be in the thick of things. It meant that Wright was not only trying to hold the centre of the England defence together but also acting as a cover for the brilliant youngster from Old Trafford.'

BILLY: There was a lot of good-natured ribbing of Stanley Matthews over his goal. His last goal for England had been eight years earlier, also against Northern Ireland and also at Windsor Park. Jackie Blanchflower, Danny's brother and always a quick wit, asked: 'Why does he always pick on us?' Danny himself came into the dressing-room after the match and told Stanley that he had been a schoolboy spectator in short trousers when he scored his last goal. 'You'll have a long beard by the time I score the next one,' said Stanley, with that poker-faced humour of his. Danny had a magnificent match, and it was clear the Irish were getting a powerful team together for their World Cup challenge.

CAP NO 79
Wales, Wembley, 14.11.56. England won 3–1
Ditchburn   Hall   Byrne R   Clayton   Wright*   Dickinson
Matthews   Brooks¹   Finney¹   Haynes¹   Grainger

Highlights: This Home Championship match was wrecked by an injury to Welsh goalkeeper Jack Kelsey, who was carried off after being knocked out diving at the feet of Tom Finney. The incident came while the Welsh supporters were celebrating an eighth-minute goal from John Charles, who rose above Billy Wright's challenge to head in an Ivor Allchurch corner. Right-back Alf Sherwood took over in the Welsh goal, and from then on England were dominant despite the stirring efforts of John Charles to turn the tide. Second-half goals from Johnny Haynes, debutant Johnny Brooks and the versatile Tom Finney at centre-forward gave England an undistinguished victory. This was England's seventh successive win at Wembley. *The Wright Cuttings Book* (*Daily Express*): 'Billy Wright felt the heat of the dragon's breath on his neck when the magnificent John Charles outjumped him to head Wales into the lead. Any other player might have crumbled, but the England captain rolled up his sleeves and did not give the Welsh centre-forward another glimpse of goal. But what might have happened had Wales been allowed to bring on a substitute goalkeeper following the unfortunate injury to Jack Kelsey? It robbed the spectators of an even match.'

BILLY: The subject of whether substitutes should be allowed was again a major talking point. Wales started full of fire and were obviously going to give us a difficult afternoon, but then the injury to goalkeeper Jack Kelsey robbed them of their rhythm. They also had Mel Charles as a hobbling passenger for much of the match, and we were handicapped by injuries to Colin Grainger and Johnny Haynes. It would have made sense to at least allow substitute goalkeepers, but the powers-that-be refused to follow the lead of the continental clubs who were using substitutes more and more. It would be another nine years before they at last saw sense and allowed substitutes.

CAP NO 80

Yugoslavia, Wembley, 28.11.56. England won 3–0

Ditchburn   Hall   Byrne R   Clayton   Wright*   Dickinson
Matthews   Brooks[1]   Finney   Haynes (Taylor T[2])   Blunstone

Highlights: Johnny Haynes was heavily tackled by Yugoslav right-back Belin in the thirtieth minute, and was unable to continue. It had been agreed beforehand that substitutes would be allowed in the case of injury and Tommy Taylor came on in place of the limping Fulham player. England had taken a thirteenth-minute lead when Johnny Brooks fired the ball high into the net after taking a neat pass from Haynes. England dominated throughout the second half and Taylor scored twice, while his Manchester United team-mate Roger Byrne had a penalty saved by world-class Yugoslav goalkeeper Vladimir Beara. Stanley Matthews ran the Yugoslav left-back into such a state of confusion that he finally resorted to rugby-tackling him in a bid to stop his dribbling runs. *The Wright Cuttings Book* (*Daily Mirror*): 'Proof of Billy Wright's supremacy is that Yugoslavia's centre-forward was rarely allowed to test Tottenham goalkeeper Ted Ditchburn. The Wolves Wonder was in complete control of the penalty area.'

BILLY: We would have had half a dozen goals but for the magnificent goalkeeping of Beara. He had been a ballet dancer before switching to football, and was one of the most supple and stylish goalkeepers I ever saw. The Yugoslavs had no idea how to contain Stanley Matthews, and after he had been rugby-tackled he said, 'For a minute I thought the game had been switched to Twickenham.'

CAP NO 81

Denmark, Molineux, 5.12.56. England won 5–2

Ditchburn   Hall   Byrne R   Clayton   Wright*   Dickinson
Matthews   Brooks   Taylor T[3]   Edwards[2]   Finney

Highlights: England's World Cup campaign got under way with this convincing victory over Denmark on Billy Wright's home ground of

Molineux. The match was distinguished by a hat-trick from Tommy Taylor and two spectacular goals from his Manchester United team-mate Duncan Edwards, who played at inside-left in place of the injured Johnny Haynes. Edwards scored with two booming long-range shots, had another shot wondrously saved and nearly uprooted a post with another thunderbolt from a free-kick. England had been drawn in a three-team group with Denmark and the Republic of Ireland, and this convincing performance underlined why they were rated among the favourites for the World Cup. *The Wright Cuttings Book* (*Daily Herald*): 'Playing as if he owned Molineux (which some Wolves fans think he should), Billy Wright was rock solid at the heart of the England defence.'

BILLY: It was as if Manchester United had taken over Molineux! Roger Byrne was the outstanding player in our defence, and up front Tommy Taylor and Duncan Edwards showed the power that had taken United to the top of the First Division in defence of their title. Duncan was a leg-pulling rascal off the pitch. His room-mate Tommy Taylor had just started smoking a pipe, and while he was not looking Duncan unscrewed the bowl, removed the stem and pushed a matchstick down it. All the lads were in on the joke except Tommy. I was called in as the stooge. 'Tommy,' I said, 'I'm thinking about trying a pipe. Is it easy to get it lit?' Dear old Tommy said in his Yorkshire accent, 'No trouble at all. Here, I'll show you.' There were five minutes of priceless comedy as Tommy sucked on his pipe until his cheeks were sunken and his face blue with the effort. This was just the sort of harmless fun that helped to generate the club spirit that Walter Winterbottom and I were so keen to encourage.

CAP NO 82
Scotland, Wembley, 6.4.57. England won 2–1
Hodgkinson   Hall   Byrne R   Clayton   Wright*   Edwards[1]
Matthews   Thompson T   Finney   Kevan[1]   Grainger

Highlights: Duncan Edwards snatched victory for England six minutes from the end with a blistering 25-yard shot that thumped into the net off a post. The Scots had got off to a flying start when Sheffield United goalkeeper Alan Hodgkinson had to pick the ball out of his net just a minute into his debut. He was beaten by a snap shot from Clyde winger Tommy Ring after he had intercepted a pass meant for Stanley Matthews. Derek Kevan, making his debut in place of Johnny Haynes, equalised in the 62nd-minute with a diving header from a Colin Grainger cross. Scottish fans were convinced they were robbed when Willie Fernie bundled the ball into the net after it had been dropped by Hodgkinson following a jolting Lawrie Reilly shoulder charge. The Dutch referee ruled that the goalkeeper had both feet off the ground when contact was made. Tommy Docherty was the pick of the Scottish players, giving a powerhouse performance in midfield and completely shutting out his Preston team-mate Tommy Thompson, who was winning his first cap for six years. The winning goal was set up by Matthews, who beat two defenders before squaring the ball into the path of Edwards. He hit a fierce first-time shot wide of goalkeeper Tommy Younger. *The Wright Cuttings Book* (*Observer*): 'Billy Wright gave an exceptional performance in the middle of the England defence. As well as keeping the dangerous Lawrie Reilly under lock and key, the England captain found time to help his defensive colleagues with superb covering work. It is no coincidence that England's run of fine results follow Wright's switch to centre-half. He plays there as to the manner born, and it has brought new confidence and cohesion to the England rearguard.'

BILLY: Big Derek Kevan was one of Walter Winterbottom's most controversial choices. He was a lumbering, inelegant player who used to take some terrible stick from the press. But talking as a centre-half who often had to mark him in club matches I can vouch for the fact that he was a real handful. He was all arms and legs and very difficult to tie down. He did not have the poise of a Tommy Taylor or the power and positional sense of a Nat Lofthouse, but he was so awkward and determined that he could unsettle the most disciplined of defences with his unorthodox approach.

CAP NO 83

Republic of Ireland, Wembley, 8.5.57. England won 5–1

Hodgkinson   Hall   Byrne R   Clayton   Wright*   Edwards
Matthews   Atyeo²   Taylor T³   Haynes   Finney

Highlights: A second successive Tommy Taylor hat-trick – all his goals coming in the first half – and two from John Atyeo crushed an outgunned Irish team in this second of England's four World Cup qualifying matches. This was, sadly, to be the last match in which Jeff Hall and Roger Byrne were to partner each other. Jeff contracted polio and died on 4 April 1959. Born in Scunthorpe on 7 September 1929, he started his career as an amateur with Bradford Park Avenue before becoming a regular in Birmingham City's defence. He would have had, statistically, the best individual England record of any player but for the 2–1 defeat by Wales in 1955. In seventeen matches he was on the beaten side only once. England won twelve of the games and drew four. Roger Byrne was his partner in every game. *The Wright Cuttings Book* (*London Evening Standard*): 'Irish centre-forward Dermot Curtis, John Atyeo's clubmate at Bristol City, was virtually shut out of the game by the immoveable Billy Wright. He managed to get the better of the England captain just once when he headed in a second-half consolation goal from a centre by Arsenal whippet Joe Haverty.'

BILLY: England were rock solid at full-back when Jeff and Roger were together. They were the perfect balance for each other, and both were strong, reliable people both on and off the pitch. Roger and his Manchester United team-mates Tommy Taylor and Duncan Edwards were back playing at Wembley just three days after the FA Cup final in which they were surprisingly beaten 2–1 by Aston Villa. All three felt strongly that Villa's goal in the sixth minute should not have been allowed. Villa goalscorer Peter McParland had collided with goalkeeper Ray Wood, who was carried off with a fractured cheekbone. From then on United were totally disjointed, with centre-half Jackie Blanchflower having to play in goal. Yet another debate started about the need for a substitute law.

CAP NO 84

Denmark, Copenhagen, 15.5.57. England won 4–1

Hodgkinson   Hall   Byrne R   Clayton   Wright*   Edwards
Matthews   Atyeo[1]   Taylor T[2]   Haynes[1]   Finney

Highlights: This World Cup qualifier was to prove the international swansong of 'Mr Football' Stanley Matthews, who was retired from the world stage at the age of 42 and 22 years after the first of his 54 caps. Denmark took the lead in the 25th minute, with Johnny Haynes equalising just before half-time. It was not until the final fifteen minutes that England got on top against a brave Danish team briefly reduced by injury to ten men. Tommy Taylor scored twice to take his haul in four matches to ten goals. Taylor's double strike came either side of a 75th-minute goal by John Atyeo, who rose at the far post to head in a Johnny Haynes centre. *The Wright Cuttings Book* (*The People*): 'There was to be no fairytale victory for the Danes against an England team in which Billy Wright was at his miserly best, giving nothing away.'

BILLY: We had no idea that this would be Stanley's final England game, otherwise we would have carried him off shoulder high, as would have been only right for one of the greatest footballers of any time. Even at 42, there were many who considered his England career had been finished too early. Just his name on the team sheet would have given us a psychological advantage when we played in the 1958 World Cup finals. A year before this match Wolves had met Blackpool in a vital First Division game, and manager Stan Cullis switched me to left-back to mark him. 'You know his play better than anybody,' said Stan. 'Keep him as quiet as possible.' Easier said than done! Despite all my years with a close-up view of the Matthews magic, I had no idea how to read him. He succeeded in giving me a lesson in the art of making a left-back look foolish and flat-footed. I just could not make any contact with him. He did not spare me, and my tongue was hanging out at the end of a match in which I chased his shadow.

CAP NO 85

Republic of Ireland, Dalymount Park, 19.5.57. Drew 1–1

Hodgkinson   Hall   Byrne R   Clayton   Wright*   Edwards
Finney   Atyeo[1]   Taylor T   Haynes   Pegg

Highlights: England, needing a point to qualify for the World Cup finals, were rocked and shocked by a third minute goal from Dublin-born winger Alf Ringstead. He crashed a loose ball wide of his Sheffield United team-mate Alan Hodgkinson to send the capacity crowd in Dalymount Park wild. From then on England struggled to make any impact against an inspired Irish defence in which Bournemouth goalkeeper Tommy Godwin and Millwall centre-half Charlie Hurley were outstanding. The game was into its last minute when Tom Finney fired over a perfect cross for John Atyeo to head a superbly taken equaliser that gave relieved England a passport to Sweden. David Pegg, who came in for the injured Stanley Matthews, won his only cap before becoming one of the victims of the Munich air crash. *The Wright Cuttings Book* (*Daily Sketch*): 'Luckily for England, Billy Wright was at his majestic best in the centre of the defence, otherwise the Irish would have been celebrating a famous victory and England would have been left wondering whether they had let the plane tickets to the World Cup finals in Sweden slip from their grasp. As it is, Wright can now look forward to leading England into a World Cup challenge that will be the strongest yet.'

> BILLY: John Atyeo's goal saved us a lot of embarrassment, and a hammering from the press. The selectors rewarded John by never selecting him again! He returned to Bristol where he created new goal scoring and appearance records for City before concentrating full-time on his teaching career. He eventually became a headmaster, which he had always been on the football pitch. We were in great heart when we left Ireland, and looking forward to making a strong challenge for the World Cup.

There was recognition of Billy's international standing when he was named runner-up to Real Madrid maestro Alfredo di Stefano as the

European Footballer of the Year for 1957, and he was in the top ten for three successive years. Now all thoughts were centred on the World Cup, with England among the favourites to lift the coveted trophy.

But there was a tragedy on the horizon that would catapult English soccer into a state of deep and tearful mourning.

Who won what in 1956–57

First Division: Manchester United, 64pts. Runners-up: Tottenham, 56pts.

Manchester United record: P42 W28 D8 L6 F103 A54 Pts64

Manchester United squad: Wood, Foulkes, Byrne*, Colman, Jones, Edwards, Berry, Whelan, Taylor, Viollet, Pegg. Also; Blanchflower J (11), Charlton (14), McGuinness (13). Top scorer: Whelan (26). Manager: Matt Busby.

Second Division: Leicester City, 61pts. Runners-up: Nottingham Forest 54pts.

Third Division (South): Ipswich, 59pts. Runners-up: Torquay, 59pts.

Third Division (North): Derby County, 63pts. Runners-up: Hartlepools, 59pts.

FA Cup final: Aston Villa 2, Manchester United 1

Aston Villa: Sims, Lynn, Aldis, Crowther, Dugdale, Saward, Smith, Sewell, Myerscough, Dixon, McParland[2].

Manchester United: Wood, Foulkes, Byrne, Colman, Blanchflower J, Edwards, Berry, Whelan, Taylor[1], Charlton, Pegg.

Top First Division marksman: John Charles (Leeds), 38 goals.

Footballer of the Year: Tom Finney (Preston).

Scottish champions: Rangers, 55pts. Runners-up: Hearts, 53pts.

Scottish Cup final: Falkirk 2, Kilmarnock 1 (after a 1–1 draw).

European Cup final: Real Madrid 2, Fiorentina 0 (Madrid).

European Footballer of the Year: Alfredo di Stefano (Real Madrid); runner-up Billy Wright (Wolves).

SEASON 1957–58:
The Saddest Day

Billy's 34th birthday on 6 February 1958 developed into the saddest day of his life; the day that brought English soccer to its knees. It was the horrific date in history when an aircraft carrying the Manchester United team home from a European Cup tie in Belgrade crashed on takeoff after refuelling at Munich.

Eight players and eight journalists were among the 23 passengers and crew killed when the snow-covered Elizabethan airliner ploughed through a perimeter fence as the pilot made a third attempt to get off the ice-bound airport runway.

The eight players who lost their lives were Roger Byrne, Geoff Bent, Eddie Colman, Mark Jones, David Pegg, Tommy Taylor, Liam Whelan and, fifteen days after the crash, Duncan Edwards.

It was the day that the Manchester United team died, and when the heart was ripped out of the England World Cup squad.

BILLY: How can I ever forget that terrible day! I was feeling nice and chirpy as I made my way back from training on the bus. I had a little Ford by then, but used to lend it to my landlady's son, Arthur Colley, so that he could drive to work. Arthur and I shared the same birthday – February 6th. So that morning we had had our usual routine of singing 'Happy Birthday' to each other, and I left the Colley house with a smile on my face. I was sitting daydreaming on the bus after our training session when I spotted a billboard outside a newsagent's that screamed, 'Man United Air Crash!' I jumped off at the next stop and bought the *Wolverhampton Express & Star*. The stop-press story was a first report that the Manchester United plane had crashed on takeoff. It said that many were feared dead, but at that stage there were no names. Over the course of next couple of hours we slowly learned the horrible facts. As well as the players, many of my good friends among the football writers had perished. I remember them so well – Alf Clarke, Don Davies, George Follows, Tom Jackson, Archie Ledbrooke, Henry Rose, Eric Thompson and my dear old England buddy Frank Swift, who was travelling as a reporter for the *News of the World*. Along with everybody else, I spent the next 24 hours almost permanently weeping over the cruel loss of so many friends and colleagues. If there could be such a thing as good news from an incident like this, we heard that young Bobby Charlton had escaped unhurt and that Sir Matt Busby and Duncan Edwards were injured but likely to live. So it was more tears two weeks later when that young giant Duncan finally lost his battle for life. That hurt more than anything, because he represented the future of our game. Big Dunc, as we called him, was at least three years short of his peak, and he could already be rated in the 'genius' bracket. It was all so tragic, and away from the personal sadness there was the wider repercussions that our national football team had been dealt a mortal blow. Yes, you could say that was a birthday I would rather forget.

A measure of the effect the crash had on the England football team can be found in the statistics. From beating world champions West Germany at Wembley in 1954, England had won sixteen and drawn eight of twenty-five internationals. After Munich and up to Billy's 105th and final game, England won just six and drew six of twenty international matches.

You do not need to be a football expert to realise that this record would have been greatly improved had Roger Byrne, Duncan Edwards and Tommy Taylor been available for selection. Their loss meant that England had been weakened in every department; defence, midfield and attack. No team in the world could have afforded to lose three such key players and still have hoped to make an impressive impact in the World Cup finals.

On the domestic front, Billy led Wolves to the first of two successive League championships. They scored 103 goals, and conceded just 47. No team had a better defensive record, and only Manchester City scored more. They found the net 104 times and managed to let in 100 goals at the wrong end! Like everything else that season, the Wolves triumph was overshadowed by the darkness and despair of the Munich air crash. Three of the players who were doomed to lose their lives were in the England team that started the 1957–58 season with a resounding win over Wales in Cardiff...

CAP NO 86

Wales, Ninian Park, 19.10.57. England won 4–0
Hopkinson   Howe D   Byrne R   Clayton   Wright*   Edwards
Douglas   Kevan   Taylor T   Haynes[2]   Finney[1] +1 own goal

Highlights: Wales were in trouble from the moment early in the game when left-back Mel Hopkins passed the ball wide of goalkeeper Jack Kelsey and into his own net. Missing the powerful influence of the absent John Charles, Wales caved in to two goals from Johnny Haynes and a brilliant strike from Tom Finney. Goalkeeper Eddie Hopkinson, right-back Don Howe and outside-right Bryan Douglas – the 'new Matthews' – all made impressive debuts. There was another debutant. Middlesbrough's Harold Shepherdson was having his first match as trainer, a job he would hold for sixteen years. *The Wright Cuttings Book* (*Daily Mirror*): 'Playing with calm composure, Billy Wright did not put a single foot wrong in yet another perfect performance.'

BILLY: Shep, as we called him, became a vital right-hand man to Walter and then to his successor, Alf Ramsey. He was the best-organised person I ever came across, and used to arrive in the dressing-room with so many medical supplies that he was like a mobile chemist's shop. I was impressed by the debut performance of young West Bromwich Albion defender Don Howe at right-back and noticed how disciplined he was both on and off the pitch.

It was background knowledge I was happy to have when I later made him one of my major signings for Arsenal.

CAP NO 87
Northern Ireland, Wembley, 6.11.57. England lost 3–2
Hopkinson   Howe D   Byrne R   Clayton   Wright*   Edwards[1]
Douglas   Kevan   Taylor T   Haynes   A'Court[1]

Highlights: Skipper Danny Blanchflower and goalkeeper Harry Gregg were carried off shoulder high by celebrating Irish fans after this unexpected victory that ended England's sixteen-match unbeaten run. Burnley schemer Jimmy McIlroy gave Ireland a first-half lead with a penalty shot that hit a post and then went into the net off the back of goalkeeper Hopkinson. The penalty had been conceded by Billy Wright with one of the few fouls he ever committed in an England shirt. Liverpool winger Alan A'Court, making his debut in place of the injured Tom Finney, equalised soon after half-time before McCrory and Simpson – with a goal hotly disputed by England – put the Irish 3–1 clear. Duncan Edwards pulled back a goal, but Ireland went on to their first victory over England since 1927 and the first on English soil since 1914. Doncaster Rovers goalkeeper Harry Gregg, later to join Manchester United and survive the Munich air crash, had a game to remember, making at least half a dozen crucial saves. *The Wright Cuttings Book* (*Daily Mail*): 'We have become so accustomed to seeing Billy Wright in complete command that it came as a shock to see him struggling to cope with the lively Irish attack. The award of a penalty against him seemed harsh, and in the press box we could not think of the last time that he had conceded as much as a free-kick.'

BILLY: The third Irish goal was at least two yards offside and we could not believe it when the linesman's flag stayed down. Welshman Mervyn Griffiths, an outstanding referee, was the man in charge. I thought he was wrong to award a penalty against me after a tackle that I thought was firm but fair. These two grumbles apart, I hold up my hands and admit that Northern Ireland deserved their victory. There were so many Irishmen on the pitch at the end that I thought the game had been transferred to Belfast. They had an enormous celebration. Let's face it, they had been waiting a long, long time for it!

CAP NO 88

France, Wembley, 27.11.57. England won 4–0

Hopkinson   Howe D   Byrne R   Clayton   Wright*   Edwards
Douglas   Robson R²   Taylor T²   Haynes   Finney

Highlights: Bryan Douglas had a storming game, and three of the four England goals came from his crosses. Bobby Robson, winning his first cap, scored two goals as did Tommy Taylor. Tragically, they were to be his last for England. The game was so one-sided that it was almost reduced to French farce, with England hammering in twenty shots to none from France in the last twenty minutes. Only one of them produced a goal, Bobby Robson hitting the back of the net at the end of a seven-man movement to underline his arrival as a force in international football. *The Wright Cuttings Book* (*Daily Mirror*): 'One word sums up Billy Wright's performance as captain and centre-half against France: "*Magnifique!*" '

BILLY: I can remember as clearly as anything Walter Winterbottom saying to me at the after-match banquet, 'Bill, I think we have a team that could make a really telling challenge for the World Cup.' Little did we know then that we would never be able to field that side again. Even more than thirty years on I get choked just thinking about it. Two other things stick out in my memory, apart from the devastating performance by Bryan Douglas who teased and tormented the French defence in the manner of Stanley Matthews. Don Howe received a telegram in the dressing-room before the kick-off. It was from his father, telling him his mother had died. Don was distraught and wanted to withdraw, but his father insisted he should play because that was what his mother would have wanted. The referee was a highly respected Russian official called Nikolai Latychev. While he was refereeing the match, somebody broke into the dressing-room and stole his wallet and passport. The terribly embarrassed Football Association reimbursed him, and the Foreign Office were called in to see that he was able to get home without any fuss. From then on, security at Wembley was tightened up.

CAP NO 89
Scotland, Hampden Park, 19.4.58. England won 4–0
Hopkinson   Howe D   Langley   Clayton   Wright*   Slater
Douglas¹   Charlton R¹   Kevan²   Haynes   Finney

Highlights: Bobby Charlton, a Munich survivor, electrified the first of his 106 England appearances with a classical goal when he connected with a Tom Finney cross on the volley to send it flashing into the Scotland net from the edge of the penalty area. His wonder strike came in the 62nd minute after Bryan Douglas had headed England into a first-half lead and then laid on the first of two goals for Derek Kevan. Fulham's Jim Langley made a commendable debut in place of the sadly missed Roger Byrne, with Wolverhampton's Bill Slater taking on the impossible job of following Duncan Edwards. The nearest Scotland came to scoring was when a Jackie Mudie header hit the bar midway through the second half, by which time England were sitting on a cushion of three goals. Kevan wrapped it up for England fifteen minutes from the end after Johnny Haynes, Bobby Charlton and Bill Slater had cut open the Scottish defence with a procession of precise passes. *The Wright Cuttings Book* (*The People*): 'Nobody is going to miss the great Duncan Edwards more than Billy Wright, but the England captain performed as well as ever against the Scots. He was obviously comfortable with his cultured clubmate Bill Slater alongside him.'

BILLY: Nobody who saw it would ever forget Bobby Charlton's first goal for England. We all agreed in the dressing-room after the match that we had never seen a football struck harder. When you think that just a few weeks earlier he had been found still strapped to his seat away from the wreckage of the crashed plane at Munich it was nothing short of a miracle. This was the start of the Bobby Charlton legend, and I felt privileged to be on the same pitch as him to witness it. As skipper, I had taken Bobby under my wing, but he was such a mature nineteen-year-old that he took everything in his stride. I agreed with his marker, Tommy Docherty, who said afterwards: 'This boy is going to be worth a million pounds.' Remember that this was at a time when the record transfer fee was the £65,000 that Juventus had paid Leeds for John Charles the previous season.

CAP NO 90
Portugal, Wembley, 7.5.58. England won 2–1
Hopkinson   Howe D   Langley   Clayton   Wright*   Slater
Douglas   Charlton R²   Kevan   Haynes   Finney

Highlights: Two goals from Bobby Charlton – the second, a scorching shot similar to that which rocked the Scots – rescued England from the brink of defeat. Portugal created enough chances to have won the game, but their finishing was feeble. Jim Langley failed to score from the penalty spot, one of only two misses throughout his career. It was the fourth penalty miss in a row in an international match at Wembley. *The Wright Cuttings Book* (*Daily Mirror*): 'When Portugal applied the pressure in the second half, Billy Wright was a steadying influence as several of his colleagues started to flap.'

BILLY: Just four days earlier, Bobby Charlton had suffered the disappointment of defeat when playing for Manchester United against Bolton in the FA Cup final. He showed what character he had by returning to Wembley and producing a magnificent performance, crowned with his two superbly taken goals. Yes, as The Doc said, he would one day be worth a million pounds. I had not seen such a wonderful home-grown talent since, well, Duncan Edwards.

CAP NO 91
Yugoslavia, Belgrade, 11.5.58. England lost 5–0
Hopkinson   Howe D   Langley   Clayton   Wright*   Slater
Douglas   Charlton R   Kevan   Haynes   Finney

Highlights: All the confidence and cohesion built up in the England team pre-Munich had disappeared, and they found this World Cup warm-up match in Belgrade too hot to handle in more ways than one. The match was played in a heat wave with temperatures in the high nineties, and three of the Yugoslav goals came in the last ten minutes with several of the England players close to exhaustion. The match was a personal nightmare for Jim Langley, who was run ragged by three-goal right-winger Petacavic. It was a particularly testing trip for Bobby Charlton. He was back in Belgrade where the Busby Babes had played their final match. The last leg of the flight had meant landing at and taking off from Munich. *The Wright Cuttings Book* (*Sunday Pictorial*): 'Jim Langley was given such a roasting that Billy Wright was forced to try to cover for him, and this meant he was leaving inviting holes for the Yugoslavs to exploit.'

BILLY: This was the match when it really dawned on us just how much we had gone back since the Munich air crash. We were disjointed and totally lacking any sort of team pattern. If anything, the final scoreline flattered us. It did severe damage to our confidence with the World Cup finals so close. Poor Jim Langley was run off his feet by his winger, and he was never selected for England again. We were very subdued in the dressing-room afterwards, and all Walter Winterbottom could bring himself to say was, 'Well, at least we've got the bad game out of our system. Now let's focus on doing much, much better in the World Cup.'

CAP NO 92
USSR, Moscow, 18.5.58. Drew 1–1
McDonald   Howe D   Banks T   Clamp   Wright*   Slater
Douglas   Robson R   Kevan¹   Haynes   Finney

Highlights: For this final match before the World Cup finals, Eddie Clamp came in at right-half to make an all-Wolves half-back line with clubmates Billy Wright and Bill Slater. Colin McDonald took over in goal and Bolton's tough-tackling Tommy Banks was called in at left-back. After the jolting defeat in Yugoslavia, England gave a much more disciplined performance in the new Lenin Stadium and a Derek Kevan goal just before half-time gave them a draw against a Russian side rated one of the best in Europe. England might have won but for the goalkeeping of the great 'Man in Black', Lev Yashin, and the intervention of the woodwork when first Tom Finney and then Derek Kevan struck shots against a post. The shock after the match was that Brian Clough, Middlesbrough's untried goal master, was told he was not needed for the World Cup squad. Cloughie had scored 42 goals in League and Cup matches that season and was in red-hot form. Cloughie made no secret of his displeasure. *The Wright Cuttings Book* (*Daily Express*): 'The Wolves element brought strength and stability to a defence that had been torn asunder in Belgrade, and Billy Wright was back to his commanding best.'

BILLY: It made no sense to us that the selectors decided to leave behind not only Brian Clough, but also the vastly experienced Nat Lofthouse and the living legend Stanley Matthews. Lofty had been in devastating form in the FA Cup final against Manchester United when his two goals virtually won the trophy for Bolton. The selectors could also have considered the young Chelsea whiz kid Jimmy Greaves. For some reason they chose to take only twenty players, when 22 were allowed in each squad. We arrived in Sweden just two days before the kick-off to the tournament, and we found we didn't have a proper training ground. I think it fair to say we were not the best-prepared team going into the finals.

CAP NO 93
USSR, World Cup, Gothenburg, 8.6.58. Drew 2–2
McDonald   Howe D   Banks T   Clamp   Wright*   Slater
Douglas   Robson R   Kevan¹   Haynes   Finney¹

Highlights: Tom Finney coolly placed a penalty wide of Russian goal-keeper Lev Yashin six minutes from the final whistle to give England a draw in their opening World Cup match against a Russian team much changed from the side they had played in Moscow the previous month. The Russians had led 2–0 with twenty minutes to go, and it looked all over for England until Bryan Douglas created a goal for Derek Kevan. After Finney had scored the equaliser from the penalty spot, a furious Lev Yashin got hold of the referee and spun him around like a top. Incredibly, he was allowed to stay on the field. He was protesting over the award of the penalty because he considered the tackle had been made outside the box. In the closing moments a crushing tackle on Finney damaged his knee and put him out of the rest of the tournament. *The Wright Cuttings Book* (*Daily Telegraph*): 'Playing a true captain's role, Wright was prominent in stopping a series of Russian attacks with perfectly timed interceptions.'

> BILLY: Lev Yashin, who was to become a good friend, was very lucky to stay on the pitch after his manhandling of the referee. After spinning him around, he threw his cap at him. It was like a scene out of a silent comedy. This wild behaviour was completely out of character for Lev. Losing Tom Finney was a severe blow, particularly as in our next match we were meeting the favourites, Brazil.

CAP NO 94
Brazil, World Cup, Gothenburg, 11.6.58. Drew 0–0
McDonald   Howe D   Banks T   Clamp   Wright*   Slater
Douglas   Robson R   Kevan   Haynes   A'Court

Highlights: This was the only World Cup match in which eventual champions Brazil failed to score, and it was due mainly to the defensive tactics worked out by Walter Winterbottom's assistant Bill Nicholson, who had watched their opening match against Austria. The Brazilians were not allowed to get into their smooth rhythm. The nearest they got to breaking down the disciplined England defence was when Vava rocked the crossbar with a shot from twenty yards. Bill Slater played a key role in what was a triumph for England, sticking close to their ball-master Didi and not giving him room to produce his devastating passes. The result forced the Brazilians to rethink, and they were persuaded to call up two exceptional but untested individualists: Garrincha and Pelé. The rest is World Cup history! *The Wright Cuttings*

Book (*London Evening News*): 'We had heard so much about the brilliance of the Brazilian forwards, but they were knocked out of their rhythm by an England defence in which Billy Wright was magnificent. He and his Wolves team-mates Eddie Clamp and Bill Slater were immoveable objects, and at full-back Don Howe and Tommy Banks refused to concede an inch.'

BILLY: We were delighted with our performance, and Bill Nicholson quite rightly got a lot of praise for his tactics. It was no surprise when he later emerged as one of the greatest of all club managers at Tottenham. My clubmate Bill Slater finished the match with bruises on the inside of both knees where he had kept banging them together to stop Didi pulling off his favourite trick of threading the ball through an opponent's legs.

CAP NO 95
Austria, World Cup, Boras, 15.6.58. Drew 2–2
McDonald   Howe D   Banks T   Clamp   Wright*   Slater
Douglas   Robson R   Kevan¹   Haynes¹   A'Court

Highlights: England, needing to beat Austria to qualify for the quarter-finals, were trailing 1–0 at half-time to a thunderbolt of a goal scored from thirty yards by left-half Koller. Johnny Haynes equalised ten minutes into the second half, and then the Austrians regained the lead following a corner. The ball was cleared to Koerner, who beat goalkeeper Colin McDonald with another long-range shot. Derek Kevan, whose bulldozing tactics had brought him severe criticism, pulled England level again ten minutes from the end after running on to a Johnny Haynes pass. Five minutes later they celebrated what they thought was a winning goal after Bobby Robson had breasted down the ball and shot all in one sweet movement. The referee ruled that Kevan had obstructed the goalkeeper. This draw meant England had to play off against Russia, their third meeting in a month. *The Wright Cuttings Book* (*The Times*): 'England might well have lost but for some valiant defending by Billy Wright.'

BILLY: We were fuming over Bobby Robson's disallowed goal. Derek Kevan's challenge on the goalkeeper would have been perfectly acceptable in the English league. There was a different interpretation of the rules by Continental referees. We were fully expecting Bobby Charlton to be called in for his World Cup debut for the deciding match against the Russians.

CAP NO 96
USSR, World Cup, Gothenburg, 17.6.58. England lost 1–0
McDonald   Howe D   Banks T   Clayton   Wright*   Slater
Brabrook   Broadbent   Kevan   Haynes   A'Court

Highlights: Chelsea winger Peter Brabrook came in for his debut along with Wolves inside-forward Peter Broadbent, but Bobby Charlton was left kicking his heels on the touchline. Brabrook almost became an instant hero with a shot that struck the Russian post and then bounced into Yashin's hands. In the second half he had a goal disallowed before the Russians scored the winning goal when Ilyin's shot went in off a post to put England out of the World Cup. *The Wright Cuttings Book* (*Sunday Express*): 'No blame for England's depressing World Cup exit can be laid at the door of Billy Wright, who has been heroic in his attemps to keep our hopes alive.'

BILLY: That defeat by the Russians was one of my lowest moments in football. I knew in my heart that this would be my last World Cup, and we had let ourselves down. When we arrived back in England, Walter Winterbottom was met at the airport by his young son, Alan, who asked the question on the lips of thousands of football fans: 'Daddy, why didn't you play Bobby Charlton?' I know that Walter had wanted to, but he was outvoted by the selectors who thought Bobby was too young. They should have watched what the Brazilians did. They introduced a seventeen-year-old youngster called Pelé, and his presence turned them from a good side into a great one.

Brazil beat host nation Sweden 5–2 in a memorable final in Stockholm.

The Swedes took a 1–0 lead in the fourth minute through Nils Liedholm, later to become one of the world's finest coaches. It was the first time Brazil had been behind in the tournament. They hit back with purpose, giving full rein to their 'samba soccer' on a rain-sodden surface. Vava equalised in the ninth minute and scored again in the 30th minute, both goals created by the ball-playing Garrincha.

Ten minutes into the second half, the young prodigy Pelé produced a moment of magic that signalled that here was a glittering talent for all to enjoy for years to come. Positioned with his back to the goal at the heart of the Swedish penalty area, he caught a high, dropping ball on his thigh, hooked it over his head, whirled round close-marking centre-half Gustavsson in time to meet the ball on the volley and to send it powering into the net. It was pure poetry from Pelé.

Mario Zagalo, destined to manage the 1970 World Cup winning team, beat two defenders before shooting Brazil's fourth goal in the 77th minute. In the hectic closing stages Agne Simonsson reduced the lead before Pelé put the finishing touch with a deftly headed goal from Zagalo's centre.

Brazil had introduced a new formation to football: 4–2–4. They illuminated a tournament in which Wales and Northern Ireland did the United Kingdom proud by reaching the quarter-finals. England were left wondering what might have been but for Munich, which threw a shadow over English football that was to last for years.

BILLY: If there was consolation for us, it was that we were the only team to hold the eventual champions. Brazil were a wonderful advertisement for football, and every player in Sweden was talking in wonder about the potential of Pelé. But when it came to the inquest into England's comparative failure I did not think enough was taken into account of the effect the Munich disaster had on us. How much better might we have performed had we had the likes of Roger Byrne, Tommy Taylor and the irreplaceable Duncan Edwards in our line-up? I also thought the selectors should have been bolder and given young Bobby Charlton a World Cup debut. I think he would have shaken the best defences.

Who won what in 1957–58

First Division: Wolves, 64pts. Runners-up: Preston, 59pts.

Wolves record: P42 W28 D8 L6 F103 A47 Pts64

Wolves squad: Finlayson, Stuart, Harris, Clamp, Wright*, Flowers, Deeley, Broadbent, Murray, Mason, Mullen. Also: Slater (14), Wilshaw (12), Booth (13). Top scorer: Murray (29). Manager: Stan Cullis.

Second Division: West Ham United, 57pts. Runners-up Blackburn Rovers, 56pts.

Third Division (South): Brighton, 60pts. Runners-up: Brentford, 58pts.

Third Division (North): Scunthorpe, 66pts, Runners-up: Accrington Stanley, 59pts.

FA Cup final: Bolton Wanderers 2, Manchester United 0

Bolton: Hopkinson, Hartle, Banks, Hennin, Higgins, Edwards, Birch, Stevens, Lofthouse², Parry, Holden.

Manchester United: Gregg, Foulkes, Greaves, Goodwin, Cope, Crowther, Dawson, Taylor E, Charlton, Viollet, Webster.

Top First Division marksman: Bobby Smith (Tottenham), 36 goals.

Footballer of the Year: Danny Blanchflower (Tottenham).

Scottish champions: Hearts, 62pts. Runners-up: Rangers, 49pts.

Scottish Cup final: Clyde 1, Hibernian 0

European Cup final: Real Madrid 3, AC Milan 2 (Brussels, after extra-time).

European Footballer of the Year: Raymond Kopa (Real Madrid).

ROMANTIC INTERLUDE:
It's All About Joy

In 1958 and in his 35th year, Billy Wright finally found there was more to life than just football. The discovery hit him like a streak of lightning, and came to him in the shapely form of one of the singing Beverley Sisters, who had captivated audiences all over the world with their stunning stage presence and perfect close harmonies.

There were (and still are) three Beverley Sisters. Beautiful twins Teddie and Babs always flanked Joy, and it was 'the one in the middle' who took Billy's eye when he used to watch them in their regular television appearances.

I am a rather worn, word-weary sportswriter who has probably reported a game or two of football too many (a sort of Stamford Bridge too far), and I am to romantic literature what Barbara Cartland was to long-distance lorry driving. So to save using syrupy phrases, I turn to the lady who brought sudden light to Billy's blinkered existence for the true story of the only real love in his life: Joy Beverley.

In what is essentially a football book, I have relied on Joy to help me cover the extremely personal side of Billy's life. This is when I hope to introduce you to the Billy Wright that only his closest friends got to know.

More than 40 years on from their first meeting, Joy recollected everything with detail as clear as if it had been the day before yesterday. 'Billy would bring the England team to the London Palladium the night before an international at Wembley,' she recalled. 'It was almost like a second home for the Beverley Sisters in those days. We used to introduce the team from the stage, but we did not get to meet them individually because they would have to dash off for an early night before their match.

'In the Easter of 1958 we were appearing in Wolverhampton. My son Vince, then nine years old, was on his school holidays and so we were together. Howard Jones, a singer who was appearing on the bill with us, told me that his friend, "the great Billy Wright, captain of England and Wolves," lived nearby, and he asked if he could take Vincent to meet him. Billy had agreed to give him a tour of Molineux and show him all his football trophies and medals.

'I gave my permission because Vincent was crazy about football, and was a keen supporter of Arsenal. He was so excited to think he was going to meet the captain of England.

'I had no intention of joining them, and much to my surprise Billy came back to our hotel to collect me and drive me to his house. It was 13 April 1958, a date carved in my heart. One look into his blue eyes and I had my first glimpse of heaven. We fell in love at first sight, a love which was to last the rest of our lives.'

As Joy, still vivacious and attractive all these years later, relived the fateful day, she held one of Billy's photo albums open at a page from the late 1950s. There was a close-up of blond Billy smiling, and she tapped it with her index finger.

'That's how he looked the first time I saw him,' she said. 'He brought romance into my life, always tender and thoughtful. Everything that any woman would want in a man. He cared about feelings and considered everyone.'

Billy had gone steady with several girls and had often walked young ladies home in the gentlemanly manner of the era, but he had sworn to himself never to make any commitment that could interfere with his football. He had a formidable ally in his landlady Mrs Colley, who never encouraged him to bring a member of the opposite sex to what Billy considered his second home. He was invariably described in the newspapers as an 'eligible bachelor'.

BILLY: There was a firm belief in those days that sex and football did not mix. I remember Stan Cullis telling me after I had hit a poor patch of form that I should steer clear of personal appearances and be careful about the people I socialised with. There was a clear meaning between the lines that I should give ladies a wide berth. Obviously there were girls who I had grown to like, and I went steady with a couple of them but nobody was special enough to make me want to, so to speak, take my eye off the ball. Football meant everything to me, and I followed the Cullis code right up until I met Joy. In truth, I engineered our meeting. When I realised just who Vincent was, I plotted so that I could get to meet his mother. I had often watched the Beverley Sisters singing on television, and, yes, it really was' the one in the middle' who always took my eye. The second we met I knew she was the one for me.

A little matter of an England tour and the 1958 World Cup finals got in the way of the romance. 'We wrote to each other every day, and Billy telephoned every evening,' Joy recalled. 'We were so happy and in love, and it was only a matter of time before the press found out about it.'

The unacceptable face of my otherwise wonderful profession of journalism rose from the gutter. One newspaper dragged up the painful side of Joy's brief first marriage to an American musician, and Billy got after-midnight calls from Fleet Street newshounds chasing his comments as he attempted to sleep in the England team hotel headquarters on the outskirts of Gothenburg.

For the first time, reporters found that our hero could put his tongue to Anglo-Saxon words. 'I had never been so angry in my life,' Billy told me. 'It was a disgraceful invasion of privacy. I was not concerned about myself, only about Joy. She was having her past raked over just because we had fallen in love with each other. For one of the few times in my life I was ready to biff reporters on the nose.'

With their secret love now out in the open, Billy and Joy's reunion at Heathrow Airport on his return from the World Cup became public property, and the newspapers were full of photographs of them kissing and cuddling. They were hounded wherever they went by a posse of photographers and reporters.

A new football season was beckoning and Joy was fulfilling a summer singing engagement with The Bevs down on the south coast in

Bournemouth. 'We had already sworn ourselves to each other,' Joy said, 'and so it was no surprise when Billy asked me to marry him. What was a surprise was that he went down not on one knee but on *both* knees to propose. Of course I said "yes" and we decided on a very quiet register office wedding.'

It was so secret that Billy did not let on to his mentor Stan Cullis, his landlady Mrs Colley, Walter Winterbottom or any of his Wolves or England team-mates.

They set the date for Sunday 27 July 1958, and booked Poole Register Office, six miles from where the Beverley Sisters were appearing in the Bournemouth summer show. So that it did not come as a complete shock to their closest friends and relatives, they sent telegrams on the Saturday afternoon warning them to "expect a big and wonderful event".

Inevitably, their secret leaked out and when they drove into Poole the town had come to a standstill. 'We drove there in two cars,' Joy remembered. 'My Mum, Dad, and the twins in one car and Billy and myself following on in our car, with Billy at the wheel. It was the biggest shock of our lives when we got to the brow of the hill leading down to the register office to find the road jammed. I said to Billy, "We've chosen a good day for it. I wonder what's going on?" I honestly had no idea that these thousands of people were there to see us. The penny only dropped when they started cheering and waving.'

The police estimate was that there were up to eight thousand extra visitors to Poole that day. Billy and Joy were mobbed going into and coming out of the register office, and one of the twins, Teddie, lost a shoe in the mêlée.

Forty-four years on I can reveal how the secret got out. Step forward Dave Lanning, the high-octane voice of darts and speedway on television. 'Thanks to your biography on Billy I have the chance to clear my conscience,' Dave told me. 'Back in 1958 I had just completed my National Service and was the lowest form of life in the reporters' room of the *Poole & Dorset Herald*. One of my duties was a regular visit to the Poole Register Office to check on births, deaths and marriages. It was run by a fussy, sniffy, archetypal civil servant who wore high collars and funereal suits. He was infuriatingly punctilious in releasing only the barest bones of information. He regarded all newspapermen with deep suspicion, and he treated me like the nosy, gutter-press reptile that I was.'

Not pausing for breath, my old mate 'Lipalong' Lanning continued, 'On the Saturday lunchtime before Billy and Joy were due to go through with their secret ceremony, I was in the Branksome Railway Hotel enjoying a brown ale and a game of table skittles when I was summoned to take a telephone call behind the bar. Blow me down if it wasn't old Tight Lips from the register office. He was bursting with a secret that he couldn't keep, and whispered conspiratorially down the blower, "You might just be interested to know that tomorrow morning I am conducting a ceremony by special licence between a William Ambrose Wright and a lady whom I believe is a well-known vocal performer."

'Once I had recovered from the heart-stopping shock of being handed this scoop by a man who would not normally give me the time of day, I called the local freelance – the late Les Cluett – and he in turn passed it on as an exclusive to legendary Fleet Street news editor Victor Sims of what was then the *Sunday Pictorial*. I was paid eight guineas for the tip, which was then twice as much as I was earning a week.

'Years later, when dear Billy was then championing my cause as a commentator with ITV, I told him my secret. He fell about laughing, but added, 'If I had known of your involvement at the time I would have kicked you in the cobblers!"'

So it was now Mr and Mrs Billy Wright. The Beverley Sisters had a hit song that had the line, 'Lord help the mister who comes between me and my sisters...' But Billy never came between them, more like he became part of them. Joy sang of her Mr Wright, and he was often called on stage for a token appearance.

BILLY: Nobody could ever separate those girls and I never ever tried. They welcomed me as part of their tightknit family, and I was more than happy to fit in with them. It was quite an experience and at times almost unsettling to be in their company. They always seemed to know what the other sisters were thinking, particularly the twins Teddie and Babs. Time and again they would say the same things together. It was like listening to a stereophonic conversation. The biggest eye-opener for me was the time and effort they put into rehearsals. They would practise nonstop until they had got their harmonies just perfect. In its way, it was just as demanding as our training sessions at Wolverhampton.

Our Billy found himself enjoying the show-business spotlight, pushing aside his natural shyness. Those of us close to him were able to spot Joy's influence in his change of dress sense, and a new confidence and buoyancy in his personality. 'Something I discovered,' said Joy, 'was that he was quite a heart-throb with the girls. I was amazed how many women told me that I was lucky to have him and to make sure I looked after him. It was as if they loved him almost as much as I did. It was wonderful getting to know each other after what had been a whirlwind romance. We shared a love for music, and I think I got to know every note of Billy's vast collection of opera records. He in turn came to watch us perform at every opportunity. I know this sounds corny, but you could have set our love to music. The arrival of Vicky and Babette made our happiness complete.'

I have mentioned Joy's son, Vincent, almost in passing, which is negligent of me. Billy looked on him as the son he never had, and Vincent was always pleased to call Billy his dad. The football writer in me was concerned about how Vincent would view this book. He is a walking encyclopaedia on football facts and figures, and is a respected sports journalist who sub-edits at the posh broadsheet end of the market. Both Joy and Billy were always proud of his achievements in what can be the sinking sands of the newspaper world, and I wanted him to be happy that I was doing his adopted dad justice.

Nervously, I handed Vince the manuscript for him to give not only a sub-editor's assessment but also the judgement of a son. I am relieved to report that he gave the thumbs up, and that is all that matters to me. I know that if I pleased Vince, I would have made Billy satisfied with what was going to be his autobiography. An old hack is happy.

The Billy and Joy fairy story reached another golden chapter on 5 April 1959 when their first daughter, Victoria, was born in the London

Clinic. She arrived on the very day that Billy became the first footballer in the world to be selected for his 100th international cap. New mum Joy was let out of hospital to watch her husband play for the first time. A Hollywood scriptwriter with an overcreative imagination – or even a Dave Lanning – could not have made it up.

It was more than luck that Vicky arrived early. 'My gynaecologist, Mr Schleyer-Saunders, was a football fan and wanted to make sure that both of us could get to Wembley to see Billy play in the most important match of his life,' Joy told me. 'He gave me a special drink that helped bring Vicky's birth forward. It was worth it just to see the look of delight on Billy's face when he noticed us, the Bevs, looking on from near the Royal Box at Wembley. The memory will live with me forever.'

We will return to Joy and Billy's personal life away from football in a later chapter. But now, after this romantic interlude, it is back to our hero's football career and the final shots for club and country.

SEASON 1958–59:
The Final Curtain

Do you think Home Secretary David Blunkett could one day persuade David Beckham to hang up his boots? It seems far-fetched, but it was the man who held that prestigious post in the Harold Macmillan government who convinced Billy that it was time to retire.

Journey with me back to the year of 1959. It was a beautiful summer's day and June was busting out all over in the garden of the imposing Stansted Hall, Essex, home of Home Secretary RA 'Rab' Butler, one of the most distinguished politicians of his generation.

The previous day Billy had heard he was to be made a Commander of the British Empire for his services to football, and the previous month he had played his 105th international match in an England shirt. The month before that he had led Wolves to their second successive League championship. He was on top of the world.

Billy and his lovely wife of eleven months, Joy, were being shown around the Stansted Hall garden by Mr Butler, who had invited them over for the opening ceremony of a new stand at his local Halstead football club.

BILLY: Suddenly, Mr Butler turned the conversation to the subject of retirement. There had been conjecture in the press about how long I would carry on playing. I was 35 and was considering at least another season or two before I hung up my boots. 'The timing for retirement is so important,' he said. 'I speak as somebody who once got it wrong. I had four years as chancellor of the

186

exchequer. For the first three years I was proud of my record but then for the next twelve months I had to take unpopular measures. If I had stepped down after three years I would have been hailed as a successful chancellor, but one more year changed many opinions about the job I had done. Take advice from me, Billy, and don't leave retirement too late. You have set standards that should never ever be lowered.' I took his advice on board, and then after struggling to conquer the hills in our pre-season training I went to see Stan Cullis to discuss my future. He made it clear that he would be looking to gradually move George Showell into the centre-half position. It was as clear a hint as I could expect that one of my most respected mentors felt I was past my best.

Billy decided there and then that the time was right to retire. He could have collected a fat fee from any national newspaper for the exclusive news. But, showing the loyalty that was his trademark, he contacted his friend on the *Wolverhampton Express & Star*, Phil Morgan, and gave him the story.

Phil revealed that his final match would be the public pre-season practice match at Molineux between the first team and the reserves on 8 August 1959: The Colours v The Whites. An astonishing crowd of more than twenty thousand turned out for what was a fairly meaningless match. They were all there to say a fond farewell to their hero, Wolverhampton's man for all seasons. For the rest of the country, it was goodbye to an England hero for all seasons.

CAP NO 97
Northern Ireland, Windsor Park, 4.10.58. Drew 3–3
McDonald   Howe D   Banks T   Clayton   Wright*   McGuinness
Brabrook   Broadbent   Charlton R[2]   Haynes   Finney[1]

Highlights: Northern Ireland and England concocted a thriller on a waterlogged mudheap of a pitch. Bobby Charlton, playing at centre-forward, scored with two thunderbolt shots to add fuel to the arguments that he should have been let off the leash in the World Cup. The Irish bravely led three times through Cush, Peacock and Casey as they searched for their first victory over England in Belfast since 1927. Bobby Charlton's two equalising goals sandwiched England's second goal by Tom Finney. This was a memorable milestone for the Preston plumber. It was his thirtieth goal for England, a new all-time scoring record. *The Wright Cuttings Book* (*Daily Mirror*): 'Thank heavens for Billy Wright. It was his tackling that kept England in the game when Jimmy McIlroy and Danny Blanchflower were looking set to completely dominate proceedings on a pudding of a pitch.'

BILLY: Two Manchester United youngsters took the eye. Twenty-year-old Wilf McGuinness, another of the Busby Babes, won the first of what would surely have been many England caps but for a broken leg virtually ending his career in 1961. Wilf, later to have an awkward spell in charge at Old Trafford, would have been on the Munich flight but for staying behind in Manchester for a cartilage operation. The star of the match was Bobby Charlton, and it revived the question that had been asked so many times in Sweden; 'Why oh why was he not selected for at least one game in the World Cup?' Only the selectors knew the answer to that one.

CAP NO 98
USSR, Wembley, 22.10.58. England won 5–0
McDonald   Howe D   Shaw G   Clayton   Wright*   Slater
Douglas   Charlton R[1]   Lofthouse[1]   Haynes[3]   Finney

Highlights: This was hollow revenge against the Russians for the defeat in the match that really mattered in the World Cup. Johnny Haynes, the pass master, turned goal snatcher with his one and only international hat-trick. Four of England's goals came in the second half as goalkeeper Belaev, deputising for the injured Lev Yashin, flapped under nonstop pressure from the lion-hearted Lofthouse, who had been recalled after two years in the international wilderness. He revealed a flash of his old power with a crashing left-foot shot for the fifth goal despite a Russian defender having a handful of his shirt. Bobby Charlton's goal came from the penalty spot. Ronnie Clayton, who was eventually to succeed Billy as skipper, had an outstanding game with his driving performance from midfield, and Graham Shaw made a sound debut at left-back. *The Wright Cuttings Book* (*Daily Express*): 'As Billy Wright approaches his historic soccer century of caps, he will look back on this match with tremendous self-satisfaction. He was a colossus in the middle of the defence and made the Russian centre-forward seem about as redundant as a Tory in the Kremlin.'

BILLY: The BBC television *Sportsview* team, led by Kenneth Wolstenholme, had been campaigning to have Johnny Haynes replaced. When they reported the match and Johnny's hat-trick, they appeared in front of the cameras in sackcloth and ashes. This was notable as Tom Finney's 76th and final game for England. No better player ever wore the white shirt. I was proud to have him as a colleague and as a friend. He left the stage quietly when what he deserved was a farewell of fireworks and praise for all he had achieved for England. Tommy was as modest as they come, and he should have received better treatment from the selectors who just suddenly ignored him after an injury and a run of bad form.

CAP NO 99
Wales, Villa Park, 26.11.58. Drew 2–2
McDonald   Howe D   Shaw G   Clayton   Wright*   Flowers
Clapton   Broadbent²   Lofthouse   Charlton R   A'Court

Highlights: Like Johnny Haynes, Peter Broadbent was more a schemer than a scorer. But, standing in for the injured hat-trick hero, he twice netted equalising goals against a spirited Welsh team. Arsenal winger Danny Clapton was given the impossible job of following Tom Finney. He performed with spirit, but no player could stand comparison with the Preston footballing master. Wales had taken a fifteenth-minute lead through Derek Tapscott, who gave Billy Wright a tough time at the heart of the defence. Broadbent neatly lobbed the ball over goalkeeper Jack Kelsey to make it 1–1 just before half-time. Despite the handicap of having injured skipper Dave Bowen as a passenger on the wing for much of the game, Wales continued to press forward in search of their first victory over England for 23 years. Ivor Allchurch restored their lead with a shot on the turn in the 70th minute. England struck back for a second equaliser when Broadbent rose at the far post to head in a centre from Alan A'Court. *The Wright Cuttings Book* (*Sunday Pictorial*): 'Billy Wright made it 99 not out against Wales, but it was a nervous nineties performance. His tackling lacked its usual bite, and his passing left something to be desired.'

BILLY: The old guard were gradually being stood down. This was the final England appearance for Nat Lofthouse. It made no sense that he had been left out of our World Cup squad. He finished with a record-equalling 30 international goals from just 33 matches. Only Tommy Lawton rated ahead of him as a centre-forward in my time with England. He used to terrorise goalkeepers in an era when the shoulder-charge was still accepted as a legitimate weapon. Who can ever forget his treatment of Manchester United goalkeeper Harry Gregg in the 1958 FA Cup final? A few years later, the shoulder-charge that put Harry and the ball into the net would have brought Lofty an instant dismissal. For Bolton, it brought them their second decisive goal. It's a different game now.

CAP NO 100
Scotland, Wembley, 11.4.59. England won 1–0
Hopkinson   Howe D   Shaw G   Clayton   Wright*   Flowers
Douglas   Broadbent   Charlton R¹   Haynes   Holden

Highlights: An historic day for our hero Billy Wright when he became the first footballer in the world to win 100 international caps. A closely fought game was won for England by an acrobatic header from Bobby Charlton after Bryan Douglas had sent over a precise centre in the 62nd minute. At the final whistle, the England skipper was carried shoulder high to the Wembley dressing-room by his team-mates Don Howe and Ronnie Clayton. Johnny Haynes collected a painful memento of Billy's historic match when a fierce tackle by Dave

Mackay left him with a broken little finger on his left hand, and Bryan Douglas limped through much of the game with damaged knee ligaments. Bolton winger Doug Holden won the first of his five caps, and played with pace and fire against a Scottish defence in no mood to concede an inch. Dundee goalkeeper Bill Brown was the man of the match, denying Bobby Charlton a hat-trick of goals with magnificent saves. It was a performance that convinced Tottenham manager Bill Nicholson that he should sign Brown for Spurs, and he became a key man in their double year of 1960–61. *The Wright Cuttings Book* (*Sunday Express*): 'Carried in triumph the length of the Wembley pitch, Billy Wright was given the sort of ovation reserved only for true sporting gods. One day his 100 caps record will be beaten, but no player will ever match the effort and enthusiasm that he put into each of the games. Billy has given blood, sweat and tears ... now it was his turn for the cheers. Every Scottish player made a point of shaking his hand. He is admired and respected far beyond English boundaries.'

BILLY: The greatest day of my England career. Everything went to perfection, and it was particularly special to be able to pick out Joy and her twin sisters Teddie and Babs in the crowd as I led the team on to the pitch. Joy had given birth to our first daughter, Victoria, just six days earlier and 'Mum' had been allowed out of hospital to watch the game. The Scots did their best to spoil my party by playing their hearts out, as they always do at Wembley. But my team-mates were determined to mark the occasion with a victory. Bobby Charlton scored yet another crackerjack goal to underline that he was a young genius at the game. I was snowed under with just thousands of telegrams and congratulatory messages, and the celebrations went on for days. Legendary German team manager Sepp Herberger came over to London specially to present me with a giant silver candlestick on behalf of the West German FA, and at a civic reception in Wolverhampton I was given a silver rose bowl by the Mayor and another one by the Wolves suppporters. From the Football Association I received a magnificent silver salver emblazoned with flags of all the countries I had played in, and the Irish FA presented me with a beautiful collection of Waterford crystal. The National Sporting Club threw a dinner for me, and gave me a huge cocktail cabinet, and then – the greatest honour of them all – I was invited to Buckingham Palace for a private lunch with the Queen and the Duke of Edinburgh. As I looked around the Palace dining room I could not quite believe that all this was happening to a lad from Ironbridge. And I owed it all to the great game of football.

CAP NO 101
Italy, Wembley, 6.5.59. Drew 2–2
Hopkinson   Howe   Shaw G   Clayton   Wright*   Flowers
Bradley[1]   Broadbent   Charlton R[1]   Haynes   Holden

Highlights: England were reduced to ten men when Ron Flowers went off with a broken nose with England leading 2–0. The goals were scored in the first half by Manchester United team-mates Bobby Charlton and Warren Bradley, a schoolmaster who was making his debut on the right wing. By the time Flowers returned to the defence seventeen minutes later the young, experimental Italian team had drawn level. The Italians were fielding the first all home-born team for 25 years following a ruling from FIFA that in future teams could not include players capped by another country. *The Wright Cuttings Book (Daily Herald)*: 'There is a distinct sign of a creak in the old Wright bones, and the question has to be asked: "How much longer can England expect to be carried on his wide shoulders?"'

BILLY: There was an embarrassing start to the game. When they stood to attention before the match the Italian players were astonished to hear the banned Mussolini-era national anthem being played. This had been replaced after the war. I think every Italian restaurant in Britain must have been short of staff because Italy had thousands of supporters in the crowd, and they whistled and hooted as the anthem was played. But for some cracking saves by our goalkeeper Eddie Hopkinson the Italian fans would have had a victory to cheer. I knew my international days were drawing to a close, and I was determined to try to enjoy the last moments.

CAP NO 102

Brazil, Rio de Janeiro, 13.5.59. England lost 2–0

Hopkinson   Howe D   Armfield   Clayton   Wright*   Flowers
Deeley   Broadbent   Charlton R   Haynes   Holden

Highlights: England's first match of a four-game summer tour was a minor test against the new world champions in front of 185,000 screaming fans in the Maracana Stadium in Rio. Bobby Charlton and Johnny Haynes rapped shots against the post after England had gone 2–0 down to early goals against a Brazilian team that featured both Didi and Pelé in a rare appearance together. Blackpool's Jimmy Armfield was given a chasing he will not forget by Julinho in what was a baptism of fire for the Blackpool defender. He was called in to partner Don Howe in an out-of-club position at left-back. Norman Deeley, a small, direct Wolves winger, was the fourth player to wear the number seven shirt since the departure of the one and only Tom Finney. Goalkeeper Eddie Hopkinson saved two certain goals from Pelé, but could do nothing to stop a thunderbolt from Julinho, who had been picked in preference to the great Garrincha. *The Wright Cuttings Book (Daily Sketch)*: 'But for some timely interventions by the resolute Wright, the defeat could have been much more depressing. The Brazilians are from another galaxy.'

BILLY: As Eddie Hopkinson lay on the ground after being beaten all ends up by Julinho's shot, a posse of Brazilian radio commentators rushed on to the pitch to try to interview him. It is just as well that they could not translate his direct comments delivered in Lancastrian tones! We were well and truly beaten by the world champions and did well to keep their score down to just two goals. Didi and Pelé together was just about the most potent combination that any team in the world could put together. Ronnie Clayton clattered into Pelé with a tackle that led to the king being carried off on a stretcher for treatment. He soon came back, but for the rest of the game Clayton's life was made hell by the Brazilian fans who would not forgive him for hurting their idol. Shortly before he was carried off Pelé missed a sitter right in front of an open goal. He was human, after all. Of all the teams I met in international football, this

Brazilian side is the only one I would put on a pedestal with the Hungarians of 1953.

CAP NO 103
Peru, Lima, 17.5.59. England lost 4–1
Hopkinson   Howe D   Armfield   Clayton   Wright*   Flowers
Deeley   Greaves[1]   Charlton R   Haynes   Holden

Highlights: Jimmy Greaves, nineteen-year-old idol of Chelsea, arrived on the international stage with a neatly taken second-half goal, drawing the goalkeeper off his line before slotting a left foot shot just inside a post. But it was the only bright moment in a miserable England performance. The Peruvians, leading 2–0 at half-time, were helped to four goals by mistakes from a strangely lethargic England defence which had no answer to the thrusting left-wing runs of Seminario, who helped himself to a hat-trick. *The Wright Cuttings Book* (*The Times*): 'It is agonising to watch Billy Wright trying to do the things he did in the summertime of his career. Autumn is now weighing on his shoulders, and winter is around the corner. Time waits for no man, not even a football god.'

BILLY: It was good to be there to witness the start of another great England career, this time of the chirpy cockney Jimmy Greaves. At the beginning of the season I had been in the middle of a Wolves defence destroyed by Greavsie at Stamford Bridge. He scored five goals for Chelsea that day, and the press reported that he had made me consider retirement. But that was nonsense. I was not marking Jimmy, and there was not a defender on earth who could have held him that afternoon. It was one of the slickest displays of finishing I had ever seen. Many years later I was delighted to play a part in getting Jimmy's television career off the ground. He was still the same cheeky, loveable rascal as I played with when he made his England debut against Peru. His goal was the only face-saving thing of an otherwise disastrous match. In truth, we were just not in the mood for that tour after a domestic season that had left many of us feeling exhausted and in need of a rest. Looking back, it was crazy that the FA should have pitched us into a match against the world champions immediately after a demanding League season. The pasting we got from Brazil demoralised us for the rest of the tour.

CAP NO 104

Mexico, Mexico City, 24.5.59. England lost 2–1
Hopkinson   Howe D   Armfield   Clayton   Wright*
McGuinness (Flowers)   Holden (Bradley)   Greaves
Kevan[1]   Haynes   Charlton R

Highlights: England scored first through Derek Kevan, but were burned out within the hour and despite officially using substitutes for the first time were run off their feet in the last half-hour. Jimmy Greaves swept the ball into the net just after half-time, but the referee ruled it offside. Moments later Mexico snatched a second goal and from then on England were on the retreat as they struggled to breathe in Mexico's thin air. Eddie Hopkinson performed wonders in the England goal, but he was often confused by the flight of the ball. Wilf McGuinness was the first player to be substituted after half an hour. He was affected by the heat and had to go to the dressing-room for an emergency intake of oxygen. Doug Holden was the next player hit by the heat, and he was replaced in the 57th minute by Warren Bradley. *The Wright Cuttings Book (Daily Telegraph)*: 'Wright lasted better than some of his younger team-mates in high-altitude conditions that sapped the strength and stamina. This has been a miserable tour, but Wright has maintained his dignity and friendly demeanour. He is not the force he once was, but he remains a fine captain and outstanding ambassador for his country.'

BILLY: The British newspapermen covering the match reported that earthquake tremors shook the ground during the match which none of we England players felt. Perhaps their imaginations had been affected by the rarefied air. It was a match that Ronnie Clayton would never forget. He had been so badly burned while sunbathing that his back came up in a mass of blisters. They burst during the game, and in the dressing-room afterwards the Mexican doctor bathed the Blackburn skipper's back with methylated spirits. It brought tears to all our eyes, let alone Ronnie's! It was this more than anything that finally convinced the Football Association that they should follow Walter Winterbottom's advice and always travel with a team doctor. It was hardly the best organised tour. My Wolves clubmate Ron Flowers at one stage found himself sharing a hotel room with six complete strangers! We had no chance against the Mexicans. You need a minimum three weeks preparation in a high-altitude country. We went into the game after less than a week in Mexico, and within an hour we were totally exhausted from chasing around in the thin air when not properly acclimatised and under a searing midday sun. It was madness. We had suffered our third successive defeat and had now won only two of our last fourteen games. The start of our bad run could be traced back to Munich.

CAP NO 105
USA, Los Angeles, 28.5.59. England won 8–1
Hopkinson   Howe D   Armfield   Clayton   Wright*   Flowers[2]
Bradley[1]   Greaves   Kevan[1]   Haynes[1]   Charlton R[3]

Highlights: This runaway victory in Billy Wright's 105th and final match helped wipe out the memory of the 1–0 defeat by the United States in the 1950 World Cup finals, but at one stage it looked as if another embarrassment was on its way. The Americans had an early goal disallowed and then took the lead, and at 1–1 at half time the football writers were preparing head-chopping stories that were hurriedly rewritten as Bobby Charlton led a second-half goal rush with a hat-trick. The pitch, rarely used for soccer, was gravel at one end and grass at the other. England scored seven of their goals while attacking the grassy end. Charlton's first hat-trick for England on the way to an all-time record 49 goals included a penalty. The suspect American goalkeeper was beaten by four shots from outside the penalty area. The only forward who did not get his name on the scoresheet was one Jimmy Greaves! *The Wright Cuttings Book* (*Daily Express*): 'If this is to be Billy Wright's international swansong, it was a thing of sweetness and beauty for a man who has never been allowed to forget that 1950 World Cup defeat by the United States. Sensing that this will be his farewell to the England stage, let's paraphrase the Bard and say, "Goodnight sweet prince, and flights of angels sing thee to thy rest from a game you have served so well."'

BILLY: I did not know this was my last game, although it was clear that my international career was approaching its end. I was the only one left from the team humiliated by the Americans in the 1950 World Cup, and for a short period in the first half I was worried that I could be in for a repeat of the nightmare. But we finally beat them as emphatically as we should have done in Brazil all those years ago. I had started my England career playing in front of a 57,000 crowd in Belfast in 1946. The finish came in front of just 13,000 fans at the Wrigley Field in Los Angeles. But what a journey I had between the two games. I considered myself a lucky, lucky man.

BREAKDOWN OF BILLY'S 105 CAPS: Northern Ireland (13 games), Scotland (13), Wales (12), France (5), Belgium (4), Denmark (4), Republic of Ireland (4), Portugal (4), Russia (4), Switzerland (4), Italy (4), Spain (3), Austria (3), Sweden (3), Yugoslavia (3), Brazil (3), USA (3), Argentina (2), Chile (2), West Germany (2), Uruguay (2), Hungary (2), Finland (1), Holland (1), Norway (1), FIFA XI (1), Peru (1), Mexico (1).

England's record in the games that he played, including one abandoned match against Argentina:

P105   W60   D23   L21   Abandoned 1   F287   A147

He scored three international goals . . . and stopped dozens of others!

BILLY'S RECORD WITH WOLVES: League appearances, all in the First Division, 490, goals 13 (three League championship medals, 1953–54, 1957–58, 1958–59); FA Cup appearances 48, goals 3 (FA Cup winning captain 1949).

Total club appearances, including European friendlies: 541, goals 19.

This record does not include Billy's unlisted wartime games with Wolves, estimated to be around a hundred.

'I reckon I must have played more than three hundred matches during my army service,' Billy told me. 'We often used to wind up our physical training sessions with a match, and then there were all the representative games with the battalion, the army and combined services, as well as any that I was able to fit in with Wolves. I can't remember a single week going by without playing at least one match, even in the summer months when I was also able to squeeze in a lot of cricket.

'And even when I was able to get home to my digs with Mrs Colley, it was nothing but football talk with my good friends Cameron Buchanan and Alan Steen, who lodged with me and served their apprenticeships at Molineux. Cameron, Alan and Arthur Colley and I were inseparable, and always managed to keep in touch despite the war.'

It all ended where it had started in the now legendary Whites v Colours preseason match at Molineux. Young local referee Jack Taylor took charge, fifteen years before handling the 1974 World Cup final. 'Billy's last match is up there at the top of my memories along with the World Cup final,' he said. 'It was a privilege to be there on the pitch with a player who was not only a great footballer but also a great gentleman. He was a wonderful advertisement for England in general and for Wolverhampton in particular.'

For Billy, the playing was over. Now came the perils of management.

Who won what in 1958–59

First Division: Wolves, 61pts. Runners-up: Manchester United, 55pts.

Wolves record: P42 W28 D5 L9 F110 A49 Pts61

Wolves squad: Finlayson, Stuart, Harris; (from) Slater, Clamp, Wright*, Flowers, Lill, Mason (Booth), Murray, Broadbent, Deeley. Top scorer: Murray (21). Manager: Stan Cullis.

Second Division: Sheffield Wednesday, 62pts. Runners-up Fulham, 60pts.

Third Division: Plymouth Argyle, 62pts. Runners-up: Hull City, 61pts.

Fourth Division: Port Vale, 64pts, Runners-up: Coventry City, 60pts.

FA Cup final: Nottingham Forest 2, Luton Town 1

Nottingham Forest: Thomson, Whare, McDonald, Whitefoot, McKinlay R, Burkitt, Dwight[1], Quigley, Wilson[1], Gray, Imlach.

Luton Town: Baynham, McNally, Hawkes, Groves, Owen, Pacey[1], Bingham, Brown, Morton, Cummins, Gregory.

Top First Division marksmen: Jimmy Greaves (Chelsea), Bobby Smith (Spurs), 32 goals.

Footballer of the Year: Syd Owen (Luton Town).

Scottish champions: Rangers, 50pts. Runners-up: Hearts, 48pts.

Scottish Cup final: St Mirren 3, Aberdeen 1

European Cup final: Real Madrid 2, Stade de Reims 0 (Stuttgart).

European Footballer of the Year: Alfredo di Stefano (Real Madrid).

1958 World Cup final at the Råsunda Stadium, Stockholm, 29 June 1958: Brazil 5, Sweden 2

Brazil: Gilmar, Santos D, Santos N, Zito, Bellini, Orlando, Garrincha, Didi, Vava[2], Pelé[2], Zagalo[1].

Sweden: Svensson, Bergmark, Axbom, Börjesson, Gustavsson, Parling, Hamrin, Gren, Simonsson[1], Liedholm[1], Skoglund.

Stats: Top scorer: Juste Fontaine (France) 13. Total goals: 126 (3.6 per game). Attendance (35 matches) 868,000 (average 24,800); 49,747 (final). Referee: Maurice Guigue (France).

SEASONS 1962–66:
Highbury Heartache

It was the one job that former footballer Billy Wright could not resist: manager of Arsenal, the club of his boyhood dreams where he thought he would be given the time, the money and the motivation to put together a championship-challenging team. But it all ended in tears.

When he hung up his boots, Billy turned down the chance of being groomed as successor to Stan Cullis and declined offers of management jobs in the Midlands and London. He preferred the role of heir-apparent to Walter Winterbottom at the Football Association where, as a staff coach, he was appointed manager of the England under–23 and youth sides.

He had just become nicely established in his niche at Lancaster Gate when, in the summer of 1962, Arsenal came calling. Chairman Denis Hill-Wood, an Old Etonian and a hugely successful City businessman, invited him to take over as Highbury manager. It was an offer he could not refuse, even though his early instincts had been that he was not cut out for club management. His predecessor at Highbury, George Swindin, had not been a failure: he was shown the door simply because he was only a modest success compared with what was happening down the road at White Hart Lane where Bill Nicholson had been leading deadly rivals Tottenham to mouthwatering triumphs, including the winning of the League and FA Cup double.

Billy Wright and Arsenal seemed a marriage made in heaven. Football's perfect ambassador, liked and respected by everybody in the game; the rich-in-tradition, widely supported club that was a sleeping giant waiting to be shaken out of its slumber.

He arrived at Highbury with a huge fanfare, a three-year contract, a new first-team coach and a £70,000 centre-forward. He chose as his right-hand man Les Shannon, who had made a name for himself behind the scenes at Everton after a playing career with Burnley.

The centre-forward was Joe Baker, the England international with a Scottish accent whom Billy brought back into British football from Torino, where he had been in harness with Denis Law. Baker was paired in a prolific striking partnership with Geoff Strong, while pass master George Eastham provided the ammunition from midfield.

In Billy's first season in charge, Arsenal finished a respectable seventh. It was promising, but not phenomenal. The shadows lengthened from the direction of Tottenham where a Jimmy Greaves-inspired Spurs became the first British club to win a major European trophy in the Cup Winners' Cup.

Billy strengthened the side by bringing in Scots Frank McLintock and Ian Ure, and his former England team-mate Don Howe. Arsenal responded by scoring 90 First Division goals. That was the good news. The bad news was that 82 were conceded by a defence giving away goals like a charitable organisation. Eighth position was considered less than satisfactory.

The nadir was reached in the 1964–65 season when Arsenal were shocked out of the FA Cup in the fourth round by Third Division Peterborough United. Thirteenth position was a disaster.

It is when somebody is struggling rather than a success that you find a man's true character. I was ghosting Billy's weekly column in the *Daily Express* at the peak, or rather depth, of his crisis. He must have looked forward to my interviews about as much as a visit to the dentists, but never once did he make me feel anything less than welcome. Most managers in his position would have found a way of blaming the players, several of whom were continually letting him down with less than total commitment; this, despite picking up in excess of £100 a week in the seasons immediately after the maximum wage had been kicked out.

I was with Billy in his office within 48 hours of his blackest moment as Arsenal manager, the FA Cup defeat by lowly Peterborough. I waited for him to lose his temper, to thump his desk and tell me for the column how he was going to rip the team apart. 'I selected the team and I must take the flak,' he said. 'The side will be unchanged for next Saturday's League match.'

If ever Billy missed a chance to make an impact as manager this was it. He should have taught the players a lesson by dropping at least four of them, but he took the soft option of letting them prove they could only get better. They got worse that season. For a man who had served his time as a player under the rigid discipline of Major Frank Buckley and Stan 'The Iron Chancellor' Cullis, he was strangely lacking in anger and passion. Had the Wolves players let them down as the Arsenal team had done to Billy, heads would have rolled and the dressing-room walls would have been blistered with their words of wrath. 'The nearest I ever heard him get to saying anything insulting,' said Joy Beverley Wright, 'was when he described somebody as being "as nutty as a fruitcake". He just wasn't into tearing people apart. He could not see the point of it.'

Frank McLintock, an old friend of mine who was later to skipper Arsenal in their great double year of 1970–71, was one of those forgiven for the defeat at Peterborough. 'This was when Billy should have brought down the iron fist,' he said. 'But it just was not in him. He was simply too kind, too nice. We needed a manager who could give us the kick up the behinds that we deserved. I got so frustrated at our lack of success and what I saw as a lack of ambition that I asked for a transfer. Billy was terribly hurt by that. It was nothing against him personally. I always had a great affection for him. But I was hungry to win something and, to be honest, I could not see us doing it under Billy's management, and deep down I think Billy had the same feeling. He was not cut out to be a manager, but I have known few nicer human beings.'

Yes, it's that old cross that Billy had to bear throughout his career in football. He was just too nice. What an epitaph!

Billy admitted that he was haunted by Arsenal's great past.

BILLY: I got to remembering what Laurie Scott had once said about playing for Arsenal – the fact that while supporters were proud of the past it was a burden for the players who had to try to live up to it. It was even more of a load for me to carry as manager, and I got to hate the bust of Herbert Chapman in the marble halls. It was always there as a reminder of the glory years and underlined that we were winning nothing at all. I just wonder if the Arsenal board, players and supporters really ever knew how much I cared about that club? I used to get physically sick before games, and several times I quietly cried my eyes out in sheer frustration. My failure in the job was the most humiliating thing that ever happened to me, much worse than defeats by the United States and Hungary because I had to carry the blame all on my own. It was about then, I think, that I discovered how comforting a drink or three could be.

The end came for him at Highbury when all eyes were on the 1966 World Cup finals that were about to kick-off in England. Arsenal had finished the season down in fourteenth position. Joy recalled: 'We were on holiday in Sweden when Billy got a telephone call from his coach Les Shannon. He rejoined me after taking the call and looked ashen faced. "That was Les telling me he has been sacked," Billy said. "That can only mean that I'm next." Sure enough, when we got home there was a message for him to go and see the chairman ... '

I interviewed the always charming and courteous Denis Hill-Wood for the *Express* within hours of Billy's departure on 10 June 1966, and he told me: 'It was the hardest job I have ever had to do, but Billy had to go because of the intolerable pressure from outside. Our support has dwindled, and the people who pay to come to watch us play have made it quite clear they are very unhappy with our performances.

'Billy is a 22-carat-gold person, but both his position as manager and mine as chairman has become impossible. We were receiving hundreds of letters demanding his dismissal and there was growing unrest among our supporters. When I called Billy in to give him the news, he made it very easy for me. 'I know what you want me for,' he said before I could say a word. There were no hard feelings, and Billy knows that he will always be very welcome at Highbury. He is a marvellous chap.'

But there were hard feelings that Billy kept to himself. The *News of the World* offered him £15,000, the equivalent of two years' salary, to

The Billy Wright Photo Album 2

This is how Billy responded (*right*) when he spotted Joy with the Beverley Sisters in the Wembley crowd (*below*), watching him lead England out for his historic 100th international. It was Joy's first day out of hospital after giving birth to their first daughter, Victoria (*above*). Sitting with The Bevs was Joy's gynaecologist, Mr Schleyer-Saunders, who induced Vicky's birth so that her mother could get to Wembley to see Billy play for England for the first time.

Billy was happiest as a family man. He cuddles week-old granddaughter Kelly (*above right*), took the photograph of second daughter Babette (*above left*) and treated Joy's son Vincent (*above*) like the son he never had. He was a doting father (*as seen right with Vicky*), and counted the family picture (*centre right*) as his favourite photograph.

Billy had four eventful years as manager of Arsenal between the taking of these two photographs. He is on his way to Australia with The Beverley Sisters in April 1962 (*above*). On his return from watching The Bevs in concert Down Under, he was appointed manager at Highbury. The picture (*right*) – playing in the garden with Babette – was taken on the day Arsenal sacked him in June 1966.

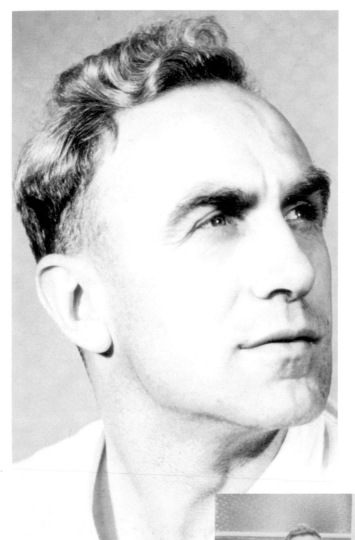

Joy's favourite photograph of Billy. 'It captures him perfectly,' she says. 'Just look at the strength of character in that face. He was so strong, honest and reliable, and this picture says it all.'

Billy and Joy were together for 36 years. 'He was the most generous and sincere man I have ever known,' she says. 'I consider myself so lucky to have had his love and companionship.'

'Lord help the mister who comes between me and my sister,' sang the Beverley Sisters. Billy, of course, never came between them, but became part of their close-knit family. He was always there to support them (*above*), and was later proud to show off The Foxes, the group in which Victoria and Babette sing with Teddie's daughter, Sasha. Seated on the left (*below*) with Vicky, Joy, Babette and Billy is the then 90-year-old mother of the Beverley Sisters, who, with her husband, formed the popular Coram & Mills musical-hall act that featured music and comedy.

This is the day in 1962 (*above*) that Billy became manager of Arsenal. He grew to hate the bust of Herbert Chapman in the marble halls of Highbury, which was always there to haunt him. It was a permanent reminder of Arsenal's great days, which Billy was never able to recapture during his generally unhappy four years in the Highbury hot seat. Joy, on the other hand, will always love the statue of Billy (*right*), which has been erected at Molineux outside the Billy Wright stand.

Billy is pictured with The Beverley Sisters and The Foxes on one of his most memorable days at Molineux, when he opened the new main stand named after him.

Billy and Joy (*above*) on the set of *This Is Your Life* after Michael Aspel had surprised him in 1987. It was the second time that Billy had been presented with the Big Red Book, the first by Eamonn Andrews in 1960.

This is what Joy describes as 'our last date' (*right*). She and Billy are pictured together at the Chelsea Flower Show in the summer of 1994.

Billy's final team photograph (*above*), taken after he had been given the honour of a place on the board of his beloved Wolves in 1990. In his retirement, after more than twenty years as a sports executive with Central Television, Billy gave more time to golf, one of his favourite pursuits. At his peak he had a four handicap, and was a regular on the pro-am circuit.

Here (*left*) he waits to tee off in the Bob Hope Classic with his partner, Gary Player.

tell his story. Joy revealed: 'I urged Billy to take it because we could have done with the money. But he just shrugged and said, "They would only be interested in the dirt." Deep down, he was very bitter over the timing of the sacking, but he kept it all to himself. I had been telling him to get out before it destroyed him, but he was a man of enormous pride and wanted to give Arsenal some of the success he had tasted at Wolves. He poured himself into the job, and was making himself ill.'

Privately, Billy told me: 'There were players who let me and themselves down by giving less than one hundred per cent. But what good was it going to do shouting about it in the newspapers? They knew who they were, and I just hope they felt at least a little guilty when I was shown the door. There was confusion at first, because Arsenal gave the impression that I had resigned. But I was never ever a quitter, and did not walk out on any job. What hurt most of all was that I knew in my heart that things were going to change for the better at Highbury. I had followed the old Wolves way of developing a youth policy and it was just about to bear fruit, but I would not be there for the harvest.'

Evidence to support Billy's appraisal was there for all to see. In 1965, Arsenal were runners-up to Everton in the FA Youth Cup; this is the competition that is a barometer for what lies ahead for clubs. The following year, just weeks before his dismissal, Billy had what he considered his most satisfying night of all at Highbury when the 'Wright Whizz kids' won the FA Youth Cup, beating Sunderland 4–1 in the second leg at home after a 2–1 defeat at Roker Park. The future looked bright, but Billy was looking at life through red and white tinted spectacles. Meanwhile, the Arsenal directors were studying the First Division table and were blind as to what glories might lie ahead.

Ironically, it was televised football that helped decide Billy's fate. A home match with Don Revie's rampaging Leeds United side was crazily rearranged for the evening of Thursday 5 May 1966. There was the little matter of the European Cup Winners' Cup final between Liverpool and Borussia Dortmund being shown 'live' on BBC television. In the press box we cynics played spot-the-crowd as just 4,544 spectators trickled through the turnstiles. This was (and remained) the lowest old First Division attendance since the First World War. Arsenal got well and truly stuffed 3–0, and it was during hushed conversations between Arsenal directors that night that it was decided that the time had come for a change of management.

'I know that settled it for certain members of the board,' Billy told me. 'But it was hardly my fault that they chose to play the match the same night as an attractive game being shown live on television. They saw the people staying away as a protest against the performances of the team, which I suppose was true to a certain extent. If only they realised, as I did, the talent that was waiting to come through.'

Here is a summary of the Wright influence on the Arsenal side that Denis Hill-Wood described as the best in the history of the Gunners. Along with goalkeeper Bob Wilson, who had first of all been signed as an amateur, six of the Arsenal double-winning squad of 1970–71 came through Billy's youth academy at Highbury: Pat Rice, Sammy Nelson, Peter Storey, Peter Simpson, Jon Sammels and John Radford. In the spring of 1966 he signed as an apprentice a youngster fresh from Holloway school, where he had been coached by Bob Wilson. His name was Charlie George.

Add to all this George Armstrong, who had been nursed along by Billy early in his career, and the influence of captain Frank McLintock and coach Don Howe, and you will see that Billy Wright's fingerprints were all over the League and FA Cup trophies.

For the record, this was the team that clinched the 'Double' at Wembley with an extra-time victory over Liverpool in the FA Cup final and a wonder goal scored by Charlie George: Wilson; Rice, McNab, Storey, McLintock, Simpson; Armstrong, Graham, Radford, Kennedy, George; substitute Eddie Kelly. It was almost the team that Billy built.

In my treasured books collection, I have a leather-bound volume presented to me by the late Denis Hill-Wood. It is a limited edition record of the Double year, autographed by each of the players and containing a hand-written inscription from the Arsenal chairman thanking me for my contribution to the successful season. All I had done was report what I had witnessed in my then role as chief football reporter of the *Daily Express*.

Billy Wright got nothing. He should, at the very least, have been given the freedom of Highbury.

On 30 July 1966 – six weeks after his sacking – England won the World Cup under the management of Alf Ramsey, who brilliantly filled the post for which our Billy had once been groomed.

By then, he was no longer in football. Billy had taken a quantum leap into the world of television.

FINAL SEASONS:
The Greatest Victory

We now move into a world away from football in our hunt for the real Billy Wright, and for the first and only time the portrait will reveal a wart or two. He was so hurt and frustrated by his failure at Arsenal that he turned his back on the game that he had always loved with an almost boyish enthusiasm. 'Whatever the offer, whatever the club, I will never go back into football,' he said. And he meant it.

He was unemployed for only a few days. Family friend Lew (later Lord) Grade decided that he was the ideal man to help bring some stardust to his fledgling ATV sports department. Under the caring wing of the then ATV executive Bill Ward, he became a presenter of weekend football programmes, working alongside the man with the mellifluous voice, Hugh Johns. He also had a brief spell in harness with former *Daily Herald* sports columnist Peter Lorenzo, with whom I later ran a sports promotions company.

'It quickly became obvious that Billy was not a natural at the microphone,' said Peter, the late father of stylish Sky Sports presenter Matthew Lorenzo. 'He gave it one hundred per cent, as with everything in his life, but he was much more comfortable off camera. He settled down to become an outstanding administrative executive.'

Billy was appointed Head of Sport for Associated Television (ATV, later reconstituted as Central Television and now Carlton). He took to this role much more positively than being Arsenal manager, and used his many contacts to give Central an edge in television sports coverage.

He proved himself a master at delegation, putting together one of the

208

strongest production teams in sports TV, including three young innovators who are today heavyweights in the television corridors of power: Trevor East, an influential force at Sky, Jeff Farmer, high-powered ITV football executive producer, and the ubiquitous Gary Newbon, who succeeded Billy as central controller of sport and outside broadcasts. He also signed a cherubic Nick Owen as a roving football reporter and, of course, had Welsh wordsmith Hugh Johns in his team as a commentator of the highest quality.

'Billy was a wonderful ambassador for ATV and then Central,' Gary Newbon told me. 'He was the perfect man to clinch a contract because people loved to meet him. Billy had a natural charm, and was a kind and considerate boss. He believed in giving people their head, and I am one of many who owe him a debt of gratitude for his encouragement and motivation. His biggest strength was that same infectious enthusiasm he always showed on the football pitch as a captain. Everybody wanted to do their best for him. He was our captain.'

Gary, king of the TV football interviewers, went a little misty eyed as he added: 'Billy not only gave me my first job in television, but also introduced me to the girl who was to become my wife. If that is not enough, he presented me with two of his caps – one for each of our twins when they were born. I know you are going to hear the word a million times when you are interviewing anybody about Billy... he really was the *nicest* person you could wish to meet.'

Andy Allan, who was managing director at Central during most of Billy's reign, said: 'Billy's effect on just about everybody he met was magical. People would come in to the office to discuss major contracts, and invariably took up half the meeting time reminiscing with Billy on his great career in football. There was not a boastful bone in Billy's body, and all those he met walked out of the office impressed by his modesty and also his natural friendliness. He worked under me, but I could never get it out of my head that he was *my* hero, and I think he had that effect on anybody from our generation who knew the first thing about football. We could not have had a better ambassador for our television company.'

At first, Billy was based in the south when making the transition into the world of television, but he was then transferred to Birmingham when the entire ATV operation was moved to the Midlands. It was the start of some dark clouds rolling into his life.

'That move to the Midlands caused us terrible heartache,' Joy Beverley Wright told me. 'By then we had two gorgeous daughters, Vicky and Babette, and I said it would be too much of a disruption for us to uproot and start a new home in Birmingham. They were studying at the brilliant Purcell School of Music at Harrow, and it would have been unfair on them to have interrupted their education. So Billy made the move up to Birmingham on his own. It meant us being separated for five and sometimes six days a week. No matter where he was Billy would call me every single evening, but a telephone is not the same as being able to touch and feel the person you love. He became very lonely living in an apartment in the Midlands, and I hold myself responsible for the problem that slowly developed, without anybody realising it. I often wonder if things would have turned out differently had I joined him with our two girls.'

I was aware earlier than most people that Billy was developing a drink problem. Sporting clubs sprouted in the 1960s and 1970s, bringing with them a lucrative after-dinner speaking circuit. I was a celebrity booker for boxing clubs run by my friends Mickey Duff, Terry Lawless and Johnny Levine, and among my regular bookings were Billy and Jimmy Greaves. Often included in my brief was the task of introducing them at the dinners, and so we sat shoulder to shoulder at the top table where the temptations to drink were difficult to ignore.

What contrasts! Jimmy was a recovering alcoholic, and could not get away from the dinner table fast enough after his always riotous speech, his words washed down with mineral water. Billy, I noticed, wanted to stay around long after the speeches were finished, thirstily reaching for the alcohol he had so conscientiously avoided throughout his playing career. He also started smoking. It was almost as if he was trying to make up for all that he missed in that fantastically disciplined first half of his life. But what nobody knew is that after those dinners and after late nights at the office Billy was then going back to his apartment and drinking alone. The bottle had become his favourite, secret companion; his crutch.

Meanwhile, Billy had signed Greavsie for his ATV sports team to start Jimmy's meteoric rise as a television personality. I was acting as Jimmy's representative in those days, and had to negotiate the contract with Billy after Trevor East, Gary Newbon and producer Tony Flanagan had campaigned for him to be their resident expert on Star Soccer. Billy was not at all sure. It was the summer of 1980 and Greavsie was then still carrying the label of 'alcoholic' and Billy worried and wondered about how his cockney accent would go down with Midland ears. 'We'll give him a three-month trial,' Billy told me. Greavsie's television career was up and running.

I have brought this Wright/Greaves episode into focus here because it is relevant to what happened a few years later. Those close to Billy could see that he was in the grip of a crisis with his drinking, and voice-of-experience Jimmy was asked to have a quiet word with him. He confidentially pointed him in the direction of Alcoholics Anonymous.

'Billy knew he had a problem,' Joy told me. 'He had a cocktail cabinet full of wines and spirit in his office and if anybody called in to see him he would use that as an excuse to pour them and, of course, himself a drink. But he was determined to beat the problem. One afternoon he booked himself into a special clinic and was away for a few weeks. I went to collect him from the clinic and could not believe the change in him. It was just like our first meeting. There was the lovely grin, his eyes were sparkling and he looked years younger. He had beaten the demons of drink and never touched another drop. Billy and I always called it his greatest victory.'

Billy had several 'lost' years, and I could fill this book with stories of his drinking escapades. But I refuse to rain on my hero, and all his old Central colleagues were equally loyal. There were many drink-related episodes – some horrendous, others hilarious – that I could have used to scar this portrait, but I prefer to concentrate on the positive aspect and the fact that he was a man who had the character and the courage to beat the bottle.

'I honestly did not think Billy could beat it,' Jimmy Greaves told me. 'It hit him in middle-age, and it's difficult when you are older to get the motivation to conquer the condition. But Billy had astonishing willpower, and got himself straightened out. All of us at Central were thrilled for him and for Joy. It was harder than anything he ever had to do in football, but he came through it with that lovely smile of his in place.'

'Joy was the rock who helped me through my crisis,' Billy confided when I congratulated him on his switch to a mineral water regime. 'It took me a long while before I realised just how dependent I had become on alcohol. It's the old story of the drinker being the last to know he has a problem. I have to be honest and admit that I completely lost it for a spell and there are a lot of blanks in my memory. The minute it sank in that the drinking was affecting my everyday life I decided I had to do something drastic to beat it. With the confidential help of some close friends and colleagues, I learned not to take a drink, just for today. I turned it around, a day at a time. But I could not have done it so quickly without the support of Joy and my family. That made all the difference. They smothered me with their love and that meant so much to me. It gave me the will to recover from what all alcoholics will tell you is an illness. I wanted to beat it for them.'

I thank Joy for giving me permission to make Billy's battle with the bottle public knowledge because I want this to be a finished portrait. The fact he conquered his problem, with few people even knowing he was in trouble, speaks volumes for that same iron will and determination that carried him through 105 international matches for England.

Joy was much more concerned about me spotlighting another phase of Billy's life and wanted to censor it: his rug-making. 'You will make him sound like a poof!' she exclaimed, which was not at all Beverley Sisters language.

Their youngest daughter, Babette, heavily expectant with a second baby to join young William as a Wright grandchild, walked in on our conversation. 'You've got to let him tell the whole story, Mum,' she said. 'It will help show what a different life it was for young footballers in Dad's day.'

Joy conceded, adding: 'Just as long as you leave your readers knowing what a unique person Billy was and his amazing contribution to the happiness of others. I have never known a less selfish person. He was one of life's true givers.'

That brought me to a question I had been meaning to ask since first stepping foot in their beautiful home on the North London/ Hertfordshire border, standing side by side to houses occupied by the lovely Beverley twins. 'Where,' I asked, looking around, 'are all of Billy's caps?' There was not one to be seen.

'Now you know what I mean about Billy being a giver,' Joy explained. 'He gave nearly all of them away to raise money for various charities, and I managed to hold on to just a few which are family keepsakes. Billy was the sort of person who would have given away his last shilling to help anybody in need.'

Other caps, along with many of Billy's mementoes, were auctioned by Christie's two years after his death. 'I was following Billy's instructions,' Joy told me. 'He was always worrying about our house being a target for burglars and said to me on several occasions, "You must auction all of this off to football people who will appreciate them. It's pointless hanging on to them after I've gone, because they will be too much of an attraction for thieves." That was typical of him, to be worrying about me after he had gone.'

When Billy retired from a consultancy role with Central Television in 1989 he was given the best possible present. He was made a director of his beloved Wolves. 'That was one of his proudest moments since his playing days,' said Joy. 'He never ever got Wolves out of his system, and to be invited on to the board by Sir Jack Hayward gave him enormous pleasure and satisfaction. The supporters welcomed him back like an old friend. Billy felt as if he had returned home.'

Sir Jack, the saviour of Wolves who turned them around with his money and motivation, took Billy's breath away when he asked him to become a director. 'I said to him in confidence, "If I buy the club, will you agree to come on the board?"' Sir Jack recalled. 'Billy was shocked into silence for a minute and then replied, "Do you really mean it?" "Put it this way," I said. "It's one of my conditions for buying the club!" His eyes lit up, and he said with tears in his eyes that it would be the greatest honour he could receive. But it was I who was honoured that he accepted my invitation.'

Billy told me that becoming involved with Wolves as a director had given him one of the greatest thrills of his life. 'I know it is an old football cliché but I really was "over the moon".' I was determined not to be just a sleeping director, and I took an interest in every development at a time when Sir Jack and the board were instigating sweeping changes. They dragged the club into the modern times when, let's be honest, just a few years earlier they were very close to going out of business. Sir Jack is a miracle worker, and I'll not hear a word said against him. He has put his money where his mouth is, and every Wolverhampton supporter owes him a debt of gratitude. He has pumped the pride back into our great club.'

His interest in the club went beyond the affairs of the boardroom. Few home reserve and youth games kicked off without him as a spectator, and he always went out of his way to give encouraging words of advice to the players before and after each match.

In his all-too-brief retirement years, Billy worked on his golf handicap which at his peak was as low as four. He also took a close interest in the launch of a new singing group, The Foxes, made up of the offspring of the Beverley Sisters and, as you would expect, perfect in their harmony and stunning in their presentation.

I went to Billy for a quote the sad day that Bobby Moore succumbed to cancer in 1992. He was distraught at the passing of the player who had been the 'Billy Wright of the 1960s', equalling Billy's record of captaining England 90 times. 'Bobby was such a lovely young man,' Billy said. 'I followed his career closely from the days when I was England Under–23 manager and he was just beginning to make the breakthrough as an outstanding prospect. I doubt if there has ever been a better reader of the game in English football. He always knew the best place to be to make the most of any situation, and he always played for the team rather than for himself. He achieved so much more than I did as England captain, leading them to the World Cup. He is a legend in the game, and he will be greatly missed both as a footballer and as a man.'

How chilling that just two years later Billy would also be struck down by cancer, and I know that my old friend Bobby would have wanted to say similar things about him. Bobby was starting out as a football apprentice at West Ham as I was beginning my reporting career on the local paper, and we were from the generation who idolised Billy.

I can just imagine the two blond gods of English football together in the soccer heaven, side by side. If they are on duty at the Pearly Gates, goodness knows how anybody will get in.

A LAST LAP OF HONOUR:
The Fantastic Farewell

Billy's last year was a painful one. It took months to diagnose that his problem was cancer. Joy lovingly nursed him through the closing weeks at their North London home. Eight days before he died – on 3 September 1994, the anniversary of the start of the Second World War that heralded such a change in his life – he had his last two visitors outside his close family.

Wolves President Sir Jack Hayward and Billy's old Central Television colleague Gary Newbon called in to say their farewells, once the diagnosis had been made that nothing more could be done to save him. Both Sir Jack and Gary were made speechless by Billy, who rather than complaining about his health apologised to them for not getting up to give them a proper welcome. 'I'm so sorry to be like this,' he said. 'Have you had a cup of tea?'

The Midlands was drenched in tears the day that he died. His funeral on 12 September 1994 was a hugely emotional affair that brought Wolverhampton to a standstill. Despite teeming rain, thousands turned out to pay a final tribute to a much-loved man who had brought honour and glory to the Midlands in general and to Wolverhampton in particular.

The skies seemed to be weeping for the loss of our hero as the pouring rain soaked the masses of people crowding the streets leading to the historic Collegiate Church of St Peter. On its way to the beautiful, thousand-year-old church, the hearse did what amounted to a lap of honour around the nearby Molineux pitch. Joy, Vicky, Babette, Vincent and the twins, Teddie and Babs, were in the leading mourners' cars as

215

the long procession briefly came to a halt outside the entrance to the Billy Wright Stand. Rain-soaked flags hung at half mast from the stand, one inscribed with the poignant Wolverhampton motto: 'Out of darkness cometh light.'

Hundreds of gold-and-black scarves had been hung on the main-gate railings by grieving supporters wanting to show their appreciation of Billy's incalculable contribution to the history of their club, and floral tributes were stacked high on the pavement outside the stadium where Billy had led Wolves through so many stirring battles. He had always played with the roar of the crowd in his ears, but now nothing could be heard except, over the loudspeaker system, the emotive sounds of 'Nimrod' from Elgar's *Enigma Variations*.

Few could hold back tears when they read the brief, heartfelt messages left with the scarves and flowers. One card read, 'So sorry you died on my wedding day – we will love you always.' Another, pinned to a scarf, said: 'I wore this all through the sixties – now I leave it with you.' Several cards said simply, 'Goodbye Sir Billy.'

Another supporter had left a can of the popular Black Country brew with the note: 'Have this one on me, Billy.'

Film from a security camera outside the ground later showed a fan wearing a Wolves shirt stopping outside the stadium long after midnight. He stripped off his shirt, put it on the railings and then, bare-chested and having made his personal statement, wandered off into the night.

More than seven hundred of Billy's closest friends and family and television colleagues packed into the church for the service. It was conducted by the Rector of Wolverhampton, the Reverend John Hall-Matthews, who along with Sir Jack Hayward's personal assistant Rachael Heyhoe Flint had been the main choreographer of the funeral. The gathering included forty members of the Former Wolves Players' Association. Seventeen of them had played with Billy during the golden years immediately after the war.

All in club blazers, they formed a guard of honour as Billy's coffin was brought into the church. It reminded those with long memories of how many of the same players had lined up at Molineux to clap Billy out on to the pitch for his final appearance in a Wolves shirt back in the summer of 1959. Just a twinkling of an eye ago.

It was as if a pack of the cigarette cards we used to collect as youngsters had been tipped out and there in life-size form were so many of the players from the glorious Wolves past. I know that in an affectionate biography like this Billy would expect me to mention every one of them. I present them here in alphabetical order:

Colin Booth, Peter Broadbent, Les Cocker, Alf Crook, Steve Daley, Fred Davies, Norman Deeley, Jack Dowen, Jimmy Dunn, Mel Eves, Ted Farmer, Malcolm Finlayson, Ron Flowers, Tom Galley, Joe Gardiner, Bill Guttridge, Gerry Harris, Kenny Hibbitt, Bobby Mason, John McAlle, Jim Murray, Geoff Palmer, Phil Parkes, Derek Parkin, John Richards, Eddie Russell, Bill Shorthouse, George Showell, Cyril Sidlow, Nigel Sims, Leslie Smith, Sammy Smyth, Barry Stobart, Eddie Stuart, Roy Swinbourne, Bobby Thomson, Dave Wagstaffe, Ken Whitfield, Bert Williams and Dennis Wilshaw.

Many of Billy's old England colleagues, including kings such as Sir Stanley Matthews, Tom Finney, Nat Lofthouse and Jimmy Greaves along with Jack Charlton, Don Howe, George Graham, Ron Atkinson and Bill Nicholson were there to say a final and fond farewell to their friend. Even though this was a sombre occasion, the crowd outside the church could not hold back polite applause in recognition of a frail Stan Cullis having made the effort to get to the service. 'Billy was always there for me,' he said. 'I want to be here for him today.'

Graham Taylor, Wolves manager at the time, was proudly in attendance with his players smartly attired in club blazers. 'Most of these lads were not born when Billy was playing,' he said. 'But they know all about the legend that is Billy Wright. He made Wolverhampton Wanderers famous around the world. Billy was such a nice, ordinary man. I say that with affection and admiration. He had managed to stay normal despite all his success. Just the name alone, Billy Wright, is inspirational.'

The last team-mates of Billy's life were the Wolves directors; he considered his place on the board as being part of a team. The directors showed their solidarity by acting as pallbearers: club president Sir Jack Hayward, chairman Jonathan Hayward, directors Nic Stones, Jack Harris, John Harris and club secretary Keith Pearson, who also read the lesson.

Sir Bobby Charlton spoke for everybody in a moving eulogy, one giant of the game remembering another. 'The first time I ever met Billy as a player was in one of my earliest games for Manchester United,' Sir Bobby told the congregation, his warm words also broadcast to the thousands standing in the rain outside. 'We were going head to head for the title. I was so hyped up by my manager, dear Matt Busby, that I actually thought that everybody in the Wolverhampton team was some sort of evil monster. Then we met in the tunnel and Billy completely disarmed me. He was the heart-throb of English football at the time, yet he came up to me to put me at my ease. He was so friendly, it taught me everything about the values which so many of you here today came to love. His record of 105 England caps was remarkable when you think that in his day there were no home and away World Cup and European Cup qualifying rounds to boost the collection. I would never have beaten his record because it would have been somewhere up around the 150 mark.'

Gerry 'You'll Never Walk Alone' Marsden was the spokesman for show business. He read the stirring 'If' poem by Rudyard Kipling, and then brought a ripple of applause from those inside and outside the church when he said: 'I often used to ask Billy why he never got a knighthood. He would reply, 'It only comes if you deserve it.' Gerry looked towards the coffin as he concluded: 'Rest in peace, *Sir* Billy Wright.'

Lying at the altar were two magnificent floral tributes: one was the crest of Wolves; the other in the shape and colours of a No 5 Wolves shirt. There was, of course, 'Abide with Me', and near the close, the recorded voices of the Beverley Sisters filled the church, beautifully singing Billy's favourite song, 'Love Me Tender'. They had sung this with the King, Elvis Presley, during a United States tour in the 1950s. Now it was exclusively for the memory of our hero, King Billy.

Most moving of all, after the Bishop of Wolverhampton, the Rt Rev Michael Bourke, had given the blessing, was the rousing sound of Ironbridge's Abraham Darby School Band and Choir (formerly Billy's Madeley School) performing the old Wolves club anthem that Billy loved so much, 'The Happy Wanderer'.

It had all started for Billy at Ironbridge; how fitting that the young generation of his hometown should have the final farewell.

Joy had placed one of Billy's caps on the coffin. She later presented it to Wolves supremo Sir Jack Hayward, who took it back to the club into which he has poured a fortune to try to revive old glories. 'Billy Wright,' he said, 'was the early inspiration for all that I have done at Molineux. His performances are stored in all our memories for ever."

'The funeral was the saddest yet most beautiful event I have ever experienced,' said Joy, who – along with the twins – dressed in black-and-gold Wolves tracksuits. 'We gave Billy the wonderful send-off that he deserved, and I am so grateful for the way the club, former players, the school and supporters put themselves out to say their farewells. Billy loved them, and they showed that they also loved him.'

Very quietly, Joy and the family later carried out Billy's last wish and scattered his ashes on the Molineux pitch where he had enjoyed so many of his happiest football times.

Wolves have done Billy's memory proud. There is the imposing Billy Wright stand that was opened during one of Billy's last visits to the ground in the summer of 1994, and on the second anniversary of his death Joy unveiled a magnificent larger-than-life statue of him at Molineux.

The bronze statue, showing Billy in his favourite role of leading out a team, was the striking work of sculptor James Butler after £50,000 had been raised following a joint appeal by the *Express & Star* and Beacon Radio, with Norman Perry as the main motivator. Old and young supporters can now gaze up in wonder at a nine-foot-high monument to a man who represented all that was best about the game of football.

Joy has a more tangible monument to Billy's massive popularity at home. It is a book of remembrance that was signed by more than 9,000 Wolves supporters, each of them leaving a brief message about what Billy meant to them. 'This,' she said, 'is for Billy's grandchildren. I want them to know just how greatly their grandfather was loved and admired.'

Only the mandarins of Whitehall and the petty, small-minded Wolverhampton County Councillors let our hero down. Deaf ears were turned to pleas for Billy to be given the knighthood he so richly deserved, and the Wolverhampton council scandalously ignored public opinion and refused to give him the Freedom of the Town that he had helped to put on the map.

The thousands who packed the streets of Wolverhampton voted with their feet on the day of Billy's funeral, and as far as they were concerned Billy not only had the freedom of their town but also of their hearts.

'Billy never once complained during his illness,' Joy told me, as in love with him now as she had been on that first exchange of glances back in the spring of 1958. 'He went to all sorts of specialists before we at last found out the cause of his trouble and by then it was too late to do anything about it. He was brave to the end, and kept saying what a wonderful life he'd had. I was so lucky to have shared so much of it with him.'

That can also be said on behalf of all those thousands of us who were so lucky to have shared his moments on the football field when, for club and country, he truly was *a hero for all seasons*.

The Things They Say About Billy

As a final flourish to the Billy Wright portrait, I have opened the paintbox to his many old friends and colleagues so that they can add a splash of colour of their choosing. Then I hand over to the most important people of all, the supporters, for their memories of a hero for all seasons. The final words will go to his family, because Billy was essentially a family man and I want this to be a lasting record for his grandchildren: Kelly, William and Babette's new baby, Emily Rose, born on 21 May 2002.

Billy's personal papers, meticulously kept cuttings books and correspondence were put at my disposal to help me collate this chapter of quotes and anecdotes, and I have mixed and shaken them with interviews of my own to make the Billy Wright quotes cocktail. It is a heady mix of tribute and trivia.

The quotes are not in any particular order, but a potpourri of the things people said about our hero during his distinguished footballing career and following his much mourned departure on 3 September 1994 at the age of 70. You are invited to add tributes or memories of your own on our special Billy Wright memorial website at www.billywright.co.uk

What the Players Say

Who better to kick-off our memories than the players who knew Billy best – his team-mates during the golden years at Molineux. Following the passing of Billy's life-long pal Jimmy Mullen in 1987, it was decided to start a Wolves Former Players' Association. The main instigator was Peter Creed, 60 years a Wolves supporter and an advertisement director of the *Wolverhampton Express & Star*, one of the finest provincial newspapers in the land. Thanks to Peter, who remains the omniscient secretary of the association, and also to the Central/Carlton television team, I have been able to collate the following tributes from Billy's old playing colleagues, all of whom were on guard of honour duty at the funeral of their captain:

BERT WILLIAMS ('The Cat', capped 24 times by England and the brilliant last line of defence for Wolves in 381 League games): 'Speaking as the proud president of our association, I know that I represent the views of all our members when I say that Billy was the most revered and respected of all our players. He was chairman of our association, and brought the same enthusiasm to that job as he did to everything he tackled. Nobody was prouder to pull on the Wolves shirt than Billy, and I swear he used to grow a couple of inches the second it was on his back. I shared his greatest and lowest moments in football. The low point was the 1–0 defeat by the United States in the 1950 World Cup when, if the ball had run for us, we would have won by four or five goals. The best moment was our victory over Honved, which helped Billy avenge the painful defeats by Hungary. A lasting memory for me is walking into the large bathroom at Wembley before the 1949 FA Cup final and finding Billy with the windows wide open listening to "Abide with Me" and saying a prayer. The traditions of the game meant so much to him.'

BILL SLATER OBE (capped by England as an amateur and a professional, a Wolves regular in 310 League matches between 1952 and 1963; later a university lecturer): 'I was very conscious of the fact that I was following a legend when I took over from Billy as Wolves captain. Wolves have not had a more loyal or more dedicated servant. We had a saying in the dressing-room, 'Show the Wright Spirit.' The Wright Spirit is the right spirit! I played with Billy in countless matches for the club and also on several occasions for England. I can count his poor games on the fingers of one hand. He was a wonderful advertisement not only for football but for the human race.'

DENNIS WILSHAW (scorer of 105 goals in 211 League games for Wolves and 10 in 12 matches for England): 'I think the best word to sum up Billy was that he was 'uncomplicated' – both as a player and as a man. In my role as a sports psychologist, I helped players come to terms with the pressures of modern football but Billy would have taken it all in his stride. Just think of the mental preparation he must have made for all those appearances for England, including the extra pressure of the captaincy. But I never saw him fazed by it, and I used to marvel at his strength in defence despite usually giving away several inches in height to his opposing centre-forward. Billy was essentially a team player, and we all tried that bit harder because our captain was always setting such a fine example.'

RON FLOWERS (a great servant for Wolves in 467 League matches and capped 49 times by England): 'I was ten years younger than Billy and he took me under his wing when I first got into the side. He was always offering words of encouragement and advice, and it was the same when I got into the England team. Billy was always there for me, supporting me on and off the pitch. When I was coming up through the Wolves junior sides, Stan Cullis used to point to Billy as the player we should model ourselves on because of his attitude and application. We could not have had a better role model.'

SAMMY SMYTH (scorer of the decisive third goal when Wolves beat Leicester City 3–1 in the 1949 FA Cup final, and a Northern Ireland international): 'Billy was my favourite footballer at all levels. He was the perfect example of the super athlete. Whenever possible we went to dances at the civic hall, and he always caught the last 10.30 p.m. bus to Claregate, where he was in digs with the Colley family. Billy used to love to play at Windsor Park where the Belfast fans always gave him a terrific welcome because of his competitive spirit. He lived for football and was committed one hundred per cent, best described in the one word, "attitude". He was from the no drinking, no swearing, no cheating school. A gentleman.'

MALCOLM FINLAYSON (Wolves goalkeeper in 179 League matches, and later a highly successful businessman; his honours included two successive League championship medals and an FA Cup winners' medal in 1960): 'I joined Wolves from Millwall and Billy helped make life easier for me on my arrival by his caring attitude and his encouragement. He was a captain who really cared about his team-mates. It was wonderful in later years to be able to be part of the Former Players' Association, and with Billy as our chairman we discovered the old spirit. Nobody can break the bond between us all, and Billy will always be a special part of our memories.'

ROY SWINBOURNE (netted 107 goals in 211 League matches for Wolves between 1949 and 1955, collected a League championship medal and scored in the momentous victories against Moscow Spartak and Honved): 'I will always deem it an honour and privilege to have played in the same team as Billy. He was an outstanding captain for Wolves and England, and an inspiration and example to us all. When I got into the team as the first of the new crop of youngsters he encouraged and guided me in my career. We would "room" together on away matches, and also on tour. When my career came to a premature end in my mid–twenties he was very supportive. A true friend indeed.'

PETER CREED (the driving force behind the Former Players' Association): 'Billy was Wolves' greatest player and skipper. Those of us fortunate to have seen all the years of his magnificent career treasure wonderful memories. In later years it was a privilege for me to be involved with Billy when he created the FPA in 1988 as a tribute to his big friend Jimmy Mullen. At that time Billy said, "Let's stick together now we're together again. We had such fun and I never want to lose the friendships I've found again here." This was so typical of Billy's caring nature, and as the founder chairman he ensured the FPA flourished. He truly loved Wolves.'

Now we switch to the memories of his international team-mates and opponents, starting off with this 1994 memory from the player Billy rated as the finest all-round footballer of his generation, the Gentle Giant of Wales …

JOHN CHARLES: 'Billy and I were both given our start in football by Major Frank Buckley. He signed Billy for Wolves and me for Leeds. We were in fits of laughter once when swapping Major Buckley stories. Both Billy and I grew up in the era when you were expected to "sir" your elders. But when I called the major "sir" he went bananas. 'Don't dare ever "sir" me, laddie,' he said. "Even my wife and daughters address me as major!" Billy remembered how the major had once massaged his players with neat whisky because it was so cold. He did the same to us at Leeds, and as with Billy he sent me to ballroom dancing lessons to improve my balance. What a character! But he got through to both Billy and me with his demands for discipline on and off the pitch. Billy developed into a remarkable centre-half, and always gave me a tough time despite the fact that I had a height advantage of about five inches. In all my time in the game I didn't meet a more sporting opponent. Hard but fair, that was Billy.'

JOE MERCER (1959 interview): 'I was Billy's skipper in his first representative match for England. It was a Victory International against Belgium at Wembley. We won comfortably 2–0 and the highlight was the way Billy, at right-half, combined with Stanley Matthews. It was Stanley who got all the headlines the next day, but I noticed how it was Billy's simple passes that continually set Stanley up. I thought to myself, "Here's a great team player." It was a view I never changed. Billy always put the team first, with Wolves and England. He's a smashing bloke and a great advertisement for our game.'

TOMMY LAWTON (1966 interview, discussing the greatest centre-halves): 'I would have to rate both Stan Cullis and Neil Franklin ahead of Billy as a centre-half, but nobody could match him for effort and determination. He played all his games with me at wing-half and he was a real driving force in midfield. His greatest asset was his ability to win the ball and then release it with passes that were always accurate. He did not go in for fancy stuff but concentrated on getting things right. It was we goalscorers who got all the glory, but Billy was as big a star as any of us.'

FRANK SWIFT (1952 interview after Billy had beaten Bob Crompton's 41-cap record): 'I had two matches as England captain before Billy, but I knew in my heart it was not ideal to have a goalkeeper as skipper. When Walter Winterbottom told me Billy was taking over I said, "You could not have made a better choice." I don't think I've ever seen Billy have a bad game. He's always in the thick of things and usually comes away with the ball. Then he finds a team-mate with a pass and England are on the attack again. We first played together for an Army side against a Scottish team at Tottenham in 1945. I was a sergeant major and he'd just been promoted to sergeant. Before the game he asked for my autograph, and I was impressed by his cheerful manner. I don't think I've ever known him be anything but cheerful and his smile lights up the dressing-room. Now I look on him as a close friend. They don't come nicer than Billy.'

SIR ALF RAMSEY (1959 interview, after Billy had announced his retirement): 'What has most impressed me about Billy is his attitude. He goes through life always trying to do the correct thing, whether it is as a player or as a person. Billy played directly in front of me for most of my appearances with England, and so I got a better view than most of his simple, yet effective way of playing the game. He had good ball control and was something of a human dynamo who was like a shield in front of me. I recall that early on in our matches together I suggested that perhaps he was watching the ball too often rather than the man. I only had to say it once, and Billy never ever committed the basic football sin again! He later became an extremely reliable centre-half who made up for his lack of height by excellent positional play. As a captain, he had a wonderful human touch, always encouraging with a quiet word. You'll never hear anyone in the game have a bad word to say about him.'

BOBBY ROBSON (1994 interview): 'When Billy took off his England shirt with the three lions I fully expected to see three lions tattooed on his heart. I came into the England team just before the 1958 World Cup, and Billy went out of his way to make me feel comfortable. He saw that as a vital part of his captaincy. I was one of the few who witnessed the angry side of Billy. He was fuming during the World Cup finals when the naughtier reporters were stirring up personal stuff about his romance with Joy. But he never let it get to him on the pitch, and always played his heart out for the team. Who knows, if it had not been for the Munich air crash Billy might easily have been the first player to lift the World Cup as England captain.'

NAT LOFTHOUSE (1994 interview): 'Billy was the *complete* captain. He was a great player and a superb motivator, particularly if you were having a difficult game. He'd be right up behind you, encouraging you and urging you on. His switch to centre-half showed just what a good football brain he had, and he could hold his own against the roughest and toughest centre-forwards without ever resorting to unfair or foul tactics. I should know because we had some great no-quarter-given battles, but at the end of them we would be the best of pals. They don't breed them like him any more.'

TOM FINNEY (1994 interview): 'I will always remember Billy as a wonderful team-mate, who had time and a smile for everybody. As a player he was a manager's dream. He won the ball and dispatched it with a minimum of fuss but with great efficiency. His tackles were so beautifully timed that he did not need to be overphysical. He was only five foot eight, but played like a giant in the centre of the defence. I am sure if you asked the supporters how tall he was they would say over six foot. That was the impression he always gave when taking on and beating centre-forwards in the air. No matter where we were in the world, Billy wore that England shirt with enormous pride.'

STANLEY MATTHEWS (1994 interview): 'Billy played the game with his soul. He gave everything he had every time he went on to the pitch, and was an inspiration to all his team-mates. I remember the first time we played together was in 1946 in a game against Belgium at Wembley. Billy arrived in his Army uniform because he was still a serving soldier and he had not long had sergeant's stripes up. The first thing he did was ask for my autograph, and I said, "But I was only a corporal!" He was switched at the last minute to right-half after being selected at inside-left. This meant he was a key supplier of the ball for me. I got out of a flu bed to play and felt like death warmed up, but Billy made my afternoon easy by following my instructions and always playing the ball to my feet. We won comfortably, and I said to Billy, "Well done. This will be the first of many England games for you, take my word for it." But who would have thought he would have gone on to play one 105 times! It was a remarkable record by a remarkable man.'

TOMMY DOCHERTY: 'I played against Billy in some out-and-out wars between the auld enemy, but never once did I see him commit a deliberate foul. I had the honour of captaining Scotland against England at Hampden in 1958 when there was an attendance of nearly 130,000 and I felt sure the Hampden Roar would frighten the England players to death. A youngster by the name of Bobby Charlton made his debut and scored a fantastic goal. We were thumped 4–0 and as I shook hands with Billy at the end I thanked him for ruining my day! Billy laughed and said that he was sure we would get our own back at Wembley the following year. That was the game in which Billy won his 100th cap, and it was Bobby Charlton who scored the vital goal again. I'll tell you this – Billy's 100th cap was the same size as his first.'

JIMMY GREAVES: 'The first time I met Billy I was a little urchin of ten-years-old. I scrambled on to the pitch from the Tottenham terraces at the end of a game against Wolves and had the cheek to ask the great man for his autograph. Most players would have cocked a deaf 'un, but he stopped and signed my programme for me. Nine years later I made my debut against Peru, and Billy was my captain and he made me feel nice and relaxed with his friendly words of encouragement. Another twenty years on Billy became my boss at Central Television, and we often found time to have a natter about our playing days. He said people always reminded him of the 1958 Wolves game against Chelsea at Stamford Bridge when I nipped past him for five goals. In fairness, he was not detailed to mark me that day, and he had the last laugh because at the end of the season, who collected the League championship trophy? William Ambrose Wright. I can't believe anybody will ever beat his record of 70 successive international matches. That says everything about his consistency and reliability.'

JOHNNY HAYNES (1989 interview after his appearance as a guest on Billy's *This Is Your Life*): 'I remember that on Billy's last tour – when we got taken to the cleaners by world champions Brazil, Peru and Mexico – the journalists travelling with us gave us some terrible stick. They went right over the top with their criticism, not making allowances for the fact that we had not been given time to acclimatise in any of the three countries. Billy, along with the rest of us, was furious about what they were writing, but he continued to treat all of the football writers with genuine warmth and politeness. That was Billy, the friendliest bloke you could ever wish to meet... and he was a bloody good footballer, too!'

DON HOWE (1994 interview): 'I grew up in Wolverhampton and Billy was my hero. When I first got picked to play for England in 1957 I was nervous on my arrival at the team hotel about going into the dining room to join such legends as Tom Finney, Duncan Edwards and Billy. He saw me hovering outside, came out and shook me warmly by the hand before leading me into the room and introducing me to everybody as if I was his brother. Two stories come to mind. After his 100th cap, Ronnie Clayton and I hoisted him up and carried him the length of the pitch and into the dressing-room. He was so modest that he wanted us to put him down, but we insisted he stay up there. I told

him that as I had carried him through the match I might as well carry
him off! I'm afraid I didn't do him justice when he bought me for
Arsenal. I broke my leg against Blackpool and he came and sat with me
in the dressing-room while the match was still going on. "Boss, you
should be out there watching," I said. "Let's just see you right first," he
said. That was Billy, always putting the concerns of others first. What
a great man, and what a great player. Don't get fooled by all that stuff
about him being too nice. He could put it about on the pitch with the
best of them when the going got tough, but he always managed to do it
without resorting to foul play. But take it from me, he was never ever
soft. When Billy tackled you, you stayed tackled.

'Don't let's lose sight of the fact that he was being groomed for the
England manager's job when he gave up his chance to come to
Highbury. It just might have been him leading England out at Wembley
for the 1966 World Cup final! Arsenal should have been more patient
with him. Let's face it, the team that Bertie Mee and I guided to the
double was largely the one that Billy had built. I will not have it that he
was a bad manager. He was an unlucky one.'

ARTHUR ELLIS (giving a referee's view of Billy when he retired in
1959): 'If every player was like Billy the life of the referee would be
easy. I refereed many matches in which he played and I can never ever
remember him protesting against a decision, although he did have the
quiet joke, saying things like, "Time you saw your optician, Arthur." It
was a delight to be on the same pitch as him. He is the man I point to
as the perfect example of the model professional footballer.'

TERRY NEILL (1994 interview): 'I was Billy's captain when he first
took over as manager at Highbury. He was like a breath of fresh air at
first, but gradually things got out of his control. The plain and simple
fact is that he was too nice to do the job properly. When you are a
manager you are at the mercy of your players. If they let you down, you
sometimes need to be unpleasant and disagreeable to get them back on
track. Billy just did not have it in him to be nasty.'

FRANK McLINTOCK (1971 interview, after he had led Arsenal to the League and FA Cup double): 'I remember bumping into Billy a couple of weeks after he had been sacked by Arsenal, and he looked years younger. I think it did him a favour getting away from the stress of the job. He was too nice to be a manager. That can't be bad to have that said behind your back!'

BOB WILSON: 'Billy signed me for Arsenal in 1963. That's the year I left Loughborough College and arrived as a PE teacher and amateur goalkeeper at Highbury. I first met Billy that same year, having skipped lectures for the day and, in a borrowed car, made my way to Islington. The first things you noticed about him was the shock of curly blond hair and his infectious smile. The late Bertie Mee, then Arsenal's physio, had arranged the meeting and Billy met me in the famous marble hall. I was awestruck by being in the company of the legendary Billy and by the ground itself. It was truly spine-chilling, and I felt as if I had walked into a cathedral.

'After that initial meeting, Billy eventually became my manager. His success could never be measured in trophies, but he undoubtedly laid the foundations of the 1971 Double team. More than half were signed by Billy.

'I can't say that he was a great football manager, but I think he was a great human being. Whatever shortcomings there may have been in management were overcome by his ability to make visitors and strangers welcome. If ever I was showing family or friends around Highbury and Billy was around, he never failed to take time out and come and say, "Hello, I'm Billy Wright. Welcome, enjoy yourself."

'Sadly, we had our fall-outs – but all player-manager relationships hinge on whether the manager is picking you or not. On one occasion Billy stood me up in front of the whole coaching staff and gave me a dreadful and humiliating dressing-down. It led to my slamming the door and with a genuine intention to walk out of Arsenal and return to teaching, or lecturing.

'One of the staff, Alf Fields, another former Arsenal player, stopped me and told me to hang on in there. You know the rest.

'There were never any hard feelings with Billy. How could you dislike such a thoroughly nice man with great humanity? By the time success came my way, Billy had lost his job, but I know he was genuinely thrilled that his early belief in me had been justified. In turn my life has been enriched by knowing the great man.'

RON ATKINSON: 'I used to clean Billy's boots when I was a kid, and he always went out of his way to thank me when most pros would have taken it for granted. We struck up quite a bond, and I became locked into the Billy Wright legend. Any youngster of my generation was in awe of him, and could reel off the names of that Wolves side that featured in those floodlit thrillers of the fifties. Billy was the player who became a household name, yet to meet him you would have thought he was the least famous and least successful. I have met a lot of so-called superstars in my life, but never one to touch Billy for humility and generosity. Boy, am I proud I used to clean his boots!'

JACK CHARLTON: 'Billy and I had Major Frank Buckley in common. He signed Billy for Wolves and me for Leeds. I think it bred in both of us a footballing philosophy that lasted throughout our careers. The major drilled into us that football was a simple game, and should be played without frills. That's the way Billy did it, and that's the way I liked to do it. When I was a kid playing street football I used to imagine I was Neil Franklin and then when he left for Colombia I became Billy Wright in those games when the coats were goalposts and you played until it was too dark to see. Some years later I was proud to inherit the England number five shirt that Billy had worn with such pride. Everybody's going to tell you that Billy was a smashing bloke. And do you want to know something? He really was.'

TERRY VENABLES: 'You know how the American college kids go in for that "All-American" stuff, with their heroes wearing the sweaters with the big initials? Well that's how Billy always came across to me – the "All-English" hero. When I was a kid of sixteen my Chelsea clubmate Allan Harris and I were invited to Lilleshall to watch the England team preparing for an international match. Billy came and introduced himself to us, as if we didn't know who he was! He talked to us about our ambitions, and gave us advice about living well and doing all the right things properly. We were in awe of him, but he had this gift for being able to put people at their ease. He really was a caring person without a touch of arrogance.'

GEORGE GRAHAM: 'While between marriages and managing Arsenal, I went shopping at Sainsburys in Cockfosters. I pushed my trolley round a corner into an aisle and collided with a trolley coming the other way. Pushing it was Billy Wright! We laughed so much we nearly fell into the trolleys. What were the odds of a current and former Arsenal manager meeting in such circumstances? We discussed the price of bread and what a pain players can be! Billy was a lovely man, and deserved better luck when he was in charge at Highbury. He was much too nice to make it as a manager, and I was determined not to make that mistake! I often see his daughters playing tennis at the David Lloyd Centre, and they are excellent at the game. There is not a Scot who did not respect Billy the footballer, and there was nobody in the game who did not respect and like Billy the man.'

GEORGE EASTHAM (the passing master Billy inherited when taking over as Arsenal manager): 'I will never forget my first meeting with Billy. I was a youngster with Newcastle, and playing against the League champions Wolves. Suddenly, this blond colossus hit me like a tank and I went over with the little matter of a broken leg. He did not show a lot of concern, and just got on with making sure Wolves won as I was shipped off to hospital. I thought what a hard blighter he was, putting it politely. The next morning a warm letter profuse with apologies arrived at the hospital. He had two sides to him. On the pitch he was totally committed to winning and could be a ruthless competitor. Off it, he was a wonderfully warm and friendly man . . . much too nice when it came to managing us at Arsenal!'

STEVE BULL (scorer of a record 250 League goals for Wolves and one of the few modern players who could look the old heroes in the eye): 'Billy had retired six years before I was born, but his legend was there to inspire us. There is not a Wolves player, past or present, who does not know about his achievements. Whenever I met him I found him modest and charming, and more interested in asking me questions than talking about himself. He was Wolves through and through.'

I close this players' section with a memory from a man Billy rated highly, both as a footballer and as a friend – Wilf Mannion. He was included in what Billy selected as his England dream team from his playing days: Frank Swift; Alf Ramsey, Roger Byrne; himself, Neil Franklin, Duncan Edwards; Stanley Matthews, Raich Carter, Tommy Lawton, Wilf Mannion, Tom Finney.

Wilf made the trip from his Northeast home to London in 1989 to take part in Billy's *This Is Your Life* tribute from Michael Aspel (this in itself was a double honour for Billy, because he is one of the few people to have been awarded two 'Big Red Books'; Eamonn Andrews had 'trapped' him in 1960).

At the after-show party, Wilf and Billy – who had both had distinctive blond hair in their playing days – reminisced about the first time they had played together for England in an official international. It was the first post-war game against Northern Ireland, and both were making their debuts. Wilf scored a hat-trick.

WILF MANNION: 'People always seem to think of Billy as a centre-half, but I remember him more as a driving wing-half. In our first game together for England I got the headlines because I scored three goals in our 7–2 victory. But Billy was the real star because he not only helped us in attack but was also here, there and everywhere in defence. As well as the match, I remember us staying in a beautiful hotel near the Mountains of Mourne, and there was a full-size billiards table in the games room. Billy and I got involved in a marathon session of billiards, with two bob at stake. What I didn't tell Billy is that I was almost professional-class at the game, but I have to say he made me work hard for my money. He was a very good potter, but I pocketed the cash! I'll tell you this – I would not have dragged all the way down here to London for anybody but Billy. He was not only a great footballer and captain, but also a great bloke.'

What the Papers Say

Billy was always a favourite of football writers, who not only appreciated his efforts on the pitch but also the way he made himself approachable and available for interviews. Following Billy's surprise retirement in the summer of 1959, the big guns of Fleet Street fired a salvo of tributes:

DESMOND HACKETT (The Man in the Brown Bowler of the *Daily Express*): 'A light has gone out on the football stage with the retirement of the British Bulldog, Billy Wright. I travelled the world with William Ambrose, and can personally vouch for the fact that English football never had a finer ambassador. He played the game the way he lives his life – with honesty, decency and total commitment. When the beautiful Joy Beverley came into his life, Billy at last found there was something in this world other than football. He will, I know, give the same commitment to his marriage that he has to the game he served so well. They will live happily ever after, which befits the fairy-tale life of King Billy.'

(Showman Des Hackett wrote before the 1954 Wolves game against Puskas-propelled Honved: 'Wolves have not a hope against Honved. If they prove me wrong I will present Billy Wright with my Brown Bowler...' Result: Wolves 3, Honved 2...and Des went into the dressing-room and crowned Billy with his famous bowler).

JL MANNING (who always had The Last Word in the *Daily Mail*): 'The greatest compliment that can be paid to William Ambrose Wright is that if he could not win by fair means, he would not try to win by foul. To play in the hurly-burly of the Football League and, more than 100 times, in the international arena and still remain a gentleman is evidence of a special person at work and at play. It takes a certain amount of courage to retire when at the top of your profession, and this is a quality that he has always had in abundance. Billy Wright, English ambassador, will be greatly missed on the football pitches of the world by friend and foe alike.'

PETER WILSON (The Man They Can't Gag of the *Daily Mirror*): 'The fact that Billy Wright has missed only three international matches since 1946 is, I would suggest, a record of consistency unsurpassed in any sport. How wise Billy is to get off the roundabout before age starts to diminish his competitive abilities. He departs in a blaze of glory, captain of his country and captain of the League champions and married to the glamorous Joy Beverley. His name and his achievements will illuminate the annals of sport for all time with the message, "Billy Wright was here!"'

GEOFFREY GREEN (*The Times*, a particular favourite of Billy's who once famously wrote: 'Billy Wright had a rare off day. He only played like one man.'): 'To measure the contribution to English football of William Ambrose Wright, you must weigh the age in which he played. After six years of World War, with all its dangers, deprivations, loss and shattering upheaval, people emerged with a universal sigh as if from a long dark tunnel. It was football that first brought a shaft of light back into our lives, and Wright came into the darkness of those immediate post-war years like a coalminer with a light shining from his helmet. He was a natural leader and we all followed as he captained England a record 90 times in 105 appearances, another record, and as he led Wolves through thundering triumphs against foreign invaders. There were more talented and more skilful players, but what he embroidered into the fabric of our lives were the values of loyalty and industry, attributes which helped pull us as a nation through those difficult years immediately after the war. Billy Wright, the man, is a human being of exemplary character. Billy Wright, the footballer, was a national treasure.'

SAM LEITCH (Scottish columnist of the *Daily Herald* and then the *Sunday Pictorial* before becoming a powerhouse executive in the world of television sport): 'Speaking as a Scot and with my tartan tongue firmly in my cheek, I am delighted to see the back of Billy Wright. He has been the scourge of we Scots for more years than I care to remember. Never once did he lead a losing England team at Hampden Park. Och, it hurt to write that. Dare I suggest that the palace got it wrong when they recently awarded him the CBE. It should have been a knighthood.'

LAURIE PIGNON (writing in the *Daily Sketch* before his switch to the *Daily Mail* where he became a legendary tennis reporter): 'It is a wise man who knows how to climb off the mountain top before he falls off. Billy Wright's decision to retire shows the same good sense that he always revealed on the football field where he was always a thought and a deed ahead of the opposition. Billy departs from playing the game, but still has much to give to football and I would like to see him one day leading the national team as manager, a job for which he will be groomed under Walter Winterbottom.'

FRANK BUTLER (respected sports editor of the *News of the World* who followed his father, James, as an exceptional sports columnist): 'English football has rarely, if ever, had a more dedicated servant than Billy Wright. If you have a son and you want to teach him about loyalty, honesty, decency and effort, then all you need do is point to Billy as the best example of how to tackle life and sport. He has chosen to retire after playing an amazing 70 consecutive matches for England and as captain of the current League champions. It takes courage and wisdom to retire at the top, and I salute my friend Billy for making a decision that is sad for our game but right for him.'

JOHN CAMKIN (then football correspondent for the *News Chronicle* before becoming an innovative executive at Coventry City): 'Billy Wright could not dribble like Matthews or Finney, head a ball like Lawton or pass like Carter, yet his contribution to English football was no less than these giants of the game. Billy became a world-class centre-half despite the handicap of being at least three inches shorter than ideal for the position. He always walked tall for England and Wolves. We football writers elected him Footballer of the Year in 1952. He was much more than that. He was the footballer of his generation.'

ALAN HOBY (colourful columnist for the *Sunday Express*): 'The Black Country became blacker with the news of Billy Wright's decision to hang up the boots that have marched to glory for Wolves and England for as long as some can remember. Greater players have pulled on the white shirt of England, but there is nobody who has been able to match the effort, efficiency and energy that Billy poured into every game. In true Horatio Nelson traditions, Billy always did his duty for his country and for his club.'

Memories have come cascading in from the generation of today's sportswriters old enough to have appreciated the special magic of Billy Wright...

IAN WOOLDRIDGE OBE (The Master, who keeps alight the flame of honest, intelligent and beautifully composed comment in the *Daily Mail*): 'My warmest recollection of William Ambrose remains the very first time I met him. I was a wet-behind-the-ears kid on the *Bournemouth Times*. One evening, strolling along the cliff tops with my inamorata of the time, I saw the great man coming in the opposite direction with a friend. I had to brace myself to approach him. I assume he must have thought I was another pestilential autograph hunter intruding on his privacy. I explained that I had just started writing a sports column on the local paper and could he please spare me a minute or two of his time – a likely story as I had no notebook or pencil and hadn't had a moment to prepare even a couple of half-intelligent questions. Billy flashed that famous smile, took me at my word, put me entirely at ease and spoke to me precisely as he would have done to Peter Wilson or Desmond Hackett, then two of the big guns of sports writing. He gave me at least ten minutes. On parting he said, "Oh, and good luck with your career." It was my first big sports interview. I walked away on air. I assumed that all great sportsmen would be as kind and courteous and as generous as that for ever but, sadly, that has not quite been the case. There was only one William Ambrose Wright.'

FRANK TAYLOR OBE (An exceptional sports journalist who won respect around the world after surviving the 1958 Munich air crash at the cost of a permanent limp. His book describing the tragedy, *The Day A Team Died*, is one of the most riveting and moving stories you will ever read. Just weeks before he passed on at age 81 in July 2002, Frank shared his memories with me): 'Billy and I had many conversations, and he used to regularly bring up two subjects. First of all, there was the famous match against Hungary when England lost 6–3 at Wembley. Billy said: "I have never been so embarrassed in all my life as when Puskas made a fool of me by pulling the ball back and then shooting the ball into the net as I tackled thin air." I was able to tell Billy that Puskas himself had told me that Billy should have been proud rather than embarrassed that day. He said that it was Billy who inspired England to battle so hard that they scored three goals against one of the greatest teams of all time. Puskas had enormous respect for Billy, as did all his opponents. The other thing that Billy liked to bring up whenever we met was his memory of Duncan Edwards as the greatest footballer of his generation. He said that with Roger Byrne, Tommy Taylor and, of course, Duncan playing England might even have gone the whole way and won the 1958 World Cup. Let's not forget that even without these three Manchester United masters, England managed to draw with the eventual world champions, Brazil. I never once heard Billy make a boastful statement, but he would always sing the praises of others. He said that in his opinion there has never been a better all-round footballer than Duncan. One master paying respect to another. They don't make them like that any more.'

JOHN SAMUEL (distinguished former sports editor of the *Observer* and the *Guardian*): 'No memory of Billy Wright is without a schoolboy gloss, of king and country, unbroken squares, colours never struck, white and old-gold shirts stained with sweat, blond head never unbowed. How many are left, I wonder, of the 100,000 who on 25 November 1953 saw that most famous of defeats, the 6–3 by which

Hungary at Wembley ripped away England's unbeaten mantle. The 29-year-old Billy had many of his 105 caps and six more seasons of international football to come. As England took up their 1–2–3–5, a formation as sanctified as a Spithead warship review, Wright was at right-half, his conversion to centre-half still a season away.

'As a young reporter with the *Brighton Argus and Sussex Daily News* I had access to county football association contacts and a pair of prized Wembley tickets. Not totally an ingenue, I had seen Derby County in their Doherty and Carter pomp demolish Brighton and Hove Albion en route to the first post-war Cup victory. Two years later, in 1948, I'd broken out of my Gloucester RAF camp, where I'd played a bit with pros, for Manchester United's epic 6–4 Cup victory over Aston Villa, then seen them beat Blackpool 4–2 in the final. Come to that, I'd been here six months earlier for the great Stanley Matthews final, Blackpool beating Bolton 4–3.

'But nothing had prepared me for the sweetness of Hungary's football as Nandor Hidegkuti swept in the first-minute goal, then another, crafted so swiftly that a baffled referee chirruped offside. Beside me on the terraces my brother-in-law's jaw sagged. We had seen nothing like it.

'England fielded two debutants in a team averaging more than 30. Some of the players barely knew each other. Amidst it all, Wright never stopped running. The blond head never dropped. The 7–1 defeat in the return match was all the more stunning, but from the ashes came the rethink that led to England's World Cup thirteen years later.

'Wright's leadership was never wanting. In the flickering black and white of the new TV age, Cullis's Wolves tenaciously met the challenge of Spartak, Honved and Real Madrid in historic floodlit adventures. In the nine seasons to 1961 they were out of the First Division's top three only once. Too many outstanding wing-halves – Wright, Slater, Clamp, Flowers? Simple. Billy a switch to centre-half, modest height notwithstanding, and never a bleat. If by the fifties and sixties an Empire was expiring, some of its heroes gave it dignity, Billy Wright chief among them.'

REG DRURY (one of the best-informed football reporters who provided the *News of the World* with a string of exclusives): 'Fleet

Street "discovered" Billy Wright at the end of the Second World War, a year before League football resumed. Sergeant Wright, as he was then, and 21 a month earlier, played for Wolves against Tottenham at White Hart Lane and was outstanding in a 4–1 victory. Despite the restricted space in the small newspapers of the day, the name Wright featured in the match reports as a "Golden Boy star of the future". He was the talk of the town. Everybody in the game in London was commenting on his potential. The following season he won the first of his caps. Fleet Street had got it right.'

DENNIS SIGNY OBE (the undisputed king of freelance football journalists, and a PR consultant to the Football League): 'Billy was peerless. A tackle he made in Wolves colours against Arsenal at Highbury in the fifties stays in my memory as the best I have ever seen. He made up yards on an opponent and whipped the ball away just as he was about to shoot. It was a different era, almost a different game. I reckon a smart-aleck referee in 2002 would have produced a red card for a tackle from behind! I remember telling Sir Stanley Matthews about the tackle. "He did that in every game he played," said Stan in a matter-of-fact way.

'Over the years I have lectured on journalism to aspiring football writers and have always contended that sports pages contain more clichés than any other part of a newspaper. How many ways can you describe a goal? It's a shot, a header, a volley, a half-volley. It's equally hard to avoid saying what everyone does when recalling Billy.

'He was a gentleman. He was courteous and friendly. He smiled. He never ducked the press, even in his most difficult and anxious times as Arsenal manager.

'My favourite recollections are not so much of Billy as a player and a manager, or with ITV but just as a family man. He always asked about my wife. When my younger son went into TV on the sports side he always asked about him and noted his progress.

'Joy helped me with road-safety initiatives when I was a newspaper editor, and I often visited her and Billy at their north London home.

'One thing I can tell you – exclusively – William Ambrose knew how to make a great cup of tea.'

PATRICK COLLINS (*Mail on Sunday* columnist and a collector of more awards for sports writing than Charlton Athletic have had hot baths): 'When I was fifteen years old, my sports-writer father took me to the annual dinner of the Football Writers' Association. After the meal and the speeches, we went to the bar. There we met Billy Wright, who had known my father for many years. He had always been a hero of mine, and I knew just about everything there was to know about him; not simply the details of his extraordinary career, but little things, like how he had felt when Major Buckley had told him he was too small for professional football. I even knew the name of his first landlady at Wolves (Mrs Colley, as I recall). But Billy didn't talk about himself; instead, he asked me about school and exams and the kind of career I hoped to follow. He actually seemed interested in me, and I remember being enormously flattered. The group at the bar grew, and notable figures like Tom Finney, Danny Blanchflower and Joe Mercer joined the company. I stood on the fringe, clutching an orange juice, but Billy made a point of introducing me to each of the great men: "This is young Pat," he would say. "He's a good friend of mine."

'I met Billy many times after this and down the years I got to know him quite well. Around twenty years later, I saw him at that same Football Writers' dinner. When the formalities were concluded, we went to the bar, where we met a young footballer of limited ability who talked about himself for twenty minutes. Billy listened patiently.

'When the young man finished his monologue, he turned to Billy. "What about you?" he asked. "Did you ever play?"

"I did," said Billy. "A long time ago."

'The young man raised an eyebrow. 'Were you any good?' he asked.

'Billy smiled. 'I was all right,' he said. 'Nothing special.'

'I was about to say something, but I kept silent. You see, you didn't argue with Billy Wright. Even when he was hopelessly wrong.'

MARTYN PRITCHARD (Buckinghamshire-based journalist with an anecdote that reveals that Billy treated all journalists, stars and starters, with equal kindness): 'As a cub reporter on the West Bromwich *Midland Chronicle*, back in 1981, I set out to interview Billy when he was Head of Sport at ITV. I missed the date of our interview. There was not one word of complaint when I finally arrived, just a gentle smile and he never once alluded to my having been something of a disorganised fool.We talked about Wolves for an hour... magic! Mr Wright was different class – a real *Boy's Own* hero and a wonderful one-club man.'

NORMAN FOX (who followed in the path of the inimitable Geoffrey Green at *The Times* and performed brilliantly; now semi-retired on the Kent coast but still writing beautifully): 'Billy was very much the star in Geoffrey Green's firmament, and he wrote some majestic pieces about him. My experiences were of meeting Billy when he had crossed over into the world of television. Like everyone else, I found him the most amazingly unassuming "superstar" you could ever meet. In particular I remember how genuinely delighted he was that his stepson Vince got a job at *The Times*. He quietly took me to one side one day to thank me warmly for encouraging him. Billy cared about people, family and otherwise. I love the story about him once telling Puskas that he really should stop eating so much or he might make himself ill in later life... fantastic when you consider how Puskas had skinned him in '53! I am working on a book to mark the 50th anniversary of the match against Hungary, and Billy's part in it all will obviously figure prominently. He was one of nature's gentlemen.'

GORDON RILEY (for many years a highly respected Shropshire journalist and a life member of the National Union of Journalists, which he joined in 1938, the same year that Billy was starting out on the football path): 'When I did a series called 'Riley Remembers' on Radio Shropshire, Billy Wright and Johnny Hancocks were two of my subjects. I had known them for some years. Johnny Hancocks was suffering from a severe stroke which had left his right side paralysed. When I interviewed him, he said Mr Cullis, and many of his old team-mates had been to see him, but Billy had not. I called Billy when he was with ATV and told him. He said, "I'll come soonest. Make the arrangements."

'Billy did not know of Johnny's plight. The reunion was poignant. They yarned about the old days and eventually it came time for Billy to go. At the front garden gate, Billy, like a gentleman, held out his hand for the handshake. Johnny grasped that hand but before releasing it, turned to us and said, "Look, I've used my right hand." It must have been magic. Johnny, although still limited in movement, returned to play bowls and I saw him later walking up the main street of Shrewsbury unaided.

'I remember Billy for being a wonderful footballer, gentleman and kind man, even when he was going through tough times in his own personal life. A Shropshire Lad of whom we are all so proud.'

PETER WATSON (former sports editor of the *London Evening News* and the *Sunday Express*, now living in retirement in Eastbourne where he spends hours polishing his golf trophies): 'I was so keen to see Billy play for Wolves when I was a schoolboy that I took a trolleybus ride and walked about a mile to get across London to see him in action against Chelsea at Stamford Bridge. This was in the days when you could reel off every team, and each player on the pitch knew the history of the club whose shirt he was proud to wear. I've forgotten the result of the match, but I was just satisfied to have seen my hero. He was only five foot eight inches tall but to my young eyes he was a giant. Years later I met him in the media world, and was just as impressed as when I saw him playing. How the game could do with his like to give some leadership today.'

STEVE GORDOS (Sports editor of the *Express & Star* in Wolverhampton, and fiercely proud of it being Britain's biggest-circulation provincial newspaper and the local paper Billy read throughout his Black Country days; Steve is without question one of the leading authorities on Wolves, and has kindly put me right on many facts and figures): 'My dad knew Billy Wright. A stallholder in Wolverhampton Market Hall, the old one not the modern monstrosity, my old man was given the name Wolfe (ideal for a Wolves fan) but was known to everyone as "Bibby". He got the nickname from a foreign nanny who could not say "baby" and always referred to him as the "bibby." As a hosier, he sold socks. Wolves players, Billy among them, were regular customers.

'Dad was a Wolves nut, who often organised away trips for fans, and he sat on the committee that arranged testimonial dinners for players. He was one of the town's personalities.

'So when, many years later, I was introduced to Billy at a quiz night at a school in Shifnal, Shropshire, his reaction was, "Bibby's lad!" and, pointing to me, he said to one of the other quiz team members: "His dad was one of the biggest rogues in Wolverhampton."

'He must have seen my face drop and quickly went on, "That was the wrong word – I mean one of the town's characters, a lovely man."

'This was, let's be honest, at the time when he was on the slide towards what is so accurately described as his greatest battle of all – against alcoholism.

'This was the man I'd watched as a kid, whose deeds loomed large in my childhood scrapbooks. I was there when he led Wolves to victory over Spartak, when he led Wolves to three First Division titles and I was at Wembley to see him play in his 100th international. Now, sadly, he was but a shadow of the superhero he once was.

'That he bounced back, beat the demon drink and was his old self by the time Sir Jack Hayward made him a Wolves director, is something for which all his many friends and fans were grateful.

'When he officially opened the stand named after him, I wrote a piece about the man accompanied by pictures of him and the Bevs at Molineux. I got a request from the club to send him the cuttings and any photographs I might have of his special night.

'I was only too happy to see to his request, as I always do with important people in the *Express & Star* circulation area. Alas, the important people don't always take the trouble to say thank you.

'However, from Billy came a lovely note – I should have kept it – saying thanks for the pictures and for what I wrote about him. He added: "You've obviously got a way with words – just like your dad."

'So he really *did* rate my old man, after all.'

DENNIS SHAW (a dear old colleague from my *Daily Herald* days, who was one of the most respected Midlands-based football writers before taking an executive role with Birmingham City): 'Billy was to me an absolute Golden Hero, the epitome of what sportsmanship was supposed to be about in our early days. I saw all the great floodlit friendlies (reported most of them for somebody or another) and everything seemed to revolve around the blond-haired guy who played every single moment of every match with one hundred per cent commitment and honesty.

'A couple of anecdotes, one against each of us. He had me presenting a one-minute run-down of the Midland team changes on his Friday night show on ATV, of which he (and he would admit it) was a not-very-good front man. On one occasion which my mates never let me forget he introduced me by saying ' ... and now over to Dennis TEAM for the SHAW changes ... '

'Move on a year or two and we were both going with the Press corps to a Wolves match in Budapest. "Hi, Bill," I greeted him at the airport. "Have you ever been to Budapest before ... ?"

'I can still see the expression of sheer disbelief on his face at the stupidity of the question. Anyone remembering the experience of England at the hands of Hungary, when Billy was captain, will know why.

'A sad memory. I was at Stamford Bridge when Chelsea beat Wolves 6–2, (five of the goals coming from a lad named Greaves with Billy unable to find him). His wonderful playing career was as good as over. There could never be another like him.'

JOHN MOYNIHAN (who reported five World Cups for the *Sunday Telegraph*; a word artist whose 1960s book *The Soccer Syndrome* is a classic that you should beg, steal or borrow...or, better still for John's royalties, buy from SportsPages!): 'Billy was a lovely man and a great footballer. I saw him first on a snowy pitch at Stamford Bridge (Christmas 1946) playing for Wolves against my beloved Chelsea team that included Billy's England team-mate Tommy Lawton. Lawton scored, but Billy with Stan Cullis (his last season as a player) dominated the match and Wolves ran out winners 2–1.

'I wrote of Billy in *The Soccer Syndrome*: "In desperation during the 1954 World Cup, England drafted Billy Wright from wing-half to centre-half and the move was a roaring success. The blond, diminutive carpet-making legend from Wolverhampton nestled into the position as though he had been living there all his life. I remember one of his last games for Wolverhampton when he was marking Tom Finney playing, himself near retirement, in a number nine role. Tom ran around like a dodgem car, but Billy was always there, squashing, without a trace of generosity, each idea served up by his rival..."

'Billy was guest of honour at a National Sporting Club dinner (at the Café Royal) in the summer of 1959 to celebrate his 100th cap for England. Among the many footballers who turned out were Jimmy Greaves, Ronnie Clayton and Jimmy Hill. Lord Brabazon said in his speech (reported for the *Evening Standard* by one John Moynihan): "Billy Wright is our hero. It is his ability to use the inside of his head as well as the outside that has made him so remarkable. Not since Romulus and Remus has there been such a distinguished Wolf."'

REG GUTTERIDGE OBE (ITV's Voice of Boxing and a life-long Arsenal supporter, and whose tea I used to make in my copyboy days on the London *Evening News*): 'I played in many golf tournaments with Billy and always found him great company. You would never believe that this was a footballing legend who had set standards of excellence that few have matched. I cannot recall him making one boastful remark about his football career, and he was also modest about his golf yet was a top-class player. He told me his one regret was that Arsenal sacked him when he felt he was on the brink of getting it right at Highbury. Billy had a rewarding career in television, but deep down I think he missed the football world and it showed in his delight when he was appointed a director at Wolves. Suddenly he was the old bubbling Billy, and he said that joining the Wolves board was "like going home" and it added twenty yards to his drives! I can think of no better role model for today's young spoiled and overpaid footballers than our Billy.'

MONTE FRESCO OBE (one of Fleet Street's finest sports photographers when with the *Daily Mirror* and now the distinguished chief executive of the top agency, Popperfoto): 'Billy was the most affable and approachable of men who, to my knowledge, never refused to cooperate with a photographer. I will never forget him joining us in Mexico for the 1970 World Cup as a member of the ITV team. He had bad experiences in the past with Mexican food, and our super *Mirror* columnist Frank McGhee elected to become his food adviser. "Just eat everything that I eat and you will be just fine," said Frank. So Billy ordered parrot-fashion everything that Frank ordered. They both spent the next 24 hours between their bed and the bathroom suffering from Montezuma's revenge! If there has been a nicer bloke in sport than Billy then I have not had the pleasure of knowing him. They threw away the mould when they made him.'

This tribute section from the press would not be complete without a Scottish view, because it was Scotland where Billy had many of his happiest days in football. I turned to a living legend in sports journalism who – in his 89th year – continues to plough the word fields as a *Racing Post* columnist...

JAMES L STEVENSON (former Scottish sports columnist with the *Daily Miror*, ex-sports editor of the northern *Daily Herald/Sun*, and for many years manager of the pioneering *Daily Mirror Punters' Club*; the first president of the Scottish Football Writers' Association in 1957): 'No one over his long spell as kingpin of England's midfield got more respect and admiration than Billy Wright when he proudly led England on to the Hampden pitch alongside Scotland's finest. And he loved it!

'The Hampden Roar from crowds well over 120,000 was a phenomenon of Glasgow's greatest venue and regarded with awe by some southerners, but not, I can tell you, by Billy when I spoke to him there after a Saturday encounter when England had been deserved winners.

'Billy told me: "I enjoy the whole setting and the noise, but it is the silence between the roars when it is our lot who are doing well that I like best!"

'Gentleman Billy, along with his lovely missus, came north several times out of season to honour Scots personalities to whom special tribute was being paid, and always the warmth of his reception proved that he was genuinely welcomed as a former adversary who was now established as a lasting friend.

'Those many this side of the border who recall the cheerful, smiling fellow who captained club and country so well will not readily forget him. Thanks for the memory, Billy...even when you were preferring silence to our legendary Hampden Roar.'

PETER YOUNG (based in Los Angeles, and the innovative, finger-on-the-pulse webmaster of one of the finest England sites on the internet at www.englandfootballonline.com): 'Billy Wright was everyone's hero in the bleak years following the Second World War. But in my family he was accorded special reverence because, so I was told, he and my paternal grandmother were born in the same house in Ironbridge. It was my grand ambition, as a young boy growing up in the Manchester area, to see Billy Wright captain England one day.

'In 1953, when I was nine, my family emigrated to Canada and four years later to the USA. The football played primarily with the feet was ignored in these strange lands, and we had to rely on the Sunday newspapers mailed by relatives for the football news. Any hope of seeing Billy Wright and England had long since left me.

'But then, one day in May 1959, as my high school French class droned along, I was summoned to the office. My father had just heard via the grapevine that England were playing the USA that very night in Los Angeles, 250 miles to the south, and he had come to take me to the match. A few hours later we arrived at the ramshackle Wrigley Field baseball park in South Central Los Angeles. And there in the flesh, his blond hair unmistakeable, was Billy Wright, England captain for ever, or so it seemed to me.

'England had a difficult time in the first half. In front of the goal they faced were the broad paths of a baseball diamond, and their passes and shots from the dirt surface went wildly awry. The USA attacked furiously and went one up. My memories of the match are dim now, but I vividly recall Billy taking command and rallying his teammates in that distinctly authoritative way he had. He had captained England in their infamous 1–0 loss to the USA at the 1950 World Cup in Brazil, and he was not going to let that happen again. England managed to equalise just before half-time, and they scored seven more goals, all unanswered, in the second half, when they passed and shot from a grass surface. Young Bobby Charlton got a hat-trick, but newcomer Jimmy Greaves went scoreless.

'More than 40 years later, that match still ranks as one of my most pleasurable experiences, all the sweeter because it came out of the blue. Only Billy Wright's remarkable longevity as England player and captain enabled my boyhood dream to become reality. It was his 105th England match, his 90th as England captain, his 70th consecutive England match, all records at the time. As it turned out, it was also his last match; he retired the following August before the season began. And so he was an England player for his entire football career, from 1946 to 1959. No one will ever match that.'

PETER ('The Poet') BATT (one of Fleet Street's great characters whose roller-coaster writing career included a long spell on the *Sun* when he was voted Sportswriter of the Year; his stunning autobiography, *Batty*, is well worth reading for anybody who thinks living is easy): 'I first saw Sergeant Billy Wright play for Wolves at Tottenham towards the end of the war when I was a young Spurs supporter. He played at inside-left and scored, and we all thought, "Who the hell is this young blond bombshell." Then he settled down to become an exceptional right-half, keeping one of my idols, Bill Nicholson, out of the England team. Later on, when working in the Midlands, I got to know Billy well socially. We drank each other under a few tables. For a bloke who never touched a drop as a player, he seemed to be making up for lost time. I was hardly the best influence on him! He was smashing company, and never once came the big "I am". Billy was the archetypal Black Country man; straight, sincere and so reliable that you could count on him in any crisis. A decade later I got to know Bobby Moore equally well, and it was amazing how alike these two great servants of English football were. Neither of them boasted and both were great ambassadors for the game and our country. I feel honoured to have watched them play, and to have had their company. I think of being with them as the summertime of my life. Great, great Englishmen.'

JEFF POWELL (award-winning sports writer with the *Daily Mail* and Boswell to the unforgettable Bobby Moore): 'I recall Bobby saying how as a youngster he studied Billy's game. Whenever Bobby talked about how he himself had no pace, could hardly head the ball and had a weak left foot he often mentioned how cleverly Billy overcame his lack of height. Thus Bobby was inspired to solve heading and pace with genius positioning and perfected the pass curved with the outside of the right foot to replicate a left-footed delivey. Bobby and Billy were two of a kind. The very best.'

And now for something completely different. This contribution comes from an old scriptwriting partner of mine with whom I used to work on the dear, departed *Daily Herald* (along with Peter Batt) in the springtime of our careers as scribblers ...

PETER CORRIGAN (the gifted chief sports columnist of the *Independent on Sunday*): 'I am delighted that you are writing a book to immortalise the great Billy – without question, one of the loveliest men I've ever met in sport. He deserves all the tributes he will undoubtedly be paid, and as a Welshman I'll just say I wish he had been born a few miles west of Shropshire.

'I will never forget how charming his wife, Joy, was despite being bombarded with calls from the likes of you and me on a daily basis in his turbulent days as Arsenal manager. My everlasting memory concerning Billy was in 1973 when he was with the media corps covering England's summer tour which included the fateful defeat in Poland that eventually led to Sir Alf Ramsey's demise. After Poland, we went to the USSR and then on to Turin to play Italy. Brian Glanville, multi-lingual, multi-talented writer and would-be footballer, had told us all to take our boots because he had arranged a match in Turin against the Italian press.

'Billy, then approaching 50, was in the team, and so was Maurice Edelston, who had played in a wartime Cup final. Ken Jones of the famous Welsh footballing family was included, along with – no relation – Peter Jones of the BBC, who had been a good-class amateur. The rest of the side was made up of willing but useless players like me, Jeff Powell of the *Daily Mail* and Reg Drury of the *News of the World*, along with, I seem to remember, Nigel Clarke, who was ghosting Bobby Moore for the *Mirror*, but could not impersonate him on the pitch.

'Anyhow, on the morning of what we thought was going to be just a kick-about game, Billy Wright happened to notice his picture in a story at the top of the main sports page of the local paper. There was this piece of about 1,000 words eulogising this great side that Glanville had put together.

'The Italian press side, the article informed us, contained five fairly recent Juventus players and there was an ex-Italian international in goal.

' "What on earth have you go us into?" we demanded of Glanville.

' "It will be good for Anglo-Italian relations," said he who could speak Italian better than most of the rest of us could speak English. He should have said "no" to this mis-match in any language he could put his tongue to.

'It was even worse than we feared when we got to the ground. There were about 4,000 spectators, and renditions of the British and Italian anthems were followed by each of us being presented with a big bouquet. The "kick about" was being given all the build-up and trappings of an international match. A ball had not been kicked and we were looking to bury Mr Glanville.

'The game was a total embarrassment, and it didn't take Billy long to realise that he was surrounded mainly by incompetents. Even approaching 50, Billy was ten times better than any other member of the team; a hundred times better than Glanville.

'Needless to say, Glanville took stick from everyone as we battled to stay in the game against vastly superior and much fitter opponents. Glanville, proud of being one of the Casuals back home in London, was playing extremely casually at left-back and in no time at all the right-winger had scored three goals.

'Billy was despairing over the performance from Glanville and, when we went in 4–0 down at half-time, he gave him a massive rollocking for failing to look after his winger. Controlling himself well, Billy suggested he would be happier if Glanville stayed in the dressing-room for the second half.

'Glanville wandered across the dressing-room to where I was sitting and said quietly: "He may have 105 caps for England but he knows nothing about zonal marking!"

'I thought I would have died suppressing the laughter but it was not a laughing matter. We went out like men to face the second-half slaughter but worse was to come. Ken Jones started to kick more than the ball and Jeff Powell decided to show how hard he was, too.

'The mood of the Italians suddenly changed. I was playing centre-forward (more Ray Charles than John Charles) and I was kicked up in the air with the ball 30 yards away. It got very nasty and the crowd were starting to climb the fencing around the pitch.

'We'd played only ten minutes of the second half when the ref blew his whistle and ran for the safety of the dressing-rooms with Billy and the rest of us gratefully racing behind him.

'I think it safe to say that Billy did not enjoy the experience. I just hope that this wasn't his last game. I doubt if he ever forgave Glanville, and in later years we had many a laugh with Billy over his lack of appreciation of the arts of zonal marking.'

In the interests of fair play for which my generation of journalists are renowned, I went to Brian Glanville for his version of events. Brian is revered and respected throughout sports journalism and also the literary world for his writing and his intellect, and his *Story of the World Cup* is the definitive history of the tournament.

BRIAN GLANVILLE: 'Before we went on to the pitch in Turin I have to say that my relationship with Billy was not very warm after I had been less than genial about his managership of Arsenal. Though I would like to mention that when he left I was so incensed, feeling that he had been betrayed by Denis Hill-Wood, that I wanted to draw a cartoon showing the Arsenal chairman stabbing him in the back with the weasel words, "I'm backing Billy Wright up to the hilt." The 1973 game that Peter Corrigan recalls was I think the nadir of our relations, though he was all smiles the next day. Least said, soonest mended. I had keenly followed Billy's career from his debut in the Victory International against Belgium at Wembley. Only recently, when selecting the best World Cup team for 1958 for a Japanese magazine, I chose Billy at centre-half.'

A PS from Norman Giller: The 1973 match (best that we draw a Turin shroud over it?) was *not* Billy's last game. Along with my then partner Peter Lorenzo and colleague Malcolm Rowley, I organised a testimonial match in 1975 for a long-serving Chelmsford stalwart called Don Walker. He was one of the loyal, unheralded band of players who had given a lifetime's service to the game with little reward. When I told Billy about the match, he immediately volunteered his services and helped us bring in the likes of Bobby Robson, Tommy Docherty, Jimmy Hill, Dave Sexton and Mike England for an All-Stars XI that drew several hundred fans to Chelmsford.

That was how Billy finished his playing career, at the age of 51 and giving his time for a relative unknown. Typical of the man.

It is not too strong a descriptive word to say that Billy was 'loved' by his colleagues in the tightknit Central Television team that he put together in Birmingham. He was so affable and easy going that he left himself open to a lot of leg-pulling, and was the victim of gags masterminded by Chris Tarrant in his madcap Tiswas days and who occupied an adjoining office.

CHRIS TARRANT: 'I was actually one of the few people who ever made Billy completely lose his rag. He had been kicked up hill and down dale by hatchet men on the football field without ever retaliating but he was once ready to tear me limb from limb. I told the story on his *This Is Your Life* show of how I pulled a prank with a toilet brush that resulted in Billy getting soaking wet, and I mean drowned-rat wet. He completely lost it and chased me around the office ready to do serious damage if he had got hold of me. But once he had cooled down and dried off he laughed it off, and was back to his usual likeable self. I don't think there is a person walking this earth with a bad thing to say about him. He was much much more than a football hero. He managed to lift everybody he met.'

Billy was famous for his malapropisms, some of them uttered on air ('Marsh went through the defence there like a knife through toast'... 'Osgood looks a new man, just like his old self...'), but he was always able to laugh at himself, a gift that has not been given to some television personalities who take themselves far too seriously. Billy was never ever guilty of that, and he was so popular that when he had his difficulties because of his drink problem his staff worked together to cover his tracks.

These are some of the memory contributions from his old television colleagues:

GARY NEWBON: 'Billy played a major part in my life both professionally and privately. He was responsible for my move from presenting sport for Westward Television in Plymouth to doing the same job for him at ATV in Birmingham. I joined him in December 1971, six months after he helped a young lady, Katie While, into the company as the editor's secretary for the local news programme. Billy played a part in matchmaking Katie and myself. We married in October 1973 and now have three children.

'When our twin boys were born in 1977 Billy gave me a couple of England caps for them on the condition that I would not give them to Laurence and Neil until they can fully appreciate them.

'Acknowledging that I was a journalist and he was a football man, Billy always gave me the freedom to run the shows and supported me all the time. He was generous and always a gentleman; a famous person who never chose to remind you of it. He had time for everyone – never forgot a name and never refused an autograph, photograph or interview.

'I took Billy's job a long time before he retired in 1989, but it had to be with his blessing. Billy was delighted for me to have the controller of sport role. We had spent a long time together at work and he told me I deserved it. He enjoyed TV but above all he loved football and his Wolves. When Sir Jack Hayward made him a director at Molineux after he retired from Central Television, Billy had five wonderful years before he lost the battle against cancer.

'I miss him. But there is always a permanent reminder for me – a wife, three great children, two of his England caps, a Molineux stand named after Billy and a wonderful statue outside the main entrance. I was proud to represent his widow, Joy, and the family on the "Statue" committee. It was my privilege to have known and to have worked alongside this very special man.'

TREVOR EAST (a high-powered backroom force at Sky Sports): 'I owe so much to Billy. He plucked me out of the obscurity of a local news agency at Derby and launched my career in television when I was a 21-year-old nobody. He was always supportive and tremendously encouraging. Even in those days at ATV and Central when we were looking at life through the bottom of a glass you could not lose respect for the man. I still chuckle at the fact that I made Billy swear on the football field, something for which he was famous for never doing during his glorious career. We were playing in a testimonial match, Billy well into his 50s. Gary Newbon was playing alongside him and charging around like a Sherman tank – a bit like his interviewing style – while Billy was all about style, poise and composure. I was showing off, trying to beat a man too many when a frustrated voice carried across the pitch, "Get rid of the ball, East. Who d'you think you are...f— Puskas!" Lovely memories. Lovely man.'

NICK OWEN (vastly experienced presenter now with BBC Midlands): 'I first met William Ambrose as an autograph hunter in 1960. It was the first footballer's autograph I ever had! He was playing in a showbiz match after his retirement in my home town of Berkhamsted in Hertfordshire. I was so thrilled to speak to him as a little boy of about thirteen and never realised that, some eighteen years later, he would give me my first job in television. I have some lovely memories of him getting his words mixed up. On one occasion, his car broke down on the M1 as he was coming to work. He told me he had to pull up on the cold shoulder! It was a privilege to work with him and I shall always be grateful for his decision to give me a chance in television. It gave me nearly two decades on national TV, presenting a huge variety of different programmes with the opportunity to travel all over the world. Bill, thank you very much.'

HUGH JOHNS (an outstanding commentator who joined ATV at the same time as Billy in 1966): 'Billy and I were joint presenters of *Star Soccer*, and we had some great times together. I know he would have been the first to admit that he was not exactly the most confident of people working to the camera and he used to call himself "Silly Billy" when his tongue got twisted. He was very self-effacing and could laugh at himself, which is a great quality and it helped him through the difficult stage of learning how to be natural in front of a camera. Not easy, I promise you.

'Billy came into his own on our many trips abroad to the major tournaments when he could open any door simply because everybody in world football knew the name Billy Wright. I recall that during the 1970 World Cup finals in Guadalajara the commentary box was right at the top of a concrete crater of a stadium. We used to have to take three breaks on the way up because each stone step was eighteen inches high, and in that rarefied air it was difficult to catch our breath. One day we decided to count the steps, and they totalled exactly one hundred and five. From then on they became known as Billy's International Steps. He was an absolutely wonderful person, who had no side to him. When you think of all the great things he achieved, he was an exceptionally modest man. I considered it a privilege to have him as a friend and colleague.'

TERRY BIDDLECOMBE (former National Hunt champion jockey and employed as the team's racing expert): 'I worked with Gary and the team for many happy years, and every week used to bring up a joint of meat from the farm for Billy. The lads said that was the only way I could keep my job! One particular Friday Billy forgot to take his meat home, and Jimmy Greaves was delegated to take it to him after he had finished a late-night stint. It was the early hours of the morning when Greavsie finally got to Billy, who was standing at his garden gate in his pyjamas guiding Jimmy towards him with a torch! The picture in my mind of England's greatest captain and England's greatest goalscorer in that situation always amuses me. Billy was a lovely lovely man, and we had some sensational times in Lorenzo's, the Italian restaurant run by Lorenzo Ferrari and which was like Billy's unofficial headquarters when he was based in Birmingham.'

BOB GILMAN (a top-ranking programme editor in the Billy Wright team): 'He was a splendid man, a good colleague and a caring person. I have only warm memories of him. We all know he had a problem with drink, but he had the character to overcome it. I think he might have been the worse for wear at his farewell party at Central. We presented him with a motorised golf buggy as a parting gift, and he decided to try it out there and then. He managed to push the wrong button and drove into the crowd. It was a startling moment, and – as usual – Billy was there laughing away with the rest of us.'

PAULINE MARSTON (who worked for Billy as his secretary when he was controller of sport at ATV in Birmingham): 'Billy was a lovely man to work for, never irritated or cross. He lived with Joy in the Southeast, but had a flat in Birmingham during the week. Bill was good at his job for two reasons. One was that because he was who he was, and everybody liked him, he used to get some wonderful guests – top sports people of that era, like Sir Alf Ramsey, Christine Janes, Anita Lonsborough and many others. The other reason was that he just had a nose for a story. He would sometimes say to me that he hadn't heard anything from, say, Derby or Moseley, or such and such cricket club, and that he just had a feeling. He would go down, usually that same day, and time and time again, he would get to the club in time to be given a major story just before it broke to the public. He would often be asked to keep it quiet for a day or two, and being Billy, he always did (a matter of honour, you see), but he would have his story ready to run as soon as he was given permission, and thus beat all his rivals. Because Billy never let down any of the people who had given him information, he was trusted, and therefore, people were always ready to talk to him.'

OLIVIA FONDYG (who followed Pauline as Billy's discreet and protective secretary): 'I was already working in the newsroom when Pauline left and I applied for her job. The partnership lasted for many happy and eventful years until Gary Newbon took over as controller. However, I always remember the interview:

'Billy: "You would like to work for me then Olivia?"

'Olivia: "Yes."

'Billy: "Okay!"

'What I discovered working closely with him is that he was a lovely man who generated a great deal of warmth and laughter to all his colleagues, and his memory still does.

'All of us who worked with Billy could tell a tale or two, but doesn't it show the love people have for his memory that no one ever does. He was a wonderful man, and that's all anybody needs to know.'

JOHN WEBSTER (former Adult Education producer at ATV and Central who later became director of televison at Sheffield University): 'Bill, as head of sport, and Tony Flanagan, head of outside broadcasts, always held court in their offices on the ground floor from where there would be frequent shouts of laughter and frantic activity, with the drinks cabinet usually open, especially if John Bromley was in town! The corner pub was the lunchtime meeting place for the regular gang. Spirits were high and the relationships between departments were warm and friendly. I proposed a series of thirteen programmes in the adult education (for leisure) category called *Rules of the Game*. The concept was that to enjoy playing and watching sport it would be enhanced by an understanding of the rules! Faced with harnessing the resources and experts to produce thirteen programmes covering all the major sports I turned to my mates Billy Wright and Tony Flanagan, and we obtained the best ratings ever recorded for an adult education series. It was a privilege to have known Billy as a friend and to have worked with him as a colleague. A great bloke – a man's man.'

BOB HALL (a highly regarded Carlton sports presenter and reporter who, with me as a witness, scored nineteen out of twenty on a Billy Wright quiz that I put on the www.billywright.co.uk website): 'I had never been to Birmingham – or indeed the Midlands – when I first took a short contract at ATV. I knew WAW was head of sport, but hadn't reckoned with my first morning. Stood as I was in the newsroom saying hello to my new colleagues, the doors at the far end of the room swung open and through walked Billy Wright. I stood open-mouthed that the man who I had only seen in a childhood *Charles Buchan's Soccer Annual* had come to life – not in old gold and black with a ball at his feet, but a man of surprisingly short stature for a world-class centre-half. Trying and failing not to stare, he smiled and came straight up to me. "Bob, heard you were joining us – welcome," and he shook my hand. Like a latter-day schoolboy in front of Michael Owen I mumbled a thank you and watched him walk off. Impressed wasn't the word.

'But Billy was forever modest, never I suspect realising just what a hero he was to so many, and what a world star he was. A letter once arrived at Molineux years after he had retired simply addressed, "Billy Wright, England." No fear of the post office losing that one!

'I was the compere on the night Wolves dedicated their main stand to him. A tear in his eye, Billy turned to me. "Isn't it marvellous," he said. I nodded. "But why me?" he asked. And the question was genuine.'

JIMMY HILL (the man who as PFA chairman did more than anybody to break the chains of soccer slavery that bound Billy throughout his career): 'I had not long left football management at Coventry to take over as head of sport at London Weekend Television when my secretary told me that Lew (later Lord) Grade was on the telephone. As he was the most powerful man in television and the boss of ATV I wondered what on earth he wanted. Tugging at my forelock, I took the telephone. "Jimmy," he said, "can you get me a couple of tickets for the Cup final?" I was speechless for a moment. "But surely as Billy Wright is your head of sport," I replied, 'you should be asking him.' There was a pause. "Oh but I couldn't possibly ask, Billy," he said. It is an anecdote that illustrates the enormous respect that Billy generated. He was a very special man.'

I wind up this media-tributes section with contributions from three giants of the broadcasting world whose names will tug at the heart-strings of all my old Fleet Street and television colleagues. Tragically, each of them passed on while this biography was being prepared.

When I was first working on the book, I took time off to collaborate with ITV's Voice of Football **BRIAN MOORE** on his autobiography, *The Final Score*. Brian and I had been close pals for years, and we often dined together with Billy, most memorably at Lorenzo's in Birmingham, an Italian restaurant where Billy and the Central Gang were legendary... and often legless! Sadly, Brian was beaten by cancer in the winter of 2001 but I know that he would want me to include this tribute wrapped in an anecdote that he gave me: 'I first met Billy when I was a starry-eyed young sub-editor on that wonderful old magazine *World Sports*. Billy came into the office for something or other in that year of 1954 when Wolves were the talk of the land because of their floodlit thrillers with the likes of Honved and Moscow Spartak. You can imagine how much in awe I was of the captain of England and of Wolves. Our editor Cecil Bear introduced me to Billy as he was showing him out of the office. I expected a perfunctory nod of the head, but instead he stood and chatted to me for five or ten minutes, asking me about my job and my ambitions. I was an absolute nobody, but here was this great man talking to me as if I was a star sports writer. It made a lasting impression on me, and as I climbed the ladder I always tried to give time to youngsters the way Billy had done for me.

'Years later we became good friends, and I ached to see him having such a difficult time as manager at Arsenal where I feel that two or three of his players did not give him the dedicated service he had a right to expect. Only those of us close to him realised the strain the job was putting on him, and he used to be physically sick before and after games. Yet his door was never closed to the prying media, and he was just as welcoming as always.

'When he crossed into my world of broadcasting I welcomed him with open arms. He knew his strengths and weaknesses, and cut back on his on-camera work after an uncomfortable opening phase to his new career. He delegated brilliantly, and I know that Gary Newbon and the team up there in Birmingham thought the world of him.

'Billy had been a great footballer, but much much more than that – he was a wonderful human being.'

These words were in my mind a year or so later when Brian's widow, Betty, and sons Richard and Simon kindly allowed me the privilege of delivering the eulogy – along with Bob Wilson and Lord Bernard Weatherill – at Brian's memorial service.

Take it from me, both Brian and Billy were wonderful human beings.

Just a week before he died in the spring of 2002, legendary football commentator **KENNETH WOLSTENHOLME OBE, DFC and Bar** responded to my request for a Billy Wright anecdote. He told me from his retirement home in Brixham, Devon: 'I had the pleasure of commentating virtually throughout Billy's entire career with England and Wolves. I can safely say that England did not have a better ambassador than Billy, who was impeccable with his behaviour and always ultra-efficient with his football. He played for the team, and encouraged everybody around him. He accepted any criticism coming his way in the same level-headed manner that he accepted praise, and was always approachable and affable. I just wonder how he would have fitted into today's game in which so many players seem to be self-centred. Billy did not even know the meaning of the word selfish. I saw him at his lowest moments, the defeats by the United States and Hungary; but never once did he let his head drop. He was a born leader, and England were very lucky to have him at what was a revolutionary time for our game. Thanks for everything, Billy.'

The last word on behalf of the media goes to the one, definitely the only **JOHN BROMLEY**. He was an exceptional sports writer whose path I followed in local East London newspapers and then on to the *Daily Herald*, with John always sending me words of encouragement as I tried (and failed) to meet his standards. John, Brommers to everybody, was a top columnist on the *Daily Mirror* before climbing off at the top of the mountain to switch to the then exciting young world of commercial television sport. He became the innovative boss of ITV sport, and along the way strengthened his friendship with Billy, whose playing career he used to report.

I wanted John to have a say in this tribute section because he knew Billy better than most. Sadly, when it came time for me to contact him for a contribution he was into the last days of a courageous two-year battle against cancer. I went ahead with my request for a quote because I thought that if I left Brommers out I would be giving up the fight on his behalf. The message sent to me from John's hospital bed through our mutual pal Reg Gutteridge was: 'I want to be included, old commander, but am not quite up to it at the moment. Get something from the cuttings!' Dear John passed on four days later. Rest easy, old friend.

This was the fitting contribution I found in Billy's cuttings book...

JOHN BROMLEY (from a *Daily Herald* interview, 1958): 'For a man who has won nearly 90 caps for his country, Billy Wright is remarkably unspoiled. With the World Cup only weeks away, I found him in a surprisingly upbeat mood considering English football is still under the black cloud cast by the Munich air disaster. 'It is important that we do our very very best for Roger Byrne, Tommy Taylor and dear Duncan Edwards,' the England captain said, sincerity shining through in every word. 'We owe it to their memories. They would not want us to just surrender. Every England player has got to try that little bit harder to make up for their tragic loss. We are all grieving, but life – and football – must go on."

What the Supporters Say

First and foremost, Billy was a man and a hero of the people. He could identify with them, and they with him. Never once did he consider himself elevated above them, even with all his success for club and country. He never lost that common touch of the footballer who learned he was to captain his country while sitting aboard a public transport bus.

This would not be a complete biography without a contribution from the supporters who shared Billy's ups and downs across all his years of service with Wolves and England. There are also many Arsenal fans who have affectionate memories of him, despite his failure to bring any trophies to Highbury, which ranked second only to Molineux as his favourite football home. I include several contributions from the younger generation who did not have the good fortune to see Billy play, but have been sufficiently moved by his legend to want to take part in the tributes. Billy would have approved of their involvement, because he always strongly believed that football belonged to the youth of the world.

Following are a cross section of the tributes that poured in when I contacted the *Wolverhampton Express & Star*, the *Shropshire Star*, Carlton TV, BBC Midlands radio, good media mates, the excellent Wolves internet site (www.wolves.co.uk), and various other websites to ask for Billy Wright stories. Out of necessity, these are heavily edited versions of the memories and tributes that appear in full on the Billy Wright website at www.billywright.co.uk, and you are very welcome to add a comment there in the special memorial book.

LAWRENCE CULLIS (Dawley, Shropshire): 'Back in 1937 I captained the Madeley Modern school football team in which Billy first started to make a name for himself. He was a year younger, but easily good enough for the senior team. Billy was an exceptionally fast runner and we called him the Ironbridge Rocket. He helped us win the Dawley Shield sprint relay cup. Fifty years later the three other members of the team, Arthur Russell, John Norry and myself, were reunited with Billy on his *This Is Your Life* show. The only surprise is that Billy won his fame as a defender, while at school he was an outstanding goalscoring forward.'

ERNEST SOUTHAN (Kinlet, Worcestershire): 'I was a schoolboy mate of Billy's, and we used to run together in the athletics team. I clearly remember trying to make him have a celebration drink at Wembley after he had captained Wolves to victory in the 1949 FA Cup final. But Billy insisted that he would only drink orange juice. That's how dedicated he always was.'

ALAN TAYLOR (Wilimington, North Carolina): 'I used to live at 32 Burland Avenue in Wolverhampton, a few doors down from Billy. As a toddler I really didn't comprehend the stature of the man known to us as "Billy". I do know that he always had time for the children on the avenue. On one occasion I crashed into his wall with my bike. He was the first there. He straightened my front wheel out, then walked me down the avenue towards my house. During the next few years I stood in awe at the Molineux watching the same Billy rise above the best to nod the ball down the field or to a team-mate. There's an old saying, "You can never go back, but you can remember"... I will. I am still in awe of "The Great One."'

CHRISTINE CLARKE (Mornington, Victoria, Australia): 'I hero-worshipped Billy when he was *the* captain and Wolves were *the* team. One day in the early 1950s – a very reserved 14-year-old schoolgirl – I worked up the courage to ask for his autograph when he was in the pavilion during a cricket match. I was extremely shy at the time and he put me at my ease with that nice smile of his. Suddenly, just as he was signing an autograph book that I had taken in for a friend, a press photographer's flashbulb went off and I nearly jumped out of my skin. I could not get away fast enough! The following week the *Wolverhampton Chronicle* published a picture of Billy signing his autograph for "an unknown admirer". Wolves continue to be *the* team for me even now I am all these miles away in Australia. My son, Ian, lives and works in Southampton and keeps me in touch with what is going on at the club where I have such fond memories of Billy and the Boys. They truly were the Golden Days.'

JOHN POWELL (Librarian and Information officer, Ironbridge Gorge Museum): 'We are very proud that Ironbridge was the birthplace of one of the world's greatest footballers. A plaque, unveiled by his widow Joy in 1998, marks the house where he was born overlooking the iron bridge in our historic town. Billy officially opened the Ironbridge Tollhouse for us in 1974, and remains a great local hero. As a Wolves season ticket holder of many seasons, I take particular pride in Billy's Ironbridge background!'

JEAN MASON (Willenhall): 'I am one of the lucky ones to have seen the great Billy Wright play and I also met him in unusual circumstances. It was during Billy's early years at Molineux. I myself was in the ATS at the time, and Billy was still a serving soldier. I came home on leave one weekend and, because I loved dancing, went to the local dance at the Wolverhampton Civic Hall. Billy was there, and I was really chuffed when he asked me for a dance. It was a 'ladies' excuse-me' and we had hardly gone a dozen steps when an attractive blonde tapped me on the shoulder and politely said, "Excuse me." Ah well, at least Billy had asked me for a dance.'

KEITH DUNN (Boston, Lincs): 'I have collected and collated many things on the life of the great Billy Wright. The most treasured thing of all came following his sad departure. When Billy died I wrote a letter to Joy Beverley care of my beloved Wolverhampton Wanderers. I thought no more about it, but then I got a fancy envelope in my post. I thought it was an invitation or an advertising gimmick. When opening the envelope I just could not believe my eyes. It was a letter from Joy Beverley, and it reduced both my wife, Shirley, and I to tears. Joy wrote about "her darling Billy" and said how kind and considerate he had always been. That letter is now framed and has pride of place on the wall in my Wolves Memorabilia room. I am a disabled person, and with not being able to work I have devoted my life to WWFC. I have supported the club now for 45 years and in that time William Ambrose Wright was, without question, the greatest of all WWFC players I have known.'

RAYMOND C F BROWN (Penn): 'As a Wolves supporter for more than 63 years, I can speak with some authority about Billy Wright the player and also Billy Wright the man. I was the public-address announcer at Molineux for thirteen years and also served as press officer, and have for many years been a match-day commentator for Radio Wulfrun, Wolverhampton's hospital radio station. The pleasure of being witness to Billy's undoubted sporting talent was only to be surpassed by the privilege of having his company. From his days as the youngest apprentice right through to becoming a director, he was always the same: courteous, humorous and kindly, and ever available to give advice and encouragement.'

CHARLIE BAMFORTH (Davis, California): 'Robert Plant, lead singer of Led Zeppelin and sex god to many, once told me in an interview about his first, and most enduring, "love affair"... for Wolves. He was four years old, sat astride his uncle's shoulders and watching the gold shirts take the field at Molineux. And the man who cemented that life-long passion for Wolves? 'Billy Wright. He turned and waved – to me, nobody else, to *me*. When Billy's *Book of Soccer* came out my mother got him to sign it – and from then on I've been friends with the captain of England and Wolves. That was such an outstanding moment in my life.'

'Billy welcomed me to his desk at the Central TV studios in Birmingham in the last week of his working life. He was a humble and patient man, perfectly happy to answer questions that he must have fielded countless times before. My article based on the interview appeared in the Wolves programme – in three separate issues, which was testimony to the depth of the story. Not long afterwards Billy became a director.'

PAUL and NICK RICHARDS (ex-Finchfield, now Christchurch, Dorset): 'My dad sat under the Molineux Street clock throughout the Golden Fifties. I find it hard to describe the enjoyment which watching Billy gave to him. Whenever we discussed football, Dad always spoke of him with fondness, admiration and wonder. 'A real footballer,' he said. And he meant it. One day, after Billy joined the Wolves board, I waited before a first-team match with my then ten-year-old son to speak with him. I thanked him on behalf of my late father for all the happiness he had given, and for coming back to Molineux. He spent time chatting to me and to my son, he signed our matchday programme, and he said, almost as if it was in confidence: 'There's only ever been one team for me, you know.' How I wished I had seen him play. Dad's life was happier because of Billy.'

SUSAN DUFFELL (Perton): 'My mother, Joyce Green, nee Matthews, was a supervisor at the local laundry used by Wolves, and she remembers very well playing footie with Billy Wright's rolled-up socks and donning the rest of his strip before it was returned to Molineux. She is 72 now and is still an ardent Wolves fan. She recalls standing in the "Cow Shed" [a terrace] and having sixpenny bets with the older men at the matches on Saturdays. Great days, great memories.'

FRANK PARDOE (Harley Warren, Worcester): 'I worked for the Football League as an assessor, looking at the match officials. I took a colleague from work, Peter Hayhurst, and his eight-year-old son, David, to a game at Molineux after Billy had joined the board. While sitting in the lounge before the game Billy came to talk to us and became interested in young David's knowledge of football. The question then arose, "How good are you?" Billy then left us, but within a minute had returned with a ball and signalled for us to follow him. Down the stairs we went, past the dressing-rooms and on to the pitch where we all had a lesson in ball control just minutes before the game was due to start. It was a never-to-be-forgotten moment for all of us.'

JEFF LYONS (Hull, Yorkshire): 'My favourite team Wolves were playing my local team Hull City at Boothferry Park. My hero was Steve Bull and after he had kindly signed a photograph for me, a steward tapped me on the shoulder and pointed. "Now there's a signature you *have* to get," he said. Yes, it was the great Billy Wright. As I asked him for his autograph, he smiled and, turning to a lady by his side, said, "You want her autograph not mine – she is far more famous than me." Of course it was his wife Joy. Billy was such a modest and unassuming man – a true great.'

BILL NEW (Didcot, Oxon): 'I have a copy of his book, *Football is my Passport*, bought for my thirteenth birthday by my mother (I am now 56), and I will always treasure that. He truly was one of the great players of all time. Wolves must always strive to keep his memory alive.'

MICHAEL J SLATER: 'In the 1980s I wrote a book on Wolves' history. My research took me to libraries, bookshops, the Football League HQ, the Football Association HQ and many other places. I never once heard or read a bad word about Billy Wright, either as a footballer or a man. Among Billy's collection of goals for Wolves was one in just twenty seconds in the 1946–47 First Division match against Everton. The ball was in the net before an opponent had even touched the ball. So the legend of Billy Wright is not just about preventing goals!'

TOMMY BARRATT (Corby, Northants): 'I am a season ticket holder in the Jack Harris stand, and I always touch Billy's statue for luck on my way into the ground before every home game.'

NEIL EVERITT (Nottingham): 'I live in Nottingham now, but used to have a season ticket on the south bank/Jack Harris stand. I am so pleased that Wolves built a stand in Billy's honour whilst he was still alive.'

CLAIRE EVANS (Bearwood, Warley): 'My only experience of meeting Billy Wright is after losing at Derby in the early nineties. My father and I stopped to talk to him about what was going wrong at the club as Billy was a director by then. He was diplomatic enough to make no dishonourable comments. I felt privileged to have met such a great ambassador not only for Wolves, but England too.'

ROGER PHILLIPS (Foxton Leicestershire): 'In 1956 we lived in Germany where my father was serving with the RAF. My mother went into the military maternity hospital in early January where my sister, Melinda, was born. The nurse looking after my mother said she was a Wolves fan and my mother said, "I use the same bus as Billy. I'll write to him and get his autograph." Not only did he send his autograph – he also sent tickets for the England vs. West Germany international to be staged in occupied Berlin the following May! My father, a pilot, wangled a flight for himself and the nurse and went to the game. England won the match with a wonder goal from Duncan Edwards. Oh, by the way, Melinda is also a season ticket holder at Molineux.'

NEIL PATERSON (Cheltenham): 'I think that the statue that bears Billy's name is one of the best of its kind. You can stand under it and imagine what it must have been like to follow him out on to the pitch, catching a glimpse of the motto on the way out of the tunnel . . . ("Out of darkness cometh light").'

JONATHAN TAYLOR (Wolverhampton): 'I became a Wolves season ticket holder in 1994 at the tender age of ten, but it was not until later in my Wolves education that I came to fully appreciate the achievements of Billy Wright. Unfortunately these circumstances were his death, and I remember the following Wolves home game against Tranmere. The minute's silence before the match was immaculately observed. Sitting in the stand named after Mr Wright, I felt that this man must have done something very special for the club and his country that all fans respected.'

ROGER WINFIELD (London): 'The third round of the Cup was the most exciting day in the football calendar. In January 1966 we (that is, Arsenal) had been drawn against Blackburn Rovers away. Billy Wright had been manager for about four years. He had found managing more difficult than playing and by early 1966 the fans and the press were becoming restless with the continuing lack of success at Highbury. At twenty to five on that Saturday in January 1966 Arsenal's season was over again for another year. Beaten 3–0 by Blackburn, the team had touched rock bottom.

'The journey home was a sombre affair. We had a struggle to get our reserved compartment, which had been occupied by fans in a less than friendly mood and we travelled in complete darkness when the lights failed. The promised buffet car was nowhere to be found. As we approached Euston I found myself standing next to the manager, yes, Billy Wright. Despite the pressure he must have been under Billy was warm and friendly to we fans who were uneasy in the company of the man most of us felt by then should be replaced.

'He thanked us for supporting the team and regretted not being able to reward us with a win. What a lovely man, I thought. I was still next to Billy as we started to walk along the platform towards the exit. There was a great deal of shouting coming from behind the barrier. I realised that a large group of Arsenal fans had assembled to meet the train and they were not in a happy mood. The cries were "Wright out. Wright out."

'I can still picture the long stretch of platform between us and the barrier. I can still hear the cries of "Wright out" getting louder and louder as we approached that barrier. Billy was walking alone. There were no club officials near him and we, the supporters, dropped behind him, whether out of respect or embarrassment I don't know. The man walked into and through this hail of abuse.

'If only, I thought, they knew what a nice man he was!'

NEIL RAPHAEL (Pickering, North Yorkshire): 'I was taken to Stamford Bridge by my father when I was six. My main memory was this determined blond defender in gold and black beating Roy Bentley in the tackle. That defender was Billy Wright and the gold and black was far more scintillating than blue and white. I was a Wolves supporter from that tackle onwards. I am a founder member of the London Wolves Supporters Club (1966). There have been many players and memories over that time but Billy Wright was the catalyst for my love of Wolves.'

NEIL SAMBROOK (Shropshire Football Association): 'In March 1989, my father, Roy Sambrook, had an operation in the Royal Shrewsbury Hospital. After visiting him one afternoon I was walking down the corridor of the hospital, when I passed someone I recognised. I turned and asked: "Excuse me Mr Wright, my dad, who is a lifelong Wolves supporter, is just recovering from an operation and it would really cheer him up if you could spare him a few minutes to say hello." Later that day I went back to visit my dad, who from a poorly state in the afternoon was now sitting up in bed and clearly in a much improved condition: "You'll never guess who I was talking to for half an hour this afternoon," he said, "No, who?" I enquired. "Only Billy Wright," Dad announced proudly. "I came round and there he was sitting on the side of the bed." Thirty minutes with Billy Wright did him more good than any amount of drugs and medicines.'

JEM MAIDMENT (Highgate, London N6): 'About five years ago I interviewed Joy – I'm a journalist – and at the end of our chat I told her I was an Arsenal fan. She then told me how Billy enjoyed his time at Arsenal even though "things didn't work out". I had an original copy of Billy's 1961 autobiography *100 Caps and All That* and told her how much I had enjoyed it. Her eyes lit up and so I told her if I could dig it out I'd send it to her. She was absolutely delighted, and even sent me a nice card thanking me. It's something of a boring anecdote but it reveals the love that existed between Billy and Joy.'

ANDY REEVES (Wolverhampton): 'Billy was a great man who loved his football and I am so proud to say that he played for Wolves. He was a footballing legend who should have been knighted.'

BOB CROCKETT (Hinckley, Leicestershire): 'My greatest thrill as a young boy was to see Billy play against Charlton in 1956, my first ever Wolves game. Billy was a true legend – a great footballer and a gentleman. When I played football at school I used to try to emulate Billy Wright and always volunteered to play centre-half. When people talk about role models he was one of the best.'

TRULS MANSSON (Stockholm, Sweden): 'The name Billy Wright is still known and respected all over the world, including my country – Sweden. He was one of the most famous players in football who inspired a young boy in Sweden, Ingvar Carlsson – later prime minister of Sweden – to become a Wolves fan. Billy Wright was a true sportsman and gentleman. A great servant to Wolverhampton Wanderers, England and to football in general.'

Norman Giller note: Truls is arguably the No 1 overseas supporter of Wolves, and his riveting website at www.trulswolves.com should be a must place to visit for Molineux fans. It has a huge following among U.K. as well as dyed-in-the-Wolves Scandinavian supporters.

JOHN JARVIS (Wigan, Lancs): 'I was privileged to be a guest of Wolves director John Harris during the Christmas period of 1993. The game was against Bolton Wanderers at Molineux. We were in the Golden Room, having just made the journey by car on the M6 from Wigan. Suddenly, the door opened, and in walked Billy. "Hello there. Hope you've all had a happy Christmas. All the best . . . ," he whispered, walking across the room smiling and into the private directors' lounge. What struck me was his civility and cheerfulness; he was clearly very ill at the time. This was a special day, in more ways than one: Wolves won by one goal to nil; and I'd met Billy Wright.'

LAURENCE FOSTER (Terenure, Dublin): 'I first saw Billy Wright play for Wolves when I was ten years old. It was the autumn of 1954 against Newcastle United and I watched with awe as he doggedly subdued the great Jackie Milburn. Five years later I was present at the memorable "Colours" versus "Whites" match at Molineux when he officially announced his retirement before the kick-off. The atmosphere was indescribable, tears mixed with admiration; and for the duration of the match there was a lump in everyone's throat because you knew that you were witnessing not only the end of an illustrious career, but the end of an era. Thank you Billy for the best childhood one could have!'

ROGER PITT (Malvern): 'My first football memories were so special; seeing the captain of England every other Saturday and watching us beat everyone under the guidance of Stan Cullis and the leadership of Billy. I remember clearly his final match when the first team and reserves formed a line as he entered Molineux to play for the last time. No home game is complete without a moment's pause at his statue as I remember "Sir Billy Wright."'

LY LIM (Singapore): 'Billy will always be my hero since he is the first player to make Wolves famous for all the right reasons. It is my hope that the current squad will be able to fire up their passion akin to what Billy had for the club to make the once mighty Wolves proud again.'

BILL MORGAN (a Wolves supporter of over 55 years): 'During the darkest days of Wolves' spiralling decline, I was invited by a friend to attend a sportsman's dinner at a hotel in Kingswinford. Among the speakers was Billy Wright. He was so upset that his beloved Wolves had slumped so badly that he actually had tears in his eyes when he predicted it would be a long journey back to the First Division. All present could not help but recognise that Billy cared so deeply about his beloved Wolves.'

GAVIN WILKES (Hereford): 'The players of today and tomorrow could learn a great deal from the way Billy played for his club and country and he should get more recognition for his achievements. Thanks for the great history Billy.'

DR ALISTAIR SURGEON FRAME (Chesterfield): 'In the early fifties, I played golf for the Birmingham University team and we were very lucky to be allowed to have Moseley Golf Club as our HQ. One weekday, Moseley were hosts to Warwickshire County Alliance Pro-am Tournaments. Billy Wright, plus his professional partner, won the tournament. The clubhouse was packed in the evening for the prize-giving ceremony. A senior old boy was giving out the prizes. He called out for Mr William Wright and his partner to come up to the platform for their prizes. When dear modest Billy went up for his prize, everyone recognised him apart from the old boy who said very clearly into the microphone, "You are Mr William Wright?" "Yes," replied Billy to huge cheers and prolonged applause.'

GEOFF WADE (Gilesgate, Durham City): 'My father took me to see my first football match as a nine-year-old at Roker Park, Sunderland. Wolves were the visitors. Billy Wright was my hero from that day on. He was a class act in a half back line of Flowers, Wright and Clamp. Yes, those were the days! My seventeen-year-old son, Mark, is a Wolves fanatic now also... stemming from the days of Billy Wright and my ramblings about the great Wolves.'

MIKE INMAN (Sydney, Australia): 'I have all Billy's books and most of the programmes for games he played in, including his last pre-season match, "Colours" versus "Whites". There were many great players for Wolves in the fifties but in my view Billy was the greatest. However, greater than his football skills, was the character of the man. To be so humble and considerate after all he achieved is remarkable.'

TOM MULLER (Corby, Northants): 'If you mention Wolves to most people they will think of Billy Wright. He is a true Wolves legend, and *always* will be.'

DUDLEY KERNICK (Stoke): 'While commercial Manager of Stoke City, I played in a charity golf tournament with Billy Wright and Derek Lymer, a golfing business friend of mine. After the game we sat down to the usual post-match presentation dinner and football stories. Finally it was my friend's turn to speak. Proud to be sitting next to the ex-captain of England, then working in television as controller of sport at ATV, Derek turned to Billy and said, "Do you know, Mr Wright, when I was twelve years old, my father allowed me out of Stoke-on-Trent for the very first time on my own. Stoke were playing Wolves at Molineux in the old First Division in the 1940s, and after the match you signed my programme." Billy, with a completely straight face, immediately replied, "Yes Derek, I did. I remember it well." This reply made his day. "Do you really, Mr Wright! I am honoured." Another life-long fan was made.'

TILLY GILBERT (Rugeley, Staffs): 'I am only thirteen years of age but I am often told about the great "hero" Billy Wright. I am a season ticket holder in his stand and he seems to me to be a great Wolves legend for today and for always.'

CHRIS CROWE (Vancouver Island, Canada): 'It was the 1955–56 season and I think it was against Newcastle United. As usual my dad had got tickets from Auntie Lil (she sold programmes on the corner opposite the Molineux Hotel). We walked down the passageway next to the south bank and reached the 'green door' on the Waterloo Road. Uncle Bill took our tickets and we were in. Dad collected his beer-crate and we hustled our way through the crowd and reached the top of the enclosure terrace. The next thing I knew I was being passed above everybody's heads towards the pitch.

'Sitting on the wall correctly (the policeman always made us sit legs in, not on the track) I was hit in the face by a football from one of the Wolves team warming up. A lot of people seemed to amass all around me but the one I remember most was Billy Wright asking if I was okay and ruffling my hair. Billy Wright actually looking at me, my hero really talking and touching me. I've bragged about it ever since.

'As we passed the players' entrance the following week Billy was leaving. He stopped and recognised me and asked if I had recovered from the knock I took on the wall. I can still recall Dad telling everyone how wonderful it was that a football legend could not only remember his son but take time to speak to him.

'My dad's passed away now and I live far away from my roots. I'm a Bushbury boy who played for and captained his school and town in the early sixties before joining the RAF. I now live in Victoria on Vancouver Island, Canada. But despite the distance and the time lapse, the memory of Billy Wright will live with me forever.'

MICHAEL DUFFY (Cannock): 'Even though I am too young to have seen Billy play I know all about the Billy Wright legend and I thank him for taking Wolves to the heights that they are today.'

DONNA BOWATER (has a special Wolves site at www.myweb. tiscali.co.uk/w3bow): 'Billy Wright, the West Stand at Molineux. Billy Wright, the statue in front of the Golden Stadium. Or at least, that's what he is to thousands of teenagers like me. For years, I've come to Molineux wondering who the legend was. Just to look at his record is to understand why this home-grown jewel came to be such a hero. I didn't witness his playing career but just by looking into the sparkling eyes of those who did as they recount to me his story gives me a window into the gentleman, the sportsman that was Billy Wright. He wasn't my hero; needless to say there are the rare individuals who play that position for me today, but, when it's my turn to pay tribute to my heroes, I hope I have as many good memories as Billy gave you. Here's to Billy Wright. Here's to your hero.'

KEITH BAKER (Stafford): 'I shall always remember the sight of Billy leading his Wolves team out on to the pitch, carrying the ball in his own inimitable way (so well reproduced in the fine statue in Waterloo Road) and somehow giving the impression to all that he was about to enjoy himself. It is my opinion that he was the best all-round half-back that England has ever produced.'

RAYMOND KYTE (Wolverhampton): 'I have appealed to Her Majesty for a knighthood for our Billy, CBE. It is my contention that Billy Wright was, and will always be, the best English footballer that ever pulled a white shirt over his head (not to mention, the old gold and black). As long as I live, I will endeavour to strive for Billy's true recognition. A knight of the realm, honoured by the monarch and all England.'

JULIAN HODGES (Manchester): 'As an unashamed Wolves supporter living in Manchester the first words I hear from any football fan, whatever the colour, when I say I'm a Wolverhamptoner is "Billy Wright". He commands respect not only throughout the country but, throughout the generations. I just wish I'd been there to see him.'

ALAN GUY (Silver End, near Witham in Essex): 'I remember meeting Billy at Corley service station on the M6 on the way to Molineux in the 1990s. My friends and I, all Wolves fans, went over and spoke to him. He was so pleased that we were travelling up from Essex to see the Wolves. Billy showed a genuine interest in us and never once gave the air of being the superstar that he will always remain. My dad and his brothers used to cycle from Wellington in Shropshire to Molineux as youngsters to watch Billy and the great Wolves side of the fifties, and they have told me many marvellous stories about him. He was very special.'

PHIL ARTHURS (Ex-Kingswinford, now Sittingbourne, Kent): 'My dad always used to say to me that Billy was one of the most complete footballers he had ever seen. Nowadays, when I walk past the tribute statue of William Ambrose Wright, I feel enormously proud that this man, this England captain, chose to represent Wolves throughout his career. God bless you Billy Wright, and my dad, for getting me hooked on one of the finest teams in England.'

NIGEL HARRIS (Springfield): 'My late grandfather, George Harris, was a Wolves supporter, and in his spare time he used to run a local Sunday league side. Billy Wright used to turn up at the local park and watch Granddad's team, encouraging them from the touchline and showing all the enthusiasm of a true football fan. We will not see his like again.'

DOUGLAS S COX (Belbroughton, Stourbridge): 'Rex Stranger, who was in the same soft-drinks business as us, was chairman of Southampton FC and a director of the Carlton Hotel in Bournemouth (I have been MD of Purity Soft Drinks for more than 56 years). Mr Stranger invited me to a match at The Dell, and he arranged for me to stay at the Carlton. I was delighted to find myself in the company of Billy Wright, who was staying there. This was in the 1950s and he was captain of Wolves and England. We got talking, and it led to Billy agreeing to lend his name to an advertising campaign for my company. His name was printed on thousands of drip mats. I paid him a fee of £20, which shows how the commercial world has changed since those innocent days. Billy was a charming man, without a shred of arrogance.'

OLIVE HARTLAND & ENID TOMKINS (The Twins, Penn, Wolverhampton): 'We were known as "The Twins" to Billy long before the Beverley Sisters came into his life. It was 1949 during a cricket match that he was introduced to us for the first time, and from that day on he never once passed us by without a kind word of greeting. We are twin sisters who have followed Wolves home and away for over 53 years and have many happy memories of Billy. He always spoke to us, and would ask with genuine interest about our journey to the match, which took a lot longer than it does today. Once, when we went to Blackpool, our mother came with us. We were hurrying to the station in snowy weather and Billy shouted, 'You should go home, Mum, and get warm instead of watching us.' He then, without being asked, arranged some tickets for us when we got to the ground.'

GEORGE MILLWARD (formerly of Lancashire, now retired in Dorset): 'I was patrolling the touchline at Ewood Park as PC 120 of the Blackburn Police in 1947 when Wolves were the visiting team. I got a close-up view of Billy, who had just been made the Wolves skipper in succession to Stan Cullis. I was so mesmerised watching him in action that I stood too long in one spot as he prepared to take a throw-in just a couple of yards from me. A fan from the terraces shouted, "Move on, or take tha' bloody helmet off so we can all see t'game." Billy gave me a great big grin, and then got on with the game. No player has since come near him for enthusiasm and honest effort.'

JUSTIN EMERY (Singapore): 'My dad, who is now 72, recalls Billy walking across the playing fields at Claregate from his boarding house. Dad used to play centre-half for Claregate United. The players would ask Billy to kick the ball back when it went out of play. He would roll it back underarm, clearly not wanting to injure himself or show off. He would then continue walking to catch his bus to go to the ground. This draws testimony to Billy's unassuming nature – unlike the modern players of today.'

ANDY PHILLIPS (Wolverhampton): 'I am too young to have seen Billy Wright play, but I do know he is and always will be respected by every Wolves fan.'

BRIAN WALKER (Bangkok, Thailand, but still a Wolves supporter): 'England played a World Cup qualifying match at Molineux in 1956, against Denmark on a Wednesday. On the Tuesday prior to the game I went with my parents to the Savoy Cinema in Wolverhampton. Sitting in the row in front of us was the entire England team. They included Busby Babes Roger Byrne, Tommy Taylor and Duncan Edwards. I was at school in those days and collected autographs. Just before the end of the film the team got up and started to leave the cinema. Armed with a pen and receipts from the Beatties store, I followed them into the foyer to try to get a few autographs. Billy made all the team sign their autographs on my Beatties receipts. What a gentleman!'

IAN PRICE (Telford): 'As a young boy my father and mother often told me of the times when they lived in Ironbridge at the bottom of Church Hill and how nice Billy was as a boy. He never forgot his roots.'

KEVIN PATERSON (Bracknell, Berkshire): 'I never saw Billy play but I can remember my granddad telling me Billy Wright stories. He clearly deserves the legend status he has now.'

PETER WELLS (Didcot, Oxon): 'I remember my mum ordering my first Wolves shirt from "Moores Gents Outfitters" in 1954. I waited so long it seemed, but it finally arrived in a box with tissue, just like a gentleman's shirt! That was it, I was King of the Heap. Down went the coats. My pals saying, "I'm Stan Matthews, I'm Tom Finney," and me – foot on the ball with arms folded – "I'm Billy Wright, captain of the Wolves." I felt so proud in my gold shirt. When I get to Molineux these days, I still feel the hairs on my neck tingle as I look in awe at the statue of the great man – who was and still remains my hero. That man who inspired me to play football until I was 40-years-old, an inspiration to us all of that era.'

TERENCE W BOWN (Axminster, Devon): 'I had the pleasure of meeting Billy and his wife, Joy, in unusual circumstances. It was in the celebrity car park at Wembley Stadium, where I was on duty as a Metropolitan Police officer. Billy, my hero since the mid-fifties, was having trouble extracting his car, and I willingly assisted him. We chatted, and the direct result was that he kindly autographed a 1940s photograph of himself that has pride of place in my Billy Wright memorabilia collection.'

JASON JONES (Coventry, Jack Harris stand): 'My grandfather continually spoke of the great days, and used to compare every player with the great man but nobody was fit to clean his boots. My grandfather is always in my thoughts and I recall how he used to tell me, "Billy Wright was the greatest man who ever lived." My grandfather never lied.'

MICHAEL SINGLETON (Kensington, London): 'I am a Chelsea supporter, and only saw Billy play once. That was one August afternoon at Stamford Bridge. It was early in the season, and the young Chelsea team – Drake's Ducklings – ran Wolves silly, with teenager Jimmy Greaves skipping through the defence to help himself to five goals. What I recall was the wonderful sportsmanship of Billy Wright. He did not once try to unfairly stop the youngster who was running him and his team-mates dizzy, and at the end he led the applause for Jimmy and warmly shook his hand. What a great sportsman.'

BRIAN BANKS (Walsall): 'I first saw Billy Wright play when I was nine years old in the 1950s. He was always a credit to football and to Wolves, and made such an impression on me that I decided to play centre-half at school in Willenhall. In my imagination I was Billy Wright, but I could never approach his ability. They don't breed them like Billy any more.'

HAROLD WHITEHOUSE (Finchfield, Wolverhampton) 'I have been a supporter of Wolves since the age of five (1933), when my father used to carry me into Molineux on his shoulders and sit me on the barrier. I had the privilege of seeing William Ambrose Wright for the first time at the end of the 1941 season. He was sixteen and playing at inside-forward. I witnessed all of Wolves floodlit friendlies, and one vivid memory for me was when Simonian, the Russian captain and centre-forward, beat Billy on the penalty spot but before he could shoot past Bert Williams, Billy had got up and taken the ball off his foot, demonstrating fantastic recovery. This memory of Billy will remain with me forever. Billy was my hero, a true sportsman and a gentleman.'

DEREK W HADEN (Gornal Wood, Dudley): 'In the early 1950s Billy came to our village to open a harvest festival at the Old Bull's Head in Lower Gornal. I am one of triplets, all boys, and we waited with a scrum of other boys in the hope of getting the great man's autograph. He did not disappoint us, and patiently gave his signature to every youngster in the queue. It would be impossible to convey to today's overpaid, less talented players just how nice and humble he was, despite having the exalted position of Wolves and England captain. He won our devotion and support for ever.'

DAVE STEVENS (Halesowen): 'When I was fourteen, I was travelling on the same train as the Wolves team. My pal and I found their compartment and stared at them through the glass. Billy saw us looking and instead of telling us to push off invited us both in to meet the team. To be in the presence of Mullen, Hancocks, Slater, Williams and, of course, "Sir" Billy, left us two schoolboys speechless for days. A year or so later my friend, Eric, became gravely ill. Billy got to hear about it and, quietly, visited him in hospital and brought real sunshine to his last few days. Eric's parents were greatly appreciative of this wonderful gesture by a true gentleman and great sportsman.'

LIONEL MORIATY (Weoley Castle, Birmingham): 'When Billy was in his prime in the 1950s, he kindly gave up his time to appear on a Brains' Trust panel at the Congregational church in Lea Road, Wolverhampton. I was in the chair and I always remember an answer he gave to a question about his attitude and approach to football: "I would never ever do anything to risk my fitness as a professional footballer," he said. "I do not drink, I do not smoke and I do not keep late nights." You could see by the shining light in his eyes that he meant every word of it. He was truly a model professional and a wonderful example to the younger generation.'

ROGER CRUTCHLEY (Walsall-born, dual Walsall – WBA fan): 'In the late sixties I became secretary of the Walsall Junior Youth League, and Billy, who was then Head of Sport at ATV, accepted my invitation to be guest of honour at our annual dinner. He gave a good address and spent ages signing autographs. I left the function at around 11.30 p.m. to return Billy to his midweek flat in Edgbaston. When I broached the tender subject of what I owed him, he got very annoyed. "You have picked me up, provided me with a nice meal, and I have met some wonderful people," he said. "I do not want anything from you." William Ambrose Wright, a gentleman of the first order.'

BRIAN GILL (Fulwood, Lancs): 'I speak as a Blackburn Rovers regular for more than 50 years. Even though he played for Wolves, Billy Wright was always one of my favourite players. While doing my National Service in the 1950s I went out of my way to see him play at Molineux. It was Wolves against Leeds and Billy was marking Welsh giant John Charles before his transfer to Juventus. What has stuck above all else in my memory is the way Billy and Big John hugged each other at the end of a no-quarter-given battle. It was a wonderful display of sportsmanship, and as a neutral in the crowd I applauded this as much as if it were match action. Billy was a great ambassador for his club and for his country, and for that I salute him.'

SCOTT COOPER (Wolverhampton): 'I am sixteen and Steve Bull was my great hero, but I don't think he was anything quite like Billy. He must have been very very special.'

BRIAN ELLINS (Bromsgrove, Worcs): 'In 1958 I was a seventeen-year-old toolmaking apprentice with a firm in Redditch. Working with me at that time was a football referee called George Hoban. He was listed to be a linesman on 8 March 1958 for Wolves v Newcastle. He had a ticket for the game that he gave to me and took me to Molineux. After the match, I was waiting for George outside on the pitch. Billy Wright spotted me standing on my own and asked if I was all right. I nodded, and he then talked about the game. He gave me that big smile of his, said "cheerio" and continued across the pitch and out of the ground, leaving me open-mouthed. There I was, seventeen years old and an ardent Wolves supporter who had just actually spoken to the captain of Wolves and England. He was an absolute gentleman. What a terrific end to a terrific day.'

ELIZABETH BARKER (Aldridge, Walsall): 'My mother watched Wolves during the halcyon days of the forties and fifties. Her cousin is none other than Bert "The Cat" Williams, who played with Billy over four hundred times. Billy was my mother's favourite player, and in those days one of the few items of memorabilia you could buy was a badge of each individual player. She always wore a Billy Wright badge. On the sad death of Billy in 1994 I was moved to write a poem in tribute, which I would like to share with you ... '

A hero among heroes
When the Wanderers reigned as kings,
Your memory we will treasure
What ere the future brings.
Your record goes before you,
Your achievements never wane,
But what we most remember
Is how you loved the game.
As Captain of your country,
Or sporting black and gold,
Your name will live on forever
It never will grow old.
In an era that was sporting,
You shone above the rest,
You always were a gentleman
You always gave your best.
So remember now our motto,
'Out of Darkness Cometh Light,'
We're proud that you belonged to us,
We'll miss you, Billy Wright

JOHN WITHERS (a retired civil servant from Penn): 'I recall an incredible match at Molineux in 1953–54. With Wilf Mannion in exceptional form, Middlesbrough rushed into a 3–0 lead. Their third goal came from a penalty given against our Billy. It was an outrageous decision, but this true sportsman just shrugged his shoulders and did not protest. The following year I saw Billy concede a penalty for which he would have got sent off in the modern game. He fisted the ball over the bar to stop a certain goal in front of more than 75,000 spectators at Stamford Bridge. Peter Sillett scored from the penalty spot, and Chelsea went on to win the League championship with Wolves in second place. In 1956 I was serving with the Royal Signals in Germany when England played the world champions Germany in Berlin. The British Army did not have access to television, but the recently reformed German Army did and a group of their NCOs kindly invited us to watch the match with them. Duncan Edwards got the headlines with a smashing goal in England's 3–1 victory, but for me Billy was the star of the match with his magnificent performance in the middle of the England defence.'

RONALD WHITCOMBE (Brierley Hill, West Midlands): 'My brother Bill, then about 38 years old, was walking along Wembley Way with his son before the kick-off to the international match in which England beat Scotland 5–1 in 1975. Suddenly, he heard somebody calling out "Billy", and he instinctively stopped and turned to find the one and only Billy Wright walking behind him. Running up to him, with a young boy in tow, was a Scottish supporter asking for Billy's autograph. He signed without hesitation, and they got chatting about past England–Scotland games in which Billy had played. Billy then made his way to the stadium, and my brother heard this conversation between the Scot and the young boy with him:

"'Dad. Dad, who's that man?"

"That my son is the one and only Billy Wright."

"Who's Billy Wright?"

"Who's Billy Wright?' the father said in a broad Scottish accent. "I'll tell you who he is. He's only the greatest centre-half England ever had. The bastard!"' '

'My brother laughed all the way to the ground, and he still does when he recalls the incident all these years later.'

ROY CADDICK (a councillor from Frinton-on-Sea, Essex): 'I was a regular at Molineux from 1944 to 1954. Week after week I saw Billy outrun, outpass and outjump his opponents. I have never known a player who was so effective every single week. It was an inspired move by Stan Cullis to switch him to centre-half. Who can forget how the comparatively short man with that distinctive blond hair consistently rose above taller centre-forwards to head the ball away?'

TERRY BARLOW (Bayston Hill, near Shrewsbury): 'I can remember as a young child playing footie with my uncles in our back garden, dashing around like someone possessed. "Carry on like that and you'll end up like Billy Wright," one of them said, and I've never forgotten it and the name Billy Wright. For at least 46 years Wolverhampton Wanderers and the name Billy Wright have been close to my heart and they always will be.'

GEORGE THOMAS (Brookmans Park): 'During the early to mid-eighties I lived opposite to Joy and Billy in New Barnet. He often passed the time of day with me. On one occasion my friend was working on my front wall. He had his young son with him, who was mad on soccer. Billy took him over to his house and showed him his caps and medals. A small matter, but it showed that Billy was a nice man as well as being a great footballer.'

DAVE KENDALL (The Cato Street Irregular): 'I was at Stamford Bridge standing in an area in front of the old main stand in the early 1960s. Just before the game started people began to cheer, clap and shout, "Good old Billy." I looked behind me and saw the great man taking a seat to watch the game. Just then a father lifted up his small son, who was holding an autograph book. A "jobsworth" in a peaked cap stepped forward to stop the lad being passed into the stand. Billy signalled to the "jobsworth" and lifted the small boy up and into the area where he was sitting. He signed the lad's book, patted him on the head and passed him back to his father. What a contrast to the present day prima donnas.'

MIKE BUCKMASTER (a Wolves fan for 51 years): 'Billy was a gentleman in all aspects of his life. He always played fairly and many of the current overpaid players could learn from him on how to conduct themselves both on and off the field. Despite being small in stature for a centre-half, to me he was (and remains) a giant.'

BILL FAULKES (Stratford-upon-Avon): 'I met Billy twenty-plus years ago. He had a presence that made one warm to him immediately. Our meeting was at a Lord's Taverners six-a-side cricket tournament at Blenheim Palace. I was part of MJK Smith's Six and we were drawn to play against a team from television's Tiswas programme, represented by, among others, Chris Tarrant, Trevor East and Billy Wright. The game was short but terrific fun and I managed to bowl out both Chris and Billy with my donkey-drop deliveries. Billy's face as I bowled him was a picture and he gave me the biggest grin I have ever seen from that day to this. What a fabulous man.'

PHIL MANNS (Hereford): 'My father, Dennis Manns, was in the Army with "Sir Billy" and this began his lifelong passion for Wolves. In 1990 my father was involved in a serious car crash, sustaining severe head injuries resulting in brain damage. While he was in a coma, my wife wrote to "Sir Billy" care of Wolves, asking if he could organise a tape of all the players, which we hoped would aid his recovery. This was subsequently done and we also received a personal letter, complete with his home address, signed photograph and free tickets to the next home match.

'This was the last game my father ever went to and despite the difficulties encountered because of his injuries, we were so happy to be able to take him to his beloved Wolves for one last time.

'He subsequently passed away six years after the accident, but we still have the letter and the photograph hangs in the hall of my own home. Billy was always a true professional and a lovely human being.'

MIKE MARTINEAU (Biggin Hill, Kent): 'I got Jimmy Greaves to sign a sports book I'd been given at Christmas 1959. In it was a photo sequence of Jimmy scoring one of the five goals he got against Wolves on 30 August 1958 in a 6–2 home win for Chelsea. Wolves went on to retain the title that season by six points from Man United. The point to make about that game was that it probably brought Billy's retirement from the international team a bit closer as Greaves destroyed him, making Billy look slow and past it. However, Billy never resorted to foul means to stop Jimmy playing. Even in such adversity his sportsmanship shone through.'

PAT EVANS (Milborne Port, Sherborne): 'As a teenage schoolgirl I supported Wolves, and lived near to where Billy Wright stayed in digs. It was always a thrill for us hero worshippers when Billy and other players travelled on the same bus from the town to our stop. Another treat was to have tea in the Copper Kettle where the players went after training. All this was a far cry from the lives of players today. I still have my autograph book with Billy's signature, "Bill Wright".'

GARY LOVATT (Wolverhampton): 'My outstanding memory of Billy is when Wolves played Honved when the stadium had been rebuilt. He stood there at the players' tunnel shaking everybody's hands as they came out. As long as I live I'll not forget the roar Billy received when he came out. It really felt like there was 50,000 in the ground again that night.'

MATT O'CONNELL (London): 'I was born in 1969 so missed seeing the great man play, yet every time I hear his name or see his marvellous statue, I go cold. Billy Wright is not only synonymous with our great Wolves club but also everything great about English football. If only I had been born 30 years earlier, if only.'

BILL POLAND (Merseyside): 'My recollection of Billy was when – playing against Everton in the fifties – he stooped to head out a rocket shot from our Tommy Eglington. Unfortunately, he did it with the top of his head. He was rushed to Walton Hospital, and they kept him in overnight. That evening I visited my wife in that hospital, and there wasn't a nurse to be seen. When I asked my wife where they all were, she said: 'Oh, some footballer was brought in injured, and they have all gone to see him.' I looked in as I left, and gave him a nod. Nice guy who often got us Evertonians mad, but, yes, a nice guy!'

STEVE STUDDS (Oxford): 'I was invited to join the Arsenal youth training scheme back in 1964 as a schoolboy player. Billy Wright was the Arsenal manager and, as an eleven-year-old, I had little idea of the pressure he was under because Arsenal were going through a rough patch. However, Billy attended almost all of our training sessions every Tuesday and Thursday evenings and encouraged, laughed and joked with all us kids from age eleven to thirteen years. I will never forget the time myself and another boy were larking around in the marbled dressing-rooms. Billy came in and jokingly grabbed us, one under each famous arm. He threw us into what seemed a gigantic wicker kit basket, shut the lid and shouted, 'Okay, Bert, the kit's packed and ready for Moscow!' I later realised, his job and health were on the line, yet he had time for us juniors. Arsenal had adopted a youth policy second to none, instigated and inspired by Billy. The fruits of all this came after Billy left. I am so proud to have met him.'

ROY TRATT: 'About ten years ago I was invited as a corporate guest to attend the Autoglass Trophy final at Wembley and was able to take my football-mad, thirteen-year-old son. As we were all leaving to take our seats for the match I spoke to fellow-guest Billy and told him that he was my first football hero. He smiled as he shook my hand and said that surely I was too young to remember him. I was 48 at the time! He then shook my son's hand and asked him who he supported. When he replied, West Ham, Billy said they were a good team and played very good football. I am sure that this brief conversation was typical of Billy. I wonder if today's millionaire footballers will ever have as much grace.'

LYN FRIEND (Barnstaple, North Devon): 'I am a librarian at Pilton Community College in Barnstaple, North Devon. My husband, Alan, has been a staunch supporter of Wolves since he was a young boy (he is now 55). Billy Wright and the Wolves football team used to come to Barnstaple and stay at the Barnstaple Road Hotel owned by the Brend Group, which is just around the corner. Mr Peter Brend, a good friend of ours, introduced my husband to Billy Wright and all the players at the time. Billy agreed to let his team train at the college. After the training Billy and the team came into my library at Pilton and had a photo shoot. One of the pictures is still in pride of place on the library notice board. Billy will be remembered by Pilton as a genuinely sincere, nice guy who spent time coaching and encouraging our footballers of the future.'

TREVOR ROBBIE (Acton, West London): 'In 1951 I was a schoolboy in Folkestone, and Wolves were in town training. I was standing at the rear of a small crowd when out came Billy Wright, my hero. I was unable to move as everybody had pushed forward to get his autograph. When he had finished signing and was about to move away, he looked up and saw me still rooted to the spot way at the back, and said, "Come here, son" and he signed my book. To me that was the measure of the man; he could quite easily have ignored little old me at the back. I am now 65 and warmed by the memory more than 50 years on.'

MALCOLM TAYLOR (Alresford, Hampshire): 'Billy always conducted himself both on and off the field in an exemplary manner. How today's players could learn from the way he approached the game.'

LES and JOHN STAITE (Bentley, Walsall): 'My Dad – an avid Wolves fan of close to sixty years – has informed me of virtually every game he saw Billy play. Old-gold-and-black blood obviously ran through his veins. Cheers Bill, all the very best wherever you are kid... Wish I'd av sin ya play, Bill.'

DAVE FINN: 'I was travelling to London by train when it stopped at Coventry and Billy got into my carriage, saying "good morning" as he sat. Being a lifelong Wolves supporter, I was in my element. We got talking and I told Billy that when I was about eight-years-old, which would have been 1956, I got his autograph. He asked where he signed and I told him it was at a charity cricket match, Wolves against Stourbridge. He smiled and said, 'You know, I played 105 times for England and had all that success with Wolves, but I always enjoyed playing cricket more than football.'''

HARRY DAVENHILL (Pelsall, Walsall): 'In my role as a Tour Guide at Molineux, I had the privilege of being the "minder" for Ferenc Puskas when Honved played Wolves to mark the opening of the new stadium. The main picture photographers wanted was Billy standing with the portly Puskas. I took Ferenc over to Billy, and one of the photographers asked them to stand closer together. As they did so, one of Billy's former team-mates shouted, "That's the nearest you ever got to him, Bill." Billy laughed louder than anybody else. What a great sportsman.'

BILL DAVIS (Prestwood): My first recollection of Billy Wright was in 1954 when my father gave me for a Christmas present the *Charles Buchan Football Annual*. The first photograph was one of Billy Wright holding the First Division trophy and from that time I became a Wolves fan and Billy my idol. Living in Dublin, it was difficult to see Billy play for Wolves but I was fortunate to see him play for England in 1957 when England knocked Ireland out of the World Cup with a last minute equaliser, and also for the Football League. There were many exceptional football players who were true gentlemen in the 1950s, each of them an example to any impressionable youngster. I believe I picked the best when I picked Billy Wright.'

RON MYATT (Great Wyrley, Staffordshire): 'My grandmother scraped together the money to surprise me with a trip to Liverpool to watch Wolves play Everton in the 1950s. Wolves lost 2–1 and I was really disappointed. At Lime Street station, we prepared for the return journey and, suddenly, the team boarded the same train. My gran disappeared and then returned, telling me to take a walk to the next compartment. I then spent five or ten minutes talking to the captain of England's football team. Billy was truly inspirational. There was no side or aloofness, just a thoroughly nice person. A few days later, I went to Molineux to try to get tickets for an upcoming match just as the players came out of the dressing-room in Waterloo Road. Despite a crowd of people being there, Billy singled me out and said "hello". The captain of England and Wolves remembering an earlier conversation with a "star-struck" kid on a train! It made me feel really something special and I have never forgotten the charm and friendliness.'

MIKE CHESTERTON (Redditch, Worcestershire): 'I was on holiday in Malta in the late 1970s and met Jimmy Mullen, Billy's lifelong friend and former Wolves and England team-mate. Never having seen Billy play, I asked Jimmy if Billy was a good player (foolish question, I know). Jimmy said: 'I'll tell you a story about Billy. I was playing with him in a particular match when I dropped back into midfield. He passed a ball to me and I passed it straight back as I was closely marked.'

'I waited for Jimmy to continue, but that was the entire story. I said politely as I could that it wasn't the greatest story I'd ever heard. Jimmy, a charismatic Geordie just smiled.

'"You mean." I said, 'that in the countless games you played with Billy for Wolves and England that was the only bad ball he gave you?'

'Jimmy nodded and smiled. "Now," he said, "you understand how good Billy was."

'It is the most simple yet most informative story I've heard, and captures the talent of Billy Wright.'

RON PARKER (Malaga, Spain): 'When I was nine or ten years old I used to go regularly to Courtolds every Saturday afternoon in the summer to watch cricket. Billy loved the game and was often there and I used to get his autograph. One day I plucked up the courage to ask him to shake my hand. He replied that it would be a great pleasure. I never wanted to wash that hand again. Many years later, in 1973, I had to go to ATV to be interviewed by Gary Newbon. By then, Billy was head of sport. Billy met me in the reception area and took me through to make-up where a girl came with a huge powder puff and told me to sit down. I protested that no way was I going to have powder on my face, but Billy explained that it was necessary because of the studio lighting and that he always had it done. I thought, 'Well if it's OK for the great man, it's OK for me!' I am retired now and live in Spain, but my heart is still with Wolves and my memories still warmed by thoughts of Billy Wright and the Golden heroes.'

DERRICK GRIFFIN (Sutton Coldfield): 'I was standing behind the goal when Wolves were beating Cardiff 9–1 in a 1955 League match when the ball went out for a goal kick. Goalkeeper Bert Williams was taking his time, as there was only five minutes left, when Billy came running up and shouted, 'Get a move on . . . we haven't won yet!' This proved what a good professional he was, giving 110 per cent and still playing to the whistle.'

GRAHAM NIGHTINGALE (Compton, Wolverhampton): 'I was nine years of age when Wolves won the FA Cup in 1949. My father was in the fire service and was on duty for the Wolves Victory Parade at the town hall on the Sunday morning. He took me to the rear entrance steps of the town hall about two hours before the team were due and said, "Stay there, don't move away." It seemed to me that everything was happening at the front of the town hall where thousands were cheering. After a long wait the team coach arrived and one by one the players and manager Stan Cullis came off. Billy Wright led the way clutching the Cup. As he walked up towards me, I reached out and touched it. Billy realised I was making the best of the opportunity, and he smiled at me and continued up the steps. All my friends later kept asking me if it was true I had touched the Cup! The Civic Banquet was held on the Monday and my dad came home and said, "here's a memento" – it was the table menu which I have treasured for over 50 years.'

JOHN HAMMOND (Hereford): 'In 1950 I was selected to play for Herefordshire Schools at Shrewsbury. When we arrived at the ground we were told Billy Wright was going to be there. After fifteen minutes I received a knock on the ankle. There were no substitutes then so I limped until half-time. In the dressing-room, I sat down very distressed. Then, to my surprise, in came Billy Wright! "Let's have a look at that ankle son," he said. "I might be able to ease it a bit for you." He brought in a bucket of cold water. "Put your foot in there. Hopefully it will ease the pain." I played the second half, my ankle a little better. I often think to myself what a wonderful thing for the captain of England to take the time to help a dejected schoolboy footballer.'

JOAN HIGGINS (Bridgnorth, Shropshire): 'My father, Len Higgins, was chairman of the schools football committee in Bridgnorth, eight or so miles from where Billy was born. I used to go regularly to the local Innage Lane playing fields to watch the matches. One Saturday in 1937 I saw the visiting Madeley Boys team run rings round our Bridgnorth side. You could not miss the Madeley centre-forward, not only because of his distinctive blond hair but also because of the fact he kept putting the ball into our net! I am now 81 and my memory plays tricks, but I am sure he scored ten goals. Of course, it was Billy Wright, and my heart missed a beat when he came close to me and I saw what a good-looking lad he was! Along with my father, I followed his career with Wolves and England and I am proud to have been there right at the start. I am still a voluntary teacher's helper, and make a point of telling six- and seven-year-olds the story of Shropshire's famous son.'

GA EVANS (Wellington, Telford): 'There were a lot of headlines being made in 1939 by Major Frank Buckley, saying that he was giving his players a monkey-gland treatment before the FA Cup final against Portsmouth. Billy Wright was then a Wolves apprentice, and one day we met in Ironbridge Road and I asked him about the treatment. He handed me a tablet and said that all the apprentices were being told to take them, rather than have the injections that the senior players were having. In my opinion, having taken it, I would say it was just a straightforward vitamin tablet. I am now 85 and continue to follow Wolves closely, with wonderful memories of Billy's days at Molineux.'

JOHN JONES (Shrewsbury): 'I knew Billy Wright when I was a schoolboy during the war and he was a corporal at Copthorne Barracks in the ITC. My father had a large garden near the barracks with many fruit trees, and we used to pick apples, pears and plums for all the physical training instructors. Billy was already a local hero, and my mother used to give me two fresh eggs to hand to Billy every Friday morning. He was a lovely man, and I used to be allowed into the barracks to watch him play football with such talented team-mates as Billy Richardson, Johnny Hancocks and Roy Brown.'

ROSALEEN PEARSON (nee Jones, Upper Astley, Shrewsbury): 'I attended the Madeley Secondary Modern School, where Billy had been a famous pupil nearly twenty years earlier. One day in 1954 he returned to visit the school and I was so excited at the prospect of meeting my Wolves hero. I dashed back to school after lunch at home to find that he had been and gone. I have always kicked myself that I did not take sandwiches that day. His widow, Joy, kindly donated one of his caps to the school. Billy was head boy at Madeley for a brief spell, and was sports editor of the school's first magazine, *The Hillsian.*'

DOUG SMOUT (Redditch): 'In the summer of 1952 I was working at the Dudley Hippodrome as a comedy unicyclist, and Billy was the celebrity compere for a week. He was a magnificent all-round sportsman, excellent at football, cricket and golf. But he could not conquer my unicycle! We posed for publicity photographs with Billy on the bike, and I had to hold him up! I used to sit in his dressing-room with him between performances, and I found out just what a lovely man he was. He had no conceit or vanity whatsoever.'

MARY BROWN (Bournemouth): 'I was fortunate enough to meet the Bevs in 1958 when the secret arrangements for Billy and Joy's wedding were taking place. At that time, my late father, Councillor Henry Brown, was mayor of Bournemouth, and the Bevs were appearing in a summer show in the town. Joy and Babs came to our hotel to discuss the Poole Register Office arrangements with my father. It was a great delight to meet them, and I have in my possession a lovely letter of thanks from them, which is in the book of press cuttings and letters of my father's very successful year as mayor of Bournemouth. Of course, the secret leaked out and Poole was absolutely jam-packed on their special day. It just proved the popularity of Billy and Joy. Yes, the Posh and Becks of their day.'

JOHN BLAKE (Bideford, North Devon): 'My mother worked in Wolverhampton during the war, and at night was an air raid warden. She told me that each warden had a young lad as their "message runner," and she was very proud to say that for a time her runner was a nice lad called Bill Wright, who became captain of Wolves and England.'

VERA WINCHESTER: 'My mother, Mrs Percy Ferriday, was head of an Infants School on Madeley Bank, Ironbridge in the 1930s and used to tell me that she taught Billy Wright to read. At dinner time, a boy would be despatched to the Infants from the Junior school next door, saying: "Can our Billy come and play?" He was six at the time and would be launching his career playing with boys up to the age of fourteen. My mother did not, of course, realise how momentous this was at the time but later, all through his many "caps" she dined out on it.'

CLIVE TRENCHARD (Hereford): 'In April 1962 I represented England at an international youth tournament in Romania. My schoolboy hero Billy Wright was our manager and a few of the players went on to make full-time careers. including Paul Madeley, Howard Wilkinson and David Pleat. Not long after we had arrived in Romania Billy knocked on the door of my hotel room. "Sorry to trouble you so early," he said, "but do you have some black shoe polish? I forgot to pack mine." He could have had the crown jewels off me! A little later that day we went to his room for the announcement of the first team selection to play Yugoslavia and he said, 'Number ten inside-left...Clive Trenchard.' I was so proud to be selected by the most respected and admired man in the game.'

JOHN BARNETT (Crewe, Cheshire): '50 years ago I was waiting with three friends on Crewe station in the hunt for autographs when I spotted a lonely figure standing on platform four. We felt it looked like Billy Wright but we knew that the Wolves on that day had been playing at home.

Having got a copy of *Billy Wright's Football Scrapbook* with me I was elected to approach the England captain and ask him if he was who we thought he was. To our delight he confirmed he really was Billy Wright. Over the next half-hour, he signed dozens of autographs and chatted away to us. He wished us all good luck, said he would have to leave and then boarded the train to North Wales. When you compare the footballers of the 1950s with today's superstars it is hard to imagine that the modern players would spend a half-hour talking to a group of teenagers.'

MRS PHYLLIS MARSH (Wednesfield, Wolverhampton): 'As a lifelong Wolves supporter, I can confirm that Billy was a gentleman on and off the field. I recall him giving a speech to an all-ladies audience in the Sir Jack Hayward Suite at Molineux when he told us that whenever they played away the Wolves players, Billy included, would make a dash for the earliest train to get them back to Wolverhampton in time for the Saturday evening dance at the Civic Hall. Happy days!'

MISS ALISON L HITCH (Aqueduct, Telford): 'I followed Billy as a pupil at Abraham Darby School, which was known as Madeley Modern when Billy went there. I was proud to be a member of the school showband that played at Billy's funeral, and the school choir sang "The Happy Wanderer". He was given the wonderful send off that this great Shropshire hero deserved.'

TREVOR T EVANS (Craven Arms, Shropshire): 'I can clearly remember the first match in which I saw Billy play. It was Wolves against Millwall at Molineux on 6 October 1945. I can be that specific because I have kept the twopenny programme! I was working as a loco fireman, and I remember the trains were chock-a-block with people going to the game, and there were more than 50,000 in the ground. Billy, playing at inside-left was exceptional. He was a great advertisement for Wolves in particular and football in general.'

JOHN DUNCAN (Brockham, Surrey): 'Back in the fifties I was a keen fan of Wolves and especially Billy Wright. My father took me, then about nine, to see Wolves play Chelsea at Stamford Bridge. After the game we waited outside in the hope of getting Billy's autograph. The players came out and went straight into their coach. I was in tears and inconsolable. My father was not beaten. He rushed us across London to the station from where he knew the team would leave. Most of the players were already on the train but Billy was saying goodbye to a blonde, who we later found out, of course, was Joy Beverley. I positioned myself between him and the ticket gate and then he walked towards me. I was rooted to the spot, tongue tied and dumbstruck, and I let my idol walk right past me. Once again I was in tears. One of the Wolves officials – none other than Stan Cullis – saw my state, ruffled my hair and took me on to the platform. We boarded the train and Billy signed my book and then took me around the carriage to collect autographs from the rest of the team. One great memory of a great footballer.'

DAVID BRAZIER (St Helens, Isle of Wight): 'I saw Billy play many times in my youth, but one incident stands out in my memory – a cameo which illustrates his sheer skill and speed of both foot and thought, not to mention his refusal to take the easy option of fouling an opponent when danger threatened. Wolves were playing at Molineux defending the North Bank end. I recall that the centre-forward was very skilful, strong and direct – it may have been Trevor Ford. Wolves were on the attack and Billy was left as the lone central defender, just inside his own half on the edge of the centre circle. Suddenly the ball broke to an opponent on the edge of his penalty area. He immediately sent a long raking ball over Billy's head and, as he did so, the centre-forward took off to chase it. The pass was of perfect weight and length. If he could have got on to it he would have had a clear run on goal, one on one with the keeper.

'Now, when the pass was struck, Billy was standing almost still, with his back to Wolves' goal. The centre-forward was facing the other way and already well into his stride, perhaps five yards short of Billy. There seemed no way, short of impeding him (which is what would happen nowadays), that Billy could prevent him getting through on goal. But, in the proverbial flash, Billy had not only turned through 180 degrees but he was running just as fast as the centre-forward, who was still a yard or two behind him.

'Then came the most amazing bit of play. Although Billy must have lost sight of the ball when he turned, as it came hurtling over his head he coolly and cleanly volleyed it back – over his head again – in the direction from which it had come. At full pelt and running toward his own goal! I have never seen anything like it since that day. What a player.'

MARTIN STEVENS (Merley, Dorset): 'My memory of seeing Billy Wright play was in a match that Wolves lost. It was against my team, Bournemouth, in the FA Cup at Molineux in 1957. It was an astonishing game during which Bournemouth's Reg Cutler collided with a goal post and it collapsed. I was fourteen at the time, and the memory has remained with me all these years because I was right behind the goal that came down. Reg recovered to score the only goal of the game. What struck me was the sporting manner in which Billy accepted defeat, and the way he kept plugging away with his one hundred per cent effort, but without resorting to foul play.'

MRS CONNIE LATCHAM (Wimborne, Dorset): 'I first saw Billy play in the 1930s when he was still a bootboy. In those days I used to support Wolves from the 'Cow Shed', and I made friends with several of the players including Bryn Jones, Tom Galley and Jesse Pye. Every Saturday we girls would go to the Civic Hall in Wolverhampton where we used to dance with the players. I can remember dancing with Billy, and I also used to have tea with him and the rest of the lads in the Copper Kettle. They were very well disciplined in those days and if any of them did take a drink in a pub late in the week they would be reported to Major Buckley. He would not stand for any nonsense. I am an Oxley girl and my heart is still with the Wolves, although these days I live in Dorset.'

ROB STOKES (Stourbridge): 'Billy was playing for Wolves in a 1950s cricket match against Coseley Cricket Club, watched by my friend, Alan, who was then five-years-old. My friend was at the time aware of the names of only two footballers, Billy Wright and Stanley Matthews. His father took him over to meet Billy and said, "Who's this Alan?" Gazing up at Billy, Alan replied: "It's Stanley Mathews!" At that, his father gave him a slap around the head, and said, "You daft little bugger. This is Billy Wright." Billy laughed and ruffled Alan's hair. "Don't you worry, young man," he said. "It's an honour to be mixed up with such a great player." He turned an embarrassing moment into one with which everybody was happy!'

JØRGEN NORBY (Denmark): 'Being 73 years old, I clearly remember the first English national team playing in Denmark after the war. Already then I was a WAW fan and Billy did not disappoint me. He was a gentleman-player, right-half, spreading horror and despair in our left side. The best ambassador England and Wolves ever had!'

CLIVE GREEN (Poole, Dorset): 'I have been a Wolves supporter from the age of eight (1946) and saw most of the home games until 1978, when I moved to Dorset. My strongest memory of Billy is, oddly, of listening to him sing "Jerusalem" at the Fighting Cocks Hotel (recently demolished) one Saturday evening following a game at Molineux around 1950/51. I was about twelve at the time, and sitting about six feet from him. I can remember that he had an excellent voice. I used to often see him queuing for the one-and-nines at the Gaumont cinema at Wolverhampton. Amazingly, he would sign autographs while patiently waiting to get into the cinema.'

BOB HOUSE (Farnborough, Hants): 'I was a young lad of eight in 1959 attending the Trosnant Junior school in Havant, Hampshire. The then headmaster was a Mr Hunt, who was also an England football referee. He invited Billy and his wife Joy to present the prizes at the school awards ceremony. Even for one so young I felt the excitement and there was a tremendous buzz throughout the school that day. They had only recenly got married and they were like royalty, a truly "golden couple". What an honour it was to have shaken hands with the England captain and his wife of Beverley Sisters fame. They both made a little boy's day very special and more than 40 years on I still mention that I shook hands with the England captain Billy Wright.'

ALFRED CAMILLERI (Sliema, Malta): 'My big wish was granted in January 1994 when I got to meet my hero Billy Wright in person. It was the day Wolves beat Crystal Palace 2–0 at Molineux, and I was fortunate enough to be a guest in the directors' box. Behind me sat Stan Cullis and in front of me Billy Wright! During half-time I had my photograph taken with Billy, Stan Cullis and another former Wolves manager, Bill McGarry. I was so excited about it that I hugged Billy, and he took it in good part. I now have an enlarged print of the photograph hanging in my study at home reminding me of that great moment in my life. I work as a sports editor with a local Maltese daily and still keep a close watch on Wolves, the team I have been proud to support all these years.'

IAN WINTER (Sports Presenter/Reporter, BBC Look East, Norwich): 'I first met Billy soon after he'd accepted Wolves' invitation to join the board of directors. I was sports editor at BBC Radio WM...he was a legend...and the club was at rock bottom. But Billy's beloved Wolves were on the way back. Under the astute management of Graham Turner, the renaissance had begun, and no one was more delighted than Billy. I was on the look-out for an expert summariser to join our commentary team at Wembley for the Sherpa Van Trophy final. Who better than Billy? Back home in the Black Country, thousands of Wolves fans who couldn't get to the game hung on his every word. The result – beating Burnley – was perfect. So too was Billy's contribution to a fantastic day. I'll never forget the joy on his face, the tear in his eye, or the incredible reception he received from countless football fans as they caught sight of the great man en route to the Wembley commentary box. Every request for an autograph or photograph was greeted with a smile and a joke. It's a pretty safe bet that most, like me, will never forget meeting with Billy Wright that day.'

DAVID BOWEN (Exeter, Devon): 'My Dad was a Wolves supporter before World War Two in Stan Cullis's playing days. In 1949 I was a nine-year-old boy living in rural south Shropshire on a farm. Wolves won the FA Cup beating Leicester City 3–1 and I did not want the year to end! All summer I practised heading a ball against one of our farm buildings, dreaming that I was like my boyhood hero, Billy Wright, playing for Wolves and England. To this day there has been no one like him. In the mid-fifties when Wolves played some of the European teams my father, brother and I would walk a couple of miles to the nearest farm of one of our friends who had a generator to make electricity and a television set to go with it. These are magic memories.'

RUSS LEAVER (Cleethorpes, Lincolnshire): 'Once, when about twelve-years-old, I attended a talk in Southend-on-Sea, Essex, where Billy Wright was the guest speaker. It must have been just after he won his 100th international cap. I still remember his slightly blond hair, nasal voice and what I now appreciate as a presence about him. You just knew he was a nice person. Nothing wrong in being "nice". I am 55-years-old now but I still remember that evening – and Billy Wright.'

IAN BAILLIE: 'In the early 1960s Billy used to appear on the children's programme Magpie encouraging young boys to always clean their football boots. I took notice! When he was a manager at Arsenal, I sent him a birthday card for February 6th. He sent a reply on Arsenal-headed notepaper with his signature thanking me. Once on a trip to Llandudno with my parents, I saw the Beverley Sisters in a shop. Joy signed a postcard of Conway Castle for me from Joy and Billy Wright. I still have the postcard and letter. These kind gestures, even at an early age, were never forgotten.'

PETER PATON (Shifnal, Shropshire): 'Thanks to Billy Wright, I got to hold the FA Cup and found a wife! In 1949 he visited my school in Bedstone, south Shropshire, and he brought the Cup with him. I was in the school first-team photographed with Billy and the Cup. Eight years later I was at the Savoy cinema in Wolverhampton with my new girlfriend Betty. I came out of the loo to find her in friendly conversation with none other than my hero, Billy! He was waiting for his landlady, the famous Mrs Colley. My girlfriend, who I was suddenly seeing in a new light, introduced me to Billy, and I was so overawed I couldn't speak. As I escorted Betty home, she explained she had known Billy, his brother Laurence and father, Tommy, all her life because they were near neighbours. With friends like that, I thought, she must be nice! We subsequently married and have lived happily ever after! We now live close to Billy's old friend and colleague Bert "The Cat" Williams, and often recall old times when Billy was the King of Molineux.'

MIKE THOMAS: 'I was eight when I discovered my hero. Wolves had just won the Cup, their captain Billy Wright also led England. It became the family joke that I talked about him so much that my mother – who also shares his birthday – laid an extra plate at teatime. Where others had invisible friends, I had Billy Wright. As a young boy growing up without a father (my father, in the RAF, was killed during the war) I could have had no better role model. He was a true sportsman, modest in success, gracious in defeat. He was very fit, he neither drank alcohol nor smoked – he even read Dickens to improve his speech-making! His principle of "leading by example" I have taken through both my sporting and my working life (an attitude sometimes not recognised in this age of delegation and "no-blame" culture!). As you can see, over 50 years later, I am still a fan. If I was writing your book, I would call it *Sir Billy*, because that is what he should have become.'

FRED CLEARY (Cape Town, South Africa): 'I remember Billy visiting what was then Rhodesia where I was working as a journalist. I took him to dinner at the Jamaica Inn, about twenty miles from Salisbury on the road to Umtali. It was owned by an Englishman, Arthur Scrutton, a former professional footballer. As we entered, Arthur, by then in late middle age, spotted the famous crop of fair hair and the handsome face of the ex-Wolves and England star. An emotional man by nature, he was so overwhelmed he could hardly speak. It was a chilly night (Rhodesian winter), so he ushered us to our seats near the fire in the main lounge and organised our drinks. With tears welling in his eyes, he looked at Billy and said, with unabashed pride: 'I never thought I would have the privilege of hosting the captain of England in my establishment. Welcome Mr Wright.' They shook hands. He said the drinks were on the house and departed, off to treasure the moment in private. A little story that captures what Billy meant to football people everywhere.'

JOHN MARSH (Bexleyheath, Kent): 'I recall in my early days supporting Charlton Athletic at the age of 12, I got to the The Valley ground early enough to witness the arrival of the Wolves team. Billy was sitting at the front of the coach alongside the driver, and as I looked up at him he winked at me. This simple fleeting moment for me as a young boy was an experience of a lifetime leaving me with an indelible memory almost fifty years later. It seemed akin to being in the company of a god.'

PETER MOSS (Christchurch, New Zealand): 'I have retired here to New Zealand after 30 years in the Metropolitan Police, and I am warmed by wonderful memories of being the duty officer in the tunnel for every Spurs home match. Billy was a favourite of mine because he always had time for a friendly chat and a smile, and never ever came the big "I am" even though he was England's greatest footballing ambassador.'

NEVILLE STOUT (West Midlands): 'What is seldom mentioned is that Billy played 90 minutes every game for his 105 England Caps and throughout every second of all his Wolves matches because he played in the days before substitutes. I saw many of his games and rarely saw him put a foot wrong.'

KEITH DABBS (Chelmsford): 'Billy was my second cousin. You will be interested to learn that he was not the first member of the wider family to play football professionally as my father, Ben Dabbs, who was his mother's cousin, played for Liverpool and Watford in the 1930s. He made both his reserve and first-team debut for Liverpool at Molineux, so the ground had special memories for him given the later success that was to come Billy's way. The family remain keen Wolves supporters, and exceptionally proud of our links with a truly model player.'

BILL POLAND (Huyton, Merseyside): 'Playing against Everton in the 1950's, Billy stooped to head out a rocket shot from our Tommy Egington. Unfortunately, he did it with the top of his head. He was carried off and rushed to Walton Hospital, where he was kept in overnight. That evening, I visited my wife in that hospital, and there wasn't a nurse to be seen. When I asked my wife where they all were, she said. "Oh, some footballer was brought in injured, and they have all gone to see him." I looked in as I left, and gave him a nod. Nice guy...often got us Evertonians mad, but a nice guy!'

CHRISTINE ILEY (Chartridge, Chesham): 'During the 1950s my first job was with Crombie Lacon & Stevens in Waterloo Road, Wolverhampton (still in practice today), and they were Billy Wright's accountants at that time. Billy was always charming, never arrogant or self-important. As junior clerk, I had to serve tea to clients. Feeling very nervous the first time I took tea into the senior partner's office, I managed to spill it but Billy just smiled and winked at me with those big blue eyes which certainly saved my embarrassment. Another time he brought the three Beverley Sisters into the offices, causing much excitement with their expensive perfume (only for the rich and famous then) filling the air of the three-storey building.'

MICK FRANCIS (Welwyn Garden City): 'Billy Wright is the reason I have supported Wolves for 45 years. Born and bred in Hertfordshire, all my friends were either Arsenal or Spurs supporters. Me being always a rebel, I didn't want to be the same as all the others, so I decided that whoever was the captain of England, I would support his club team. And I have never wavered. God bless you Billy.'

NORMAN SIBLEY (Wolves supporter): 'I still have the scrapbooks I kept from the days when Billy and Wolves were at their peak. As a goalkeeper, I idolised the great Bert Williams, but there was no question that Billy was the best outfield player for that outstanding team.'

ALTON DOUGLAS (Author of *Memories of Wolverhampton* and over 30 books on the West Midlands): 'As a warm-up comic at ATV for several years I would see Billy every Sunday after I had finished with the *Golden Shot* show. Over the years we would natter quite a lot. To give an example of his kind attitude and consideration I remember one special day at New Street Station. I spotted him some distance away, and I could see he was in a hurry. Instead of either pretending he did not see me or miming "I am in a rush" – he ran across the entire width of the

Station concourse, slapped my shoulder and said "I can't stop, mate, my train leaves in three minutes," and sprinted off again! Typical Billy.'

MAL DOWNING (Upminster, Essex): 'It was 1961 and the showbiz eleven football team were playing at Hornchurch stadium. I was thirteen years old at the time and had the job of helping players park their cars. A big Ford Zephyr car pulled into the car park and as I looked at the driver I realised it was Billy Wright. Wolves were the team I had supported since the first televised floodlit match on television in 1954 (watching it on a twelve-inch TV at my grandmother's house). I helped Billy park his car and as he got out he said, "Thanks for helping me park, son" and threw me a large Jaffa orange. I ate the orange but kept the peel in a small box and eventually threw it away mouldy thirteen years later when I was 26 years of age. That's how highly I regarded Billy Wright.'

MARK RAFFERTY (Sutton Coldfield): 'I am a 37-year-old Police Officer with the West Midlands Police with seventeen years service. I am in particular a lifelong Aston Villa supporter, a lover of all sports in general and to some degree a bit of a sporting romantic and traditionalist. In the summer of 1993 my wife and I made a failed attempt to set up and run a restaurant business based on a sporting theme. I wrote to 40 sports personalities asking if there was a small memento they could let me have to display in the restaurant. I had mostly refusals, but from Billy and Joy Wright – two people I had never met in my life – came a Mexican football shirt that Billy had collected from an opponent way back in 1959 in his penultimate game for England. It was accompanied by Billy's autograph and the note, "What a small jersey! No wonder I could not mark him!" What a great gesture from a wonderful man.'

And a final PS from **Maria Scott**, whose sister had a romance with Billy before he met Joy: 'Billy courted my sister, Jane, in the old fashioned way, but there was little chance of it leading to anything too serious. This was because Billy used to insist on bidding her goodnight early so that he could always be in bed by 10.30. That's how dedicated he was to his football.'

How to end these tributes from the supporters, who were so special to Billy? I give the final words to a teenage fan who never saw him play but who has been touched by the spirit of Billy Wright. This was the brief message left on the Billy Wright website by Brad Simpson of Berkshire: 'Billy Wright will live forever.'

What Family and Friends Say

We now come to the people who meant the most to Billy, his friends and family. Kicking off we have his 'Girl of the Century', Victoria Anne, the daughter who was born on 5 April 1959, the day he became the first footballer in the world selected for a hundredth cap...

VICKY WRIGHT: 'My Dad was the most kind, gentle, generous, loving, emotional man I have ever met. I feel the most lucky and privileged person to have been blessed with having him as a father. He gave my sister, Babette, and I constant and unconditional love. There was never a day he didn't tell us he loved us, hugged us and made us laugh. He taught us so much and has left us with a multitude of happy memories. I will be ever grateful. I love and miss him more than words can say.

'Two special memories I would like to share concern the time that I brought my baby daughter, Kelly, home from the hospital. She was his first grandchild and he was *so* proud. Dad asked if he could take her for a walk in the pram. Being a new mum, I naturally felt a little nervous letting her go, but knowing what it meant to him, I waved goodbye and off they walked into the spring sunshine ...

'Two hours later and me sick with worry, he returned with the biggest smile on his face and proudly told me how he had visited *every* neighbour in the area! All of them still tell me about this happy day in their lives and how special he made them feel. I wasn't the only one!

'A few days later I was at home feeling totally exhausted. As normal I got my daily phone call from Dad asking if I needed anything. He would always pop up to Waitrose for us all to get the shopping! Dad must have detected just how tired I was and five minutes later the door bell went and there he was, with that lovely smile.

'"Come on sweet," he said. "you sit down, I'll look after K.J." (his special nickname for Kelly Joy). We all sat on the sofa together, Dad with Kelly in one arm and me in the other. I slept, undisturbed, for an hour and a half! When I woke he said that we had not moved, I really had never felt as safe and as loved, and I will never forget this precious memory.'

Beautiful Babette arrived five years later, after Billy had started out on his adventure as manager of Arsenal. As this book was being prepared for publication, Babette was preparing for a major production of her own, with a second baby on the way. This was Babette's contribution to the Billy memories:

BABETTE WRIGHT (now Mrs Woodham): 'I miss Dad very much, our wonderful hugs, kisses and laughs we had, but I have such fantastic memories of him. I am honoured to have him as a father and as a friend and to feel he is still with me every step of the way.

'One of my memories is when Dad and I used to have our chats in the kitchen before anyone got up, and we usually talked about football, which I followed avidly. We had great discussions. His knowledge of the game always amazed me. We'd talk about the game the night before or the weekend results, while he made us a cup of tea. I still love football, and never miss my Saturday nights watching the games. I now have a son, William; named, of course, after Dad. I can see Dad in him in so many ways – his warmth, kindness and affection, and generous nature. I hope that he will follow football like me and love the game, so we can have *our* chats like Dad and I used to.

'I am so happy that you have decided to write this book. I will treasure it and read it over and over again. At last I can read about Dad's career properly, in full. It is fascinating to read the quotes from him after every game about his performance and to see the team line-ups. Dad never ever boasted about his record, but when you see it in black and white like this it makes you realise just what an incredible career he had. I hope that everyone who buys the book enjoys it too, and they can begin to really understand what a fabulous man and father he really was, in every possible way.'

We now come to the person who first brought Joy and Billy together, Joy's son Vincent. I can vouch for the fact that Billy never ever thought of him as anything but his own son, and he was bursting with pride when he told me that Vince had landed a job as a subeditor on *The Times* sports desk.

VINCENT WRIGHT: 'It was Billy's friendship, openness and honesty with the media that encouraged me to become a sports journalist when I left school towards the end of the sixties. Despite the considerable stress of managing a big club like Arsenal, I cannot remember him refusing an interview, cannot remember him not answering the telephone, which would often ring with infuriating frequency. Even at his lowest point, Billy always had time for everybody. I rather naively thought that reporters would always be treated in this helpful and courteous manner, only to discover, on my first newspaper and subsequent others, that I was profoundly mistaken. In fact, journalism was much harder than Billy made it look! Little wonder at Billy's huge popularity with the print and broadcast media and even less wonder at the countless tributes paid to him since his death seven years ago. He came into my life when I was nine and I feel privileged to have known him.'

No book on Billy Wright would be a finished product without a contribution from the two ladies he looked on as friends as well as relatives – the famous Twins of the Beverley Sisters, Babs and Teddie. This is what they had to say, jointly of course:

THE TWINS, BABS and TEDDIE: 'It was always difficult for Billy and Joy to get together as often as they wanted. They were gloriously in love and we twins were so, so happy for them. A year after they were married, we were headlining in another record-breaking season and the BBC television cameras were filming The Bevs at Great Yarmouth riding in one of the horse-drawn carriages that parade along the seafront. When the filming ended, we patted the horses and Joy suggested she'd like some manure for her new garden in the house she and Billy had just bought in London. The boot of her car was duly laden with huge stacks of the stuff. Billy came to see Joy the following day and she oversaw the transfer of the smelly load into Billy's car boot.

'Included in Billy's busy schedule the following week was the honour of a private luncheon at Buckingham Palace with the Queen herself. After his Royal audience, he drove back up to Yarmouth for another snatched romantic visit to Joy. Meanwhile, our sister had organised a second huge load of fresh manure for transferring to London. Imagine our complete horror to find the original piles still sitting steaming in the boot of Billy's car! He had totally forgotten about it.

'To this day, we laugh at the thought of our dear Billy driving his car into Buckingham Palace and parking his oh-so-fragant automobile under the Queen's window!

'We twins would just like to add that we never once had a cross word with Billy; as his sister-in-laws obviously at close quarters for 36 years this is quite remarkable. We simply saw the same sweet-natured man behind closed doors – the same person the world saw in his public life.'

SASHA (Billy's niece who runs a company called Sing and Sign which teaches babies to communicate with sign language through music): 'My lovely Uncle Billy absolutely adored his daughters Vicky and Babette. I remember when the girls and I did shows (as singing group The Foxes) in the Midlands, Billy would often come along, bringing friends and colleagues from Central TV. His eyes would shine with pride for his girls – however he was not one for flowery showbiz praise. If we asked what he had thought of our performance his favourite initial reply was, "Rubbish!" Billy's relationship with his daughters was enviable. There was no tension in their company, just gentle banter, teasing and great warmth. They miss him dreadfully and so do I. Each Easter Sunday morning, for as long as I can remember, there would be an anonymous delivery at the house I shared with Vicky and Babette. Three enormous Easter eggs in carrier bags would have been left on the doorstep, the mysterious postman gone without trace. This is only a small memory of a very big man, but for me it typifies his wonderful nature, his generosity, and most of all the love he felt for his daughters.'

NEIL WRIGHT (the son of Billy's late younger brother, Laurence): 'I have never been interested in football – the footballing gene obviously missed a generation – so I never really appreciated how much Bill and his playing career meant to the supporters. I have two main recollections of Bill and both came at the later stages of his life. The first came when he arranged for me and a few friends to join him in his stand for a Wolves game. We arrived at the ground quite late and approached the executive entrance to meet him. When I explained I was there to meet Bill the steward on the door simply replied "Yeah, you and 20,000 others!" Still doubting me, he pointed us towards the main stand entrance. Bill met me there and took me round the stand, and it was only as we were walking together that I realised just how much people revered him. We met supporters in the corridors who almost bowed to him as they shook his hand. He, of course, greeted them in his usual friendly and polite manner. It was really touching to see people's reactions to him and gave a brief glimpse of his stature in football and at Wolves.

'The second came after his death when I travelled to the ground with my mum and sister to see the tributes that people were laying in front of his stand. To see all of the pictures, cards and football stuff that people had brought in his memory was quite moving. I distinctly remember seeing a young guy who must have only been in his early twenties – he can't even have seen Bill play – standing there with tears in his eyes. It makes you wonder if the players of today could be as admired when they reach their seventies.'

RON THOMPSON (Billy's cousin from King's Norton, Birmingham, who has memories of the young Bill Wright): 'His mother – Aunt Annie to me – was my father's sister. We lived in Birmingham, and used to visit Bill's family in Ironbridge and they would come to see us in Brum. I have lovely childhood memories of us going swimming and fishing in the River Severn. I remember Bill giving me a ride on his merry-go-round which consisted of an old-type turntable which he kept under his bed. The fact that we could sit on it and be turned round indicates the age we must have been. I can confirm that as a youngster he always answered to the name of Bill with, to my recollection, only Aunt Annie calling him Billy. I am proud of my association with a man who became a legend in his own lifetime and who was never ever spoiled by his fame.'

When he joined the Wolves board as a director, Billy was delighted to find himself reunited with an old family friend, Rachael Heyhoe Flint, the former England women's cricket captain who has become a vibrant personality behind the scenes at Molineux and now sits on the main board.

RACHAEL HEYHOE FLINT: 'Billy was a family friend from way, way back. My father, Geoffrey Heyhoe, was director of physical education for Wolverhampton. In his early days Dad took "PT" lessons (it's what it was called then, physical training) at Wolverhampton Technical College evening classes. This was in the 1940s and 1950s – and the one and only Billy Wright used to attend these classes to improve his fitness. No posh gymnasiums or weight-training rooms at Molineux for the players in those days!

'My father always told me that Billy could jump higher than anyone else in his class to reach the high beam, even though many were taller. No wonder Billy was such a good header of the ball and dominating in the air.

'When I joined Wolves in 1990 as Public Relations executive – at the invitation of Sir Jack Hayward, when he bought the club – it was great to be reunited with Billy at Molineux more than 40 years on from when my father pushed him through his paces. Billy always used to call me "Flinty".

'I helped coordinate dear Billy's funeral. It was a dreadfully wet, dull day, yet the roads from Molineux to St Peter's Church were lined a dozen deep from about eleven o'clock in the morning. It was like a state funeral. There were thousands assembled, all wishing to bid farewell to their Billy. The entire pavement in front of Molineux was completely covered with flowers, tributes, scarves, flags, and children's teddy bears. They had to be stacked tidily to allow the funeral guests to arrive.

'It was a day I'll never forget. The funeral hearse arrived at Molineux and entered the big gates by the club shop. Billy did a last lap of honour around the pitch, while the PA system played Elgar's "Nimrod" from his *Enigma Variations*. Members of the club staff stood bareheaded in the stands in the pouring rain; Sir Jack and the rest of the board members plus Joy Beverley, her sisters, and Billy's family watched from the directors' box. It was a silent, tearful and enormously emotional tribute.

'The huge crowds that lined the cortege route showed the overwhelming love there was and still is for Billy Wright. Although Ironbridge-born, he was and remains "our Billy" to all Wulfrunians.'

GRAHAM KELLY (former Chief Executive of the Football Association): 'Billy and I fell in together, chatting on the steps down from Wembley after a 1990s international match when an autograph-hunter approached. The guy asked me for my signature, no doubt because he recognised my face from the telly and some fleeting, unimportant issue, completely ignoring the recipient of countless medals and 105 caps. Billy remained as charming as he always was and passed the matter off in a moment. Billy and Joy – a lovely and loving couple.'

JOHN MAJOR (who was Prime Minister when Billy died in 1994): 'Billy was one of my childhood heroes along with the likes of Stanley Matthews and Tom Finney and cricketers of the calibre of May, Hutton and Compton who led me into a lifetime's love of sport. If I close my eyes I can still see him in the black and gold of Wolves or the white of England leading the teams out on to the pitch with a pride that seemed to make him stand inches taller. He represented the best, the very, very best, of English sport.'

The biggest thrill and honour of Billy's footballing life off the pitch came when he was invited to join the Molineux board by the 'Saviour of Wolves'...

SIR JACK HAYWARD OBE: 'Although working and living overseas during the 1950s, I followed Billy's Wolves and England career very closely. I got to know him well during the 1980s when Jack Harris was chairman and used to invite Billy to travel to away matches. When I was considering buying Wolves from the Gallagher family I asked Billy if he would do me the honour of becoming a director. I clearly recall him having tears in his eyes, and he said the honour would be his. His parting words that day were, "I can't wait to tell Joy. She'll be so thrilled."

'When we started to rebuild Molineux I told him that, if he agreed, the main stand would be named after him. He protested that he was not worthy of the honour! I used to stay at the Friendly Hotel near Walsall on the eve of home Saturday matches, and used to invite Billy to join me for dinner. No matter what time I got there, Billy would always beat me to the dining table. "How long have you been here?" I would ask. "Since Wednesday," was the reply! He never used to miss a single midweek game – be it first-team, reserve or youth matches – until he became seriously ill.

'When the Queen opened Molineux I was delighted to introduce Billy to her in front of "his" stand. Her Majesty was amused!

'I was the last person outside his close family to see Billy before he died. He was weak and skeletal, yet he talked of an operation by a surgeon friend of mine "as soon as I'm fit". Not many days later, his funeral – beautifully organised by Rachael Heyhoe Flint and the Reverend John Hall-Matthews – was a very sad yet fantastic tribute to Billy from the people of Wolverhampton. They did their most famous son very proud.'

Only one person can possibly have the last word, the love and light of Billy's life ...

JOY BEVERLEY WRIGHT: 'I would just like to say thank you from the bottom of my heart to all those people who have kindly taken the time and trouble to share their memories of a marvellous man. I hope you have got as much pleasure from reading Billy's life story as I have of reliving it. He really *was* a hero for all seasons.'

Index